THE POLITICS OF HUMAN RIGHTS

UNA-USA POLICY STUDIES BOOK SERIES

The United Nations Association of the USA is a private, nonprofit organiztion dedicated to broadening public understanding of the activities of the United Nations and other multilateral institutions. Through its nationwide membership and network of affiliated national organizations, UNA-USA conducts a broad range of programs to inform and involve the public in foreign affairs issues.

The UNA-USA Policy Studies Program conducts projects involving research and analysis of a wide spectrum of policy issues of concern to the international community. The Program brings together panels of interested and knowledgeable Americans to study and make recommendations on specific problems of U.S. foreign policy and multilateral activities. As part of this process, a number of papers are commissioned from leading specialists.

The UNA-USA Policy Studies Book Series contains books based on rewritten and edited collections of some of these papers. UNA-USA is responsible for the choice of the subject areas and the decision to publish the volumes, but the responsibility for the content of the papers and for opinions expressed in them rests with the individual authors and editors.

Already published:
Disaster Assistance: Appraisal, Reform and New Approaches, edited by Lynn H. Stephens and Stephen J. Green.
The New International Economic Order: A U.S. Response, edited by David B. H. Denoon.

THE POLITICS OF HUMAN RIGHTS

Edited by
Paula R. Newberg

New York University Press • New York *and* London

Library of Congress Cataloging in Publication Data
Main entry under title:

The Politics of human rights.

  (UNA-USA policy studies book series)
  Bibliography: p.
  Includes Index.
  1. Civil rights—Addresses, essays, lectures.
I. Newberg, Paula R., 1952-   II. Series: United
Nations Association of the United States of America.
UNA-USA policy studies book series.
JC571.P64   323.4   79-1998
ISBN 0-8147-5754-5
ISBN 0-8147-5755-3 (pbk.)

Manufactured in the United States of America

CONTENTS

v

PREFACE

Many of the essays in this volume were commissioned initially as background material and analysis for a UNA-USA Policy Panel considering the role of human rights in American foreign policy. That Panel published a report of its findings in December 1979, entitled *United States Foreign Policy and Human Rights: Principles, Priorities, Practice.* The background papers were all substantially revised and rewritten for publication here, and new essays were added for this collection. Several of the authors were able to attend a day-long meeting to discuss their papers early in the revision process, held at the Harvard Law School in October 1978. To all the authors whose work is included here, this editor is grateful for their patience, goodwill, and continued interest.

During the process of commissioning papers, and later during the editing and revision period, many individuals generously offered their time and encouragement, both for general discussion and for reading. Among them, special thanks are due to: Georges Abi-Saab, David A. Bazelon, Lincoln P. Bloomfield, David Carliner, Jerome A. Cohen, Jill Conway, Asbjorn Eide, C. Clyde Ferguson, Frances FitzGerald, Gidon Gottlieb, Dennis Goulet, Stephanie Grant, Ernst Haas, Louis Henkin, Ngo Manh Lan, Anthony Lewis, Niall MacDermot, Elenora Masini, Richard Seifman, Philippe de Seynes, Henry Shue, Helmut Sonnenfeldt, Mumtaz Soysal, John B. Starr, and David Szanton.

Paula R. Newberg

vii

CONTRIBUTORS

Richard J. Barnet is a Senior Fellow of the Institute for Policy Studies in Washington, D.C.

John H. Barton is Professor of Law at Stanford University.

Graciela Chichilnisky is Associate Professor of Economics at Columbia University.

H. S. D. Cole is a Senior Research Fellow of the Science Policy Research Unit at the University of Sussex.

Joseph W. Elder is a Professor in the Departments of Sociology and South Asian Studies at the University of Wisconsin (Madison).

Richard A. Falk is the Albert G. Milbank Professor of International Law and Practice in the Department of Politics, Princeton University.

Paula R. Newberg is Director of the United Nations Association (USA) policy study, *United States Foreign Policy and Human Rights.*

Barnett R. Rubin is a doctoral candidate in political science at The University of Chicago.

Dankwart A. Rustow is Distinguished Professor of Political Science at the City University Graduate Center (New York).

Tracy B. Strong is Associate Professor at Amherst and Smith Colleges.

Sidney Weintraub is Dean Rusk Professor of International Affairs at the University of Texas and Senior Fellow at The Brookings Institution (Washington, D.C.).

Stephen B. Young is an Assistant Dean at the Harvard Law School.

Chapter 1

INTRODUCTION: DIMENSIONS OF THE PROBLEM

PAULA R. NEWBERG

In March 1974 a congressional committee—the House International Affairs Subcommittee on International Organizations and Movements—began to examine the role of human rights in U.S. foreign policy. After receiving testimony from a wide range of governmental and nongovernmental experts, that committee concluded that "protection of human rights is essentially the responsibility of each government with respect to its own citizens; however, when a government is itself the perpetrator of the violations, the victim has no recourse but to seek redress from outside his national boundaries."

Those early hearings were prelude to a charge that slowly began to change the shape of American foreign policy. Responding to what it saw as recalcitrance, if not refusal, by the executive branch to take human rights factors into account when making and executing policy, Congress took an active and enthusiastic role by enacting new laws, making the relationships between rights and foreign policy explicit in their efforts to improve respect for rights abroad. Not only do certain trade, assistance, and diplomatic benefits now hinge on the way a recipient country treats its own citizens, but the executive branch is required to report publicly its assessment of the condition of human rights in every country with which it has ties.

Concurrent with these congressional actions, the Carter administration itself has tried to articulate a foreign policy that considers human rights its guiding moral principle, giving it not only priority but visibility. As the president suggested in 1978, he regarded human rights to be the "soul" of U.S. foreign policy. Some administration figures have considered the human rights movement to be a powerful antidote to the ideological force of communism, and therefore an issue to be pursued vigorously.

As those who drafted the initial legislation were undoubtedly aware, and as this administration soon discovered, it is extremely difficult to translate principle into practice. There have been at least two major reasons for this difficulty. First, the issue of human rights intersects with almost every aspect of a government's domestic policies and therefore impinges upon virtually every parallel aspect of its relations with other countries. Rarely do governments violate human rights out of ignorance or as whim; rather, the violation of rights is often an act of desperation, perceived as necessary to maintain power and authority. Thus, in the process of orchestrating relations with a government that violates human rights, it is necessary to take into account the reasons for the violations in the affected country, the possibilities of change motivated by international pressures, and the combination of domestic factors that led to the violation of rights in the first place.

Second, principle and practice are governed by priorities. Edmund Burke, citing the differences between the philosopher and the political leader, long ago noted that whereas the philosopher is concerned with a general view of society, the statesman must combine ideas with circumstance. "Circumstances are infinite, are infinitely combined, are variable and transient ... a statesman, never losing sight of principles, is to be guided by circumstances." The configuration of interests that any one government, and in particular the government of the United States, must face are complex. It has been very hard to promote rights while maintaining a consistent and useful foreign policy in other areas. In fact, it can be argued quite persuasively that if issues concerning human rights are to take precedence in foreign policy, the entire complexion of American activities abroad may have to change. If human rights is to be one factor among many, such a change may seem less imperative, but the context in which human rights are promoted and pursued is then different. The Congress, the executive branch and the American people have yet to agree on the role the U.S. should play in the international community to promote rights, and the most useful and effective modes for combining diverse interests.

Despite their zeal in the late 1970s, Americans did not invent human rights. By treating the problem as a serious part of its bilateral policies, the United States is carrying out the earlier mandates of the United Nations, taking its guidance from the Charter, the Universal Declaration of Human Rights, and subsequent UN treaties. Although bilateral and multilateral discussions and actions have not necessarily been parallel, consistent, or harmonious on these questions in the last decade, the issue of human rights has figured prominently on the agendas of international and regional organizations and conferences.

New mechanisms have been developed in the UN as more of its members have ratified its human rights treaties; the Inter-American Commission on Human Rights of the Organization of American States has established a new charter and a court;[1] the Organization of African Unity is planning for a Human Rights Commission;[2] and interparliamentary discussions on human rights have become a regular part of U.S. and European debates. In 1975 the Final Act of the Helsinki Conference on Security and Cooperation in Europe gave human rights a formal place in the dynamics of East-West politics.[3] Throughout, nonpartisan and nongovernmental groups such as the International Commission of Jurists, the International League for Human Rights, and Amnesty International have maintained vigilant watch over governments, monitoring daily their respect for the rights of their residents.

Each of these mechanisms and procedures is one step further on the road to international and regional protections for human rights. Each incorporates sets of standards with institutions for promotion and protection. None substitutes for the protections that each state must provide to ensure that individual and collective rights are fully observed. However, their establishment and gradual improvement can supplement these national protections and provide extra protections where and when they are needed. The international movement to protect international human rights has been called a quest to speak on behalf of those who cannot speak for themselves. Where national governments have been unable or unwilling to provide adequately for their residents to exercise their rights, these multilateral institutions offer an essential service.

Despite the long-term promise offered by multilateral approaches, it should be recognized that at present many international mechanisms tend to be cumbersome, slow-moving, and politicized. They operate under difficult political constraints imposed by the diverse and often conflicting interests of their member states. Every national government is to some degree sensitive to international criticism of its domestic policies and often seeks to forestall or influence international efforts to investigate its alleged abuses of human rights. At best, the development of effective international institutions will be a long-term process requiring many more years of patience and fortitude on the part of their members, but the process has begun and some foundations have been laid for further progress.

The road during the last several years has been a bumpy one, not without hazards, missed signals, and misinterpreted directions. The problems of integrating a concern for human rights in the agendas of governments and intergovernmental organizations are rooted in disputes about the nature of rights, of political society, and of human happiness. Legislating a role for ethics in political policy cannot help but be a divisive and often incendiary activity; indeed, separating human rights as an operational dimension of foreign policy from the broader, familiar issue of morality in politics has proved to be a difficult obstacle to overcome, both domestically and internationally. It is an issue that is easier to confront in rhetoric than in action, and even then with difficulty. While human rights now appears almost automatically as an item in political debate, the tone with which it is approached is unpredictable, and the place it is given varies widely, depending on time, place, and context.

The dividing lines are recognizable. For some, human rights has become a useful weapon in the arsenals of ideological battle, be it East-West, or North-South; for others, it is an issue without politics or partisanship, a touchstone from which to begin any further action or negotiation. Some see it as an issue to be resolved independently, prior to any other; others perceive a human rights component in every aspect of economic, social, and political life. Running through almost any discussion are hauntingly familiar refrains: Just what are these rights about which we argue—which are most important and which should be considered first? How do they fit into patterns of development, growth, and social progress? Are they more important in some places than in others? Are there permissible limits to governmental authority to direct the lives of individuals, even when rights are infringed?

If there is one identifiable constant, it is that human rights are violated—purposefully and pervasively—every day. Although bilateral and multilateral political discussions may have made the violation of rights a crime to which few governments will now voluntarily admit or righteously justify, the variety and extent of human rights violations today suggest that our contemporary situation is as urgent as it has been at any time in the postwar era. More than thirty years after the Universal Declaration was accepted by the UN General Assembly, the rights of individuals and groups are violated as a consistent and even accepted part of everyday life in almost every country in the world. That simple fact remains the most compelling issue for those concerned with peace, rights, and foreign policy and motivates further scrutiny, discussion, and argument.

***

Writing about human rights, although an intractable task, has become a minor growth industry in the last several years.[4] Because questions about the nature of rights are closely intertwined with questions about political systems, legal obligations, cultural integrity, and personal morality, recent political interest in human rights has spurred—as it did thirty years ago—renewed scholarly pursuit. It therefore seems appropriate to explain this addition to an ever expanding literature by describing its place in that body of writing and suggesting where it offers new approaches.

The most direct and visible investigations about human rights concern specific countries and problems. Taking a cue from the publications of nongovernmental organizations devoted to illuminating public awareness about particular horrors, recent writings have analyzed the kinds of violations that occur and the kinds of political systems in which they occur. Although these situations do change, we now have a large if not comprehensive literature about those societies in which egregious violations take place. As an offshoot, some comparative studies—cross-cultural and cross-temporal—are also beginning to be available.

At the same time, and largely as a result of the standard-setting activities of the UN human rights bodies and specialized agencies, there is an active literature concerning the legal status of rights. The impetus for new writing seems to be three-fold: lively debate within international organizations about the status of economic and social rights, which has led to tentative explorations in jurisprudence; greater stature of international and regional treaties on human rights as well as other multilateral initiatives, which has motivated some research into comparative legal institutions; and new legal guarantees, in the United States and elsewhere, for integrating human rights into domestic and foreign policy. Because human rights has always held a special place in postwar international law, there are also some contributions to this field and its stepchild, world-order studies. In all of these areas, earlier advocacy frequently seems to have been tempered, if only slightly, to produce somewhat more dispassionate analysis.

The jurisprudence writings have been supplemented by some additions in moral philosophy. Some of these studies have a legalistic tone, whereas others are located in the mainstream of the history of philosophy; this has been largely Anglo-American, or at least recognizably based on an analytic philosophical tradition. However, with changes in world politics—notably the Islamic revolution that replaced the Shah's regime in Iran and the increased prominence of Islamic nationalism—have come investigations into the relationships between rights and cultural systems.

The present volume is a collection of essays directed toward a series of difficult—in some cases, seemingly unanswerable—questions of a different nature. They take their focus from an initial interest in American foreign policy but, for the most part, do not take current policies as their primary interest. Instead, these essays attempt to pose a series of questions that need to be considered prior to the making of specific policy—questions about the role of the state, the nature of political ideals, and the diversity of human culture. In particular, they treat the relationships between social justice and political equality, the assumptions of international assistance programs and the effects of these programs on domestic economic distribution, and the role these questions play in the process of clarifying the meaning of rights in political policy. In each essay, the relationship of the specific subject of investigation to the general issue of human rights is both clear and immediate. The questions that motivate each author vary, but each tries to pose the problems concerning human rights in unusual, and prospectively productive ways. Taken separately, each offers an analysis of problems that deserve detailed scrutiny; taken together, they propose a collection of methods and issues that not only reflect one another but reinforce common concerns and interests.

The sections of this book are divided according to the levels of analysis and questioning of their constituent essays, rather than on strict substantive similarity. How questions are phrased, the scope of the problems discussed, and the kinds of solutions or directions proposed take precedence in this volume. The analyses move from the general to the specific—or, more accurately, from macrolevel questioning to microlevel analysis. Thus, the first section sets out a series of alternative ways to interpret human rights in the context of world politics and American diplomatic history—contrasting patterns of thought and habits of belief and action—and the second section uses these analyses to develop more specific models for policy analysis. The constant shift between explicit conceptual (and practical) models for constructing political action, and the implicit attitudes that so often govern the way peoples and nations behave is itself a dialogue that is reflected in scholarly discussion as much as in daily political life. Thus, the second section moves quite naturally from a discussion of concepts to studies of the societies themselves. There is no attempt to be comprehensive here; indeed, few particular societies are discussed. The cases that have been selected demonstrate that the complex of concerns that involve human rights overlap and, in many ways, come back to reconsider basic relationships between personal or social values and the perceptions we use to judge individual and collective action.

The final section includes three essays that analyze policy problems in the fields of foreign assistance and law. These are pressing concerns for the conduct of foreign policy in the immediate future, and they form a backdrop against which the discussions of earlier chapters can be assessed. The conceptual analyses that form the bulk of this volume suggest new ways to implement current policies or new directions in which to take future actions. Therefore, the fundamental problems intrinsic to a discussion of human rights, and the problems of current policy, need to be evaluated side by side if the policy ventures of the next decade are to be useful and sensible.

Section I, comprising papers by Rustow, Strong, and Falk, poses several general questions about the kinds of world views Americans have adopted when dealing with problems of rights and sovereignty. Rustow, elaborating on some of his earlier work in development and modernization studies, suggests that once we in the United States dismiss any notion of international human rights as being identical to American constitutional rights, it becomes necessary to reassess concepts of citizenship, the nature of global order, and the changing economic relations between the United States and the rest of the world. His analysis begins with a brief exploration of the way eighteenth-century notions of power and political change have been used in the formulation of U.S. foreign policies. Noting the problems such views have created for the pursuits of foreign policy, he concludes that promoting rights as part of American foreign policy can be pursued usefully only as part of a broad, long-term framework of foreign affairs that stresses the close relations between economic and political development strategies. This is a theme that recurs later in the volume—notably in papers by Chichilnisky and Cole, Elder, and Barnet.

Strong goes on to elaborate one part of that thesis—that there is something unique to the self-image of the United States that directs its interests in rights in certain specific ways. Like Rustow, he investigates the differences between the rights of man and the rights of citizens. Noting that "a feeling of exceptionalism" has been part of American consciousness since the founding of the republic, he describes the "double genealogy" of this character, which he believes has led to peculiar and forceful interactions between this republican tradition and the notion of rights it tries to provide. His analysis of selected aspects of American history, particularly the early republic and the years surrounding the Lodge-Wilson debates about the League of Nations, suggests that these interrelations have become the basis for a style of politics that has given the current U.S. interest in human rights an intriguing, if not always fruitful, direction.

That this pattern or style of politics is but one of many possible ways to view the world—each with serious attendant difficulties—is a problem that Falk sets out to explore. He posits a series of perspectives or "logics" about the relations between individuals and states (and the theories that inform them), and he then explores the ramifications each present to those who must not only study but make policy. His working assumption is that "human rights" occupy a peculiar place in these logics of political behavior and that exploring such rights—as distinct from constitutional guarantees that define the citizen in specific political societies—can provide us with a revised perspective about compatibilities among states, international organizations, and individuals. Throughout, he suggests that each of these logics are configurations of power, interests, and beliefs that rarely exist independently; the contributions they present today are but the latest stages in the dynamic process that the concerns of world order must confront.

In Section II, several authors try to interpret contemporary problems by using the concepts, if not always the language, the earlier chapters provide. After offering a series of contrasting models for interpreting the relations between basic needs, human rights, and economic distribution, Chichilnisky and Cole conclude that, within the current North-South debate, liberal Northern economic policies are inconsistent with the North's purported concern for promoting human rights and fostering well-being. They believe that these policies not only do not achieve their intended economic goals but that these goals themselves, even if fulfilled, would contradict humanitarian interests. They suggest that, by reorienting perspectives for looking at North-South relations, the concepts of economic self-interest and global good can be reconstrued. Their recommendations complement some of Falk's analysis in Section I. In particular, some of their assumptions presume implicitly that power and interests are defined according to the views of hegemony that Falk offers. The implications for reconstruing these concepts of good and interest are thus far wider than the limited sphere of economic relations with which they are primarily concerned.

Barnet elaborates on one aspect of these considerations by investigating the ways in which the current policies of multinational corporations contradict one of the stated goals of international organizations—the right to food. After isolating the elaborate dialectic between public and private sector views of the common good, he explores some of the philosophic assumptions that lead governments to treat having food, or the access to food, as a right. He then looks at the economic conditions that leads governments to sanction or encourage corporate policies that make it difficult, if not impossible, for individuals to satisfy that right, either independently or with the aid of their own governments. His conclusions are in some ways similar to Falk's and to Chichilnisky and Cole's: that explicit policy choices must be made, by both corporations and governments, if "the rhetoric of basic needs and right to food" is to be translated into practical policy; that these choices will involve sacrifices of unknown dimensions by some countries and some corporations; but that choosing not to adopt steps to eliminate hunger is itself a violation of rights.

These choices are all extremely intricate ones to make. The levels of complexity—among competing interests, perceived values, and varying constituencies—are so numerous that a decision of any sort necessarily resonates in many quarters. Barnet's queries focus in part of the nature of responsibility and the difficulties of ascribing it among different actors. The way this is done reflects not only the choices to be made among Rustow's development strategies, Falk's logics, and Chichilnisky and Cole's models but some fundamental choices about political ideals such as justice and equality.

Continuing Barnet's concern with the right to have food, Elder looks at a particular part of that problem—the patterns of land distribution that make having food a possibility in many parts of the world—and explores some questions about the ways that redistributing land fits into global and regional notions about society and polity alike. He tries to isolate a concept of justice and legitimacy that can be used to make sense of the distribution problems that now face local governments and regional financial institutions. By locating a peculiar paradox of Western economies and Eastern society—that increasing economic inequalities in South Asia may be a result of a "unique convergence of Western values regarding equality and justice"—he begins to refine our understandings of the dilemmas that U.S. foreign policy, World Bank policy, and the local societies will continue to confront in the future. Past policies have produced consequences with many severe problems; new frameworks of legitimacy will have to contend with these new difficulties as much as with the earlier problem of distribution.

When establishing such frameworks, where do we find our initial sources of social sanction? Elder suggests that Western perceptions about Hindu culture—what that culture would and would not accept—contributed significantly to the ways the West has tried to help, or work with, Asian nations to promote rights and satisfy needs. Young takes this one step further and offers a somewhat different analysis of Western responses to foreign cultures, in this case Southeast Asia. He suggests that universal rights function in society as limits on the activities of government, where these limits are beliefs or rational principles, or the habitual operations of society. He goes on to suggest that non-Western society may not call such constraints "rights" in the same way that Western society has, but that there are functional equivalents to such rights in the religions and cultures of Southeast Asia. By examining the ancient sources of these limits, he offers some insight into the ways in which Americans can and should reform their views of Asian society as the United States seeks to promote rights abroad. His own analysis finds other, deeper problems of method and pursuit, notably the problem of incorporating the lessons of relativism into policies that are usually seen as protecting absolutes.

As Rustow points out at the beginning of his essay, "Once human rights are introduced into the workaday conduct of congressional or presidential policy ... contentious questions arise." Each chapter in this volume considers some of the policy consequences of changing perceptions of human rights; the essays in Section III look at specific policies themselves. Perhaps the two most obvious areas in which U.S. human rights policy has been refocused recently are economic assistance and international law. Weintraub examines these two "moral pillars" of American policy—what he calls "the nobler content of what is otherwise mostly an exercise in *Realpolitik*"—by evaluating the successes and failures of the human rights component of American aid programs. His paper assesses these programs in light of their explicit goals and contrasts the effectiveness of bilateral and multilateral initiatives in these areas. This approach contrasts sharply with the discussion by Chichilnisky and Cole, although both essays take economic relations as their subject. Chichilnisky and Cole see assistance as one limited and pernicious aspect of hegemonial economic policies; Weintraub, on the other hand, while criticizing the way assistance has been handled, assumes that human rights efforts are supported by aid programs and that these programs are useful and worthwhile parts of American economic endeavor. Both essays, however, agree that current policy has not been consistent, regardless of its genesis or import, and that this inconsistency has weakened American efforts on behalf of human rights.

In international law, American efforts have been more tentative, although future possibilities are quite promising. For many years, Senate opposition to ratifying the international human rights treaties was quite strong; therefore, even though the United States had played an active part in drafting these treaties in the United Nations, it has not been able to participate in many of the mechanisms that monitor human rights compliance around the world. Four of these treaties were signed by President Carter, and an earlier one by President Truman; they all now await Senate ratification. Among the most important of these documents is the American Convention on Human Rights, promulgated by the Organization of American States. Were the United States to ratify this document, its diplomacy on human rights in Latin America, both bilaterally and in the OAS, could change markedly. Barton looks at the role of this treaty in American diplomacy in this hemisphere and analyzes the likely effects of ratification. Equally important, he examines the ways in which this ratification could change diplomacy on human rights from an executive-dominated activity to a parliamentary one.

No volume of this size and scope can treat every issue on the human rights agenda comprehensively. Indeed, the essays in this volume raise far more problems—of policy, method, and substance—that they can answer. This is a quest rooted in optimism. Only by articulating hard questions in new ways, and by offering different perspectives from which to address these questions, can new debate be stimulated in fruitful and practical directions. The problems of political policy, social control, and ethics are among the most durable any modern society must confront. It is as part of an effort to propel these debates into the next decade that this collecton of essays is devoted.

NOTES

1. The American Convention on Human Rights, which sets forth standards of human rights observance for members of the Organization of American States, has entered into force. Moreover, the Inter-American Human Rights Commission is now operating and has conducted on-site investigations in a number of countries. In 1979 the Inter-American Court of Human Rights, based in San José, Costa Rica, was also established. It is affiliated with a new Institute for Human Rights.

2. In 1979 the 16th Annual Conference of the Organization of African Unity adopted a resolution calling for the establishment of an African charter on human rights and a permanent body to protect those rights. Similarly, the Union of Arab Jurists recommended at their most recent symposium that the Arab states establish a regional human rights treaty.

3. The second follow-up meeting to the Conference on Security and Cooperation in Europe (CSCE) is planned for late 1980; it is scheduled to discuss further machinery for implementing the human rights protections included in the CSCE Final Act.

4. U.S. laws on human rights can most easily be found in volumes issued annually by the Government Printing Office entitled *Legislation on Foreign Relations*. Congressional hearings on proposed legislation usually includes commentary on these provisions. For collections of international documents on human rights, see Ian Brownlie, ed., *Basic Documents on Human Rights* (Oxford: Clarendon Press, 1971), and Louis B. Sohn and Thomas Buergenthal, *International Protection of Human Rights* (Indianapolis: Bobbs-Merrill, 1973).

Among recent collections of essays and new volumes of issue analysis are:

A. I. Melden, *Rights and Persons* (Berkeley: University of California Press, 1977); Charles Fried, *Right and Wrong* (Cambridge: Harvard University Press, 1978); Henry Shue, Basic Rights: *A Philosophical Perspective on Some Foreign Policy Choices* (manuscript); Fouad Ajami, *Human Rights and World Order Politics* (WOMP Paper #4, 1978); P. G. Brown and D. Maclean, eds., *Human Rights and U.S. Foreign Policy: Principles and Applications* (Lexington: Lexington Books, 1979); D. P. Kommers and G. D. Loescher, eds., *Human Rights and American Foreign Policy* (Notre Dame: University of Notre Dame Press, 1979); B. M. Rubin and E. P. Spiro, eds., *Human*

Rights and U.S. Foreign Policy (Boulder: Westview Press, 1979); Abdul Aziz Said, ed., *Human Rights and World Order* (New York: Transaction Books, 1978); Ronald Dworkin, *Taking Rights Seriously* (Cambridge: Harvard University Press, 1978); A. Pollis and P. Schwab, eds., *Human Rights: Cultural and Ideological Perspectives* (New York: Praeger, 1979).

SECTION I

Integrating human rights concerns into the daily assumptions and actions of international affairs requires that the relationships between individuals, societies, and governments be constantly clarified and reinterpreted. The status of the individual as citizen, both as social member and as the subject of international discourse and debate is a complex and variable one; the assumptions that govern the attitudes of international organizations, national governments, and both private and public international actors change accordingly.

In this section, Dankwart Rustow tries to draw out one level of current discussion of these issues by exploring the ways in which we think of "citizens" as part of the process of economic development and social modernization. He examines the delicate dialectic between man *qua* man and man as citizen in the context of the changing functions of social groups and government in the developing world. The kinds of rights we "attach" to different conceptions of citizenship are difficult to distinguish and become even harder to conceptualize if the conception of human rights as absolute values remains a constant of international organization. Richard Falk takes this discussion one step further and investigates the assumptions that ground different views of international organization (and their concomitant perspectives about individuals and their rights). Taken together, an intriguing equilibrium develops between two pictures of the international arena: one from the standpoint of the person, the other from the standpoint of his or her surroundings. In the midst of this evolving set of understandings,

17

Tracy Strong offers an analysis of the ways in which the role of the United States has been interpreted by those who have been responsible for articulating its foreign policy during the last two centuries. This provides one more level of analysis—an image, self-conceived, of this nation pursuing its own interests, at least in part in the name of the interests of others.

Chapter 2

MAN OR CITIZEN? GLOBAL MODERNIZATION AND HUMAN RIGHTS

DANKWART A. RUSTOW

For some decades, diplomats at the United Nations and other international forums have sought to codify human rights. And for some years policymakers in Washington have sought to make the promotion of human rights a major purpose in the conduct of our foreign relations. Such efforts have run into two major controversies, one centering on the very definition of human rights, the other on the method of their global application.

Is there not something parochial about any notion of human rights based on the first ten amendments of the U.S. Constitution and the voluminous body of legislation and jurisprudence derived from them? Does not the attempt to introduce such notions into international documents and to impose them on peoples of other historical traditions smack of political arrogance and cultural imperialism? Must we not, from the very start, distinguish between particular rights as they have evolved in our own national history and more general rights that might be equally cherished and respected by Cambodians, Zambians, and Paraguayans as well as by Americans, Englishmen, or Norwegians? Specifically, should we not differentiate between basic human rights, such as immunity from torture, which are, or should be, global; political rights, such as that of freely choosing among competing candidates, which may vary

19

with the type of a country's regime; and economic rights, such as to employment, minimum income, or food, which may vary with the degree of a country's economic development? Such have been some of the more troublesome questions of definition and principle.

Once human rights are introduced into the workaday conduct of congressional or presidential policy—as in the Jackson amendment or in Jimmy Carter's first year in Washington—other, equally contentious questions arise. How high a priority should we assign to human rights, however defined, as compared with arms reduction, global defense commitments, or promotion of foreign trade? Should we boycott coffee imports from Idi Amin's Uganda, withdraw our naval forces from Ferdinand Marcos's Philippines, deny American oil-drilling equipment to the Soviets unless they release Anatoly Shcharansky or Dr. Semyon Gluzman, break off all relations with the shah's (or Ayatollah Khomeini's) Iran, or forbid Americans to invest in or to trade with South Africa? If we apply no sanctions whatever, will our policy not remain empty rhetoric? If we apply them selectively—say, against Chile but not the Philippines, against Uganda but not South Africa, against Russia but not China—will we not stand accused of hypocrisy? Or if we apply them fully to all governments that trample on their citizens' rights, will we not soon be retreating into a sanctimonious, ineffectual, and self-defeating isolation? Meanwhile, since denial of foreign aid and of trade are among the most potent weapons in our human rights arsenal, is our pressure not likely to weigh most heavily on our friends and clients rather than on our antagonists? As Henry Kissinger said recently—no doubt with partisan exaggeration—to make human rights "a vocal objective of our foreign policy involves great dangers: You run the risk of either showing your impotence or producing revolutions in friendly countries, or both."[1]

This essay, rather than answering such questions of principle and of application, will seek to suggest three perspectives from which they may be more rationally and coherently considered. The first of these perspectives derives from the eighteenth-century distinction between the rights of man and the rights of the citizen; the second from the recent and contemporary process of worldwide economic and social modernization; and the third from the future possibility of a global government of mankind.

HUMAN RIGHTS: MAN VS. CITIZEN?

The most revolutionary document of the great French Revolution was the Declaration of the Rights of Man and the Citizen. The two sets of rights, human and civic, were combined into a single document; yet the distinction between them was clear to anyone whose political beliefs had been derived—as had been those of Mirabeau, Robespierre, Jefferson, Franklin, and their contemporaries—from the postulate of a social contract. It was obvious to thinkers of the seventeenth and eighteenth centuries that men had certain rights by virtue of their mere existence as human beings; hence these basic rights were theirs even in the state of nature. But in the natural, presocial, and pregovernmental state these rights were at best precarious, and at worst their enjoyment was illusory. In Hobbe's state of nature (admittedly an extreme version) natural man could assert his most basic right to life only by killing others before he himself was killed.

To overcome the inconveniences and lurking dangers of this natural state, men band together in societies. In doing so they give up certain rights, such as that of retaliation, and acquire certain new ones, such as that of participation in the community's decisions—all for the sake of preserving more effectively the most important of the original natural rights, such as "life, liberty, and the pursuit of happiness." These were the basic, or "unalienable," human rights, and it was in order "to secure these rights" that governments were formed. When governments began grossly to violate this constitutive purpose of theirs, it was time to overthrow them and replace them with more serviceable ones.

Yet as long as governments remained true to their mission, and all the more when they had been freshly restored to it, there could be no basic conflict between the rights of the citizen of a particular country and the natural rights of humanity at large. The very proclamation of human and civic rights in Philadelphia in 1776 and in Paris in 1789 was taken to enhance the liberties not only of Americans or Frenchmen but potentially of all other peoples as well. To be sure, the method of enhancement adopted on either side of the Atlantic turned out to be almost exactly opposite. For about a century after its formation, the American republic steered clear of political entanglements overseas but freely welcomed to its shores millions who felt politically or economically oppressed (particularly if such oppression happened to take place in Great Britain, Ireland, Scandinavia, or Germany). In short, America expanded the liberty of others through the import of population. The more impetuous French, in an intense effort over a quarter century, tried to make an even more ambitious contribution through the export of armies, political ideology, and forms of government.

The universalist, expansionist mission already was implicit in the 1789 declaration. "The nation is . . . the source of all sovereignty." "The law is an expression of the common will. All citizens have a right to concur, either personally or by their representation, in its formation" (arts. 3, 5). One of man's basic human rights, that is to say, was to live in a nation-state with a representative form of government. The revolutionary implications of such statements were readily obvious to all contemporaries—the monarchs of Prussia, Austria, and Sweden, and the oligarchs of Britain and Venice, who feared for their privileges and organized military coalitions to snuff out the French revolutionary spark; and to the French and their leaders who carried their military campaigns as far as Cairo, Malaga, and Moscow and reorganized political regimes from Rome and Ragusa to Hamburg and the Hague.

In the twentieth century, declarations of rights are penned no longer by revolutionaries engaged at the peril of their lives in the overthrow of established governments but rather by the diplomatic emissaries of those very governmental establishments. Yet diplomatic rhetoric harks back to the two central themes of 1789—the rights of man and the rights of the citizen.

Thus, the Universal Declaration of Human Rights, adopted unanimously in 1948 by the United Nations General Assembly against only 8 abstentions, reiterated a lengthy catalogue of rights: not only freedom of thought, expression, and association (arts. 18–20) but also everyone's "right to take part in the government of his country, directly or through freely chosen representatives" (art. 21). The right to fair treatment under the legal system is considerably elaborated, and a detailed list of social and economic rights is added ("social security," "right to work," "standard of living," "health," "education" [arts. 22–27]). And where the 1789 declaration merely implied that all human beings had the right to be citizens of representative nation-states, that of 1948 asserts with explicit sweep that "Everyone is entitled to a social and international order in which the rights and freedoms set forth in this Declaration can be fully realized" (art. 28). One may legitimately ask how many of the governments that have adhered to the Universal Declaration since 1948 consist themselves of the "freely chosen representatives" of their people or endeavor to create conditions in which the enumerated rights and freedoms "can be fully realized." If there were even half as much fervor or military support behind this declaration as there was behind that of 1789, governments these days would be toppling from Transvaal to Siberia and from Patagonia to Polynesia.

The vast majority of the 150-odd states currently recognized as independent and represented in the United Nations are military dictatorships, party oligarchies, or personal autocracies. Fewer than a third have governments based on free elections, and fewer than half have legal systems that would meet the minimal standards of the common law or square with the notions of a *Rechtsstaat*. Thus, it is perhaps not surprising that various documents intended to provide for specific implementation of the Universal Declaration have attracted less and less support. The 1948 Genocide Convention three decades later had been adopted by 82 states and the 1966 International Convention on the Elimination of All Forms of Racial Discrimination by as many as 94. But three other documents of 1966—the International Covenant on Economic, Social, and

Cultural Rights; the International Covenant on Civil and Political Rights; and the Optional Protocol to the latter—have been endorsed by only 46, 44, and 16 member states of the UN respectively.[2]

The difficulties encountered by these sweeping mid-century declarations have encouraged a tendency to draw up shorter catalogues of rights and in that process to draw a distinction between the rights of man, to which representative democracies, communist oligarchies, and assorted tyrannies can or might commit themselves; and the rights of the citizen, which would be variously defined under each type of political system and rejected outright by some.

The Helsinki agreement is a prime example of this recent tendency, and the willingness of the Soviet and other East European governments to sign the Helsinki documents indicates the short-run tactical advantage of the novel distinction between the rights of man and the rights of the citizen. But how sound is the distinction in logic, and how tenable will it prove in the long run? Is a human being's right to freedom of opinion, to free movement and emigration, to peaceful petition, and to security from torture in the end any less subversive of dictatorship and tyranny than would be the citizen's right to print an uncensored newspaper, to be safe from arbitrary arrest, or to join with fellow citizens in choosing his rulers from among competing political parties? Conversely, without a modicum of free press and free opposition, how could torture, deportation, and arbitrary killing become known—let alone be denounced or prevented? In sum, are the more hopeful and extreme supporters of the human rights campaign in the West, and its more fearful critics in the East, correct in seeing it as the thin end of the wedge of subversion? Or can some subtler distinction between the rights of man and the rights of the citizen exorcise such dangers of political interference?

More moderate human rights supporters in the West, of course, would reject the aim of a complete change of regime in countries like the Soviet Union as wrong, dangerous, or utopian; instead they would try to develop a human rights policy that would merely soften some of the harsher aspects of the present regime. Whatever the aim, a choice of means also must be made. Are we to promote human rights by specific pressure (such as diplomatic, e.g., no recognition of post-1945 frontiers without acknowledgment of human rights; or economic, e.g., no advanced technology exports while Soviet dissidents are being persecuted)? Or must we ultimately appeal to the consciences of the Soviet and other leaders—to their commitment, or at least their recurrent lip service, to the humanitarian and libertarian elements in Marxism? And to be effective in such appeals, must we not examine our own consciences and our own performance in such matters as racial equality or economic security for all citizens?

This, in turn, raises questions of even more fundamental principle. Once the appeal is to the forum of conscience, does not the ultimate goal become the building of a global human community with its own slowly evolving social, legal, and political institutions? When we speak of human rights today, must we not try to overcome the recent distinction by thinking once again of human rights as the rights both of man *and* of the citizen? And where, except under a global human government with universal citizenship, can the rights of man and the rights of the citizen ever be fully integrated? In sum, should we not look upon all the recent international human rights documents as so many preliminary drafts of a bill of rights for the citizens of a future world state?

MODERNIZATION AND HUMAN RIGHTS

"Modernization," I have proposed elsewhere, may be defined as "widening control over nature through closer cooperation among men."[3]

For the human individual, modernization means wider physical mobility, a richer choice of consumer goods and cultural styles, more access to information, greatly enhanced opportunities for self-assertion—in sum, a vastly increased right to self-expression. In his relations with others it implies a tighter web of association, more intensive communication, greater dependence on them for both the necessities and the amenities of life, more expectations placed on others, more reliance on their predictability, and more opportunities for emulation and envy—in sum, more claims on one's fellow man, more asserted rights to specified treatment from others.

Modernization also opens up vast new opportunities for group action—and this quite regardless of whether the groups are based on voluntary association (such as corporations, parties, pressure groups, or trade unions) or on premodern tradition (such as religious hierarchies, ethnic groups, or tribes).

Political parties can organize in support of political programs and candidates for office; trade unions can fight for higher wages and shorter hours; localities can protest against the encroachment of central government. But this collective assertion of rights implies two sorts of dangers. The first is that the rights of outsiders will be disregarded or destroyed: a newspaper strike may be a good way of asserting the pressmen's presumed right to secure employment, but it deprives millions of readers of the right to be informed of the news; Basque separatism and Irish nationalism are making life nasty, brutish, and short for residents of Bilbao and Belfast. Second, even in relation to its own membership, organization is a two-edged sword. This paradox was noted sixty years ago by Robert Michels, who suggested that "organization is the weapon of the weak in their struggle with the strong"—in a book subtitled *The Oligarchic Tendencies of Modern Democracy.*[4] The weaker the workers in modern industrial society, the more they stand in need of hierarchical organization to assert their democratic rights; yet the more hierarchical the organization, the weaker the individual worker vis-à-vis the party or trade union leaders and the greater the temptation of the leaders to set aside the interests of their followers. Organization thus magnifies the conflict over the rights of individuals; it also creates a new potential arena of conflict between the organization and its individual members.

The greater scope for individual choice and variety paradoxically means, for society as a whole, a greater need for uniformity. The wider the variety of goods to be offered to the consumer, the greater the need for standardized production. The shift from written manuscripts to printed books, and from individual tutoring to universal schooling, makes necessary the standardization of vocabulary, grammar, and spelling. Even a relatively passive government in modern society will have to formulate a larger number of rules to regulate the more complex interaction of its citizenry. The rulers' ideal may be that of the night watchman (the *Nachtwächterstaat*), but there are so many more things to be watched at night! A more active political system faces many more opportunities for enhancing and repressing its citizens—or enhancing some and repressing others. Universal schooling, centralized taxation, and conscription are among the characteristic devices of modern administration, and they open up vast opportunities for influencing the minds of the young, for directing the economy, for regimenting the citizen-soldier, and for encroaching brutally on the collective rights of citizens of foreign countries.

There are at least three types of group conflicts in modern society. One type of conflict concerns social and economic equality among the classes and regions: the division of the national product, the comparative rate of development, access to education and careers, the allocation of government benefits. Such conflicts tend to become sharper in the early phases of modernization, as the rapid growth of industry pits entrepreneur against laborer or widens the economic gap between, say, São Paolo and the Nordeste, or Milan and Calabria. After this first phase, the further course of events no longer conforms to the Marxist projection of economic class conflict tearing apart industrial society and plunging it into violent revolution. This is partly because the proletarian threat of revolution acts as a self-disconfirming prophecy: social reform is hastened by conservatives such as Disraeli, Napoleon III, and Bismarck so as to prevent a repetition of the 1848 revolution or the Paris Commune. But partly, too, conflicts of allocation are intrinsically more easily solved than the second major type of conflict. Allocation is, after all, a quantitative matter. In any dispute over economic policy or social expenditure the contestants can always split the difference. In an expanding economy, the issue can even be postponed, attenuated, or evaded by converting the zero-sum game into a positive-sum game, or by giving each contestant a larger slice without having to redivide the pie.

Not so with the second type of issue which might be called issues of emotional community or group identity: religion, language, ethnicity, tribalism. These issues, contrary to a widespread liberal opinion, do not disappear in the course of modernization, and those issues that linger tend to become less tractable with time. Modern communication, I suggested, increases the need for predictability and reliability. As more people talk to each other, it becomes more important that they be able to understand each other in both the plain and the figurative sense. This makes for a major redrawing of the lines of community. In traditional society (e.g., medieval Europe or British India), the educated upper class speaks a single language (Latin, English) across the (sub-) continent; the peasantry, a series of dialects, many of which shade off into each other continuously. With the advent of modernity neither the language gap between elite and mass nor the shadings of dialects can be easily continued; and since the educated elite has more mental flexibility, the solution is not for the peasantry to learn Latin but for the Dantes, Luthers, Chaucers, and Shakespeares to develop a richer and homogeneous literary language out of the peasant vernaculars. But the new common language that unites the dialects of Germany also sets the new German language off more sharply from Danish and Dutch; similarly, the literary language of Florence, Naples, and Milan is tightly unified (more or less) at the cost of breaking up the earlier looser unity of Romance vernaculars into distinct languages of Italian, French, and Spanish. A parallel progress occurs with the expansion of modern schooling: while everyone is illiterate it matters little in what language they do *not* read or write. The eagerness of the Committee of Union and Programs after the Ottoman Revolution of 1908 to provide schooling throughout the towns of the empire hastened the secession of Albania: the lawmakers of Istanbul assumed that the language of education for all Ottoman Muslims would be Turkish; the Albanians insisted on having the curriculum in their own language.

The prevailing nationalist historiography stresses the unifying tendency of nationalism, but its divisive tendency is even more obvious. As Deutsch has calculated, the number of linguistic or ethnic groups in Europe on behalf of which some nationalist claims have been put forward went up at an exponential rate from generation to generation from the late eighteenth to the mid-twentieth century. Regional differences of economic development—the relative backwardness of Brittany and the relative advancement of the Basque region and Catalonia—can help accentuate latent linguistic differences and conflicts, and much the same goes for regional economic differences between, say, Catholic and Protestant regions of the same country (Netherlands, Switzerland, Germany). Lipset and Rokkan have rightly identified the denominational divisions of the sixteenth century as one of the major formative factors in the party divisions of Europe three and four centuries later.[5]

The difficulty with this second type of issue is that you can never split the difference. The best you can get is a pluralistic compromise, or standoff, whereby some schoolchildren are taught Flemish and some French, or some are brought up according to the precepts of Voltaire, some of Aquinas, and some of Calvin. But all too often the issue is stated in exclusive terms; unless the use of French is imposed on all residents of Montreal the English military conquest of Quebec of 1759–60 will be followed by the ultimate, linguistic conquest in our own day.

To the two categories of economic and of ethnic group conflict might be added a third category: conflict waged, and rights claimed, on behalf of human groups distinguished by their physical characteristics—men and women, adults and children, those with light and dark skin, and so forth. The struggle for equal rights here runs into what Erikson has described as the human tendency to elevate this or that subgroup into a "pseudospecies."[6] The first two conflicts mentioned are attenuated by the fact that biology draws together the sexes and that the passage of time transforms age differences, whereas social and economic divisions based on so-called race can persist indefinitely and sharpen over time.

TOWARD A GLOBAL COMMUNITY?

The revolution of modernization entered its most intense worldwide phase in the quarter century after World War II. American hegemony provided external security for most nations. An unprecedented lowering of tariff barriers among noncommunist economies made possible a far more intensive worldwide division of labor. Multinational corporations, escaping heavy taxes and high labor costs in the older industrial countries, spread their manufacturing to new locations such as Brazil, Hong Kong, South Korea, and Taiwan. The transition of about one hundred countries from colonial or semicolonial status to formal independence raised the political aspirations of their elites. Cheap and rapid air travel brought the upper classes of all countries into closer contact than ever. Cinema and television made audiences around the world vividly aware of each other's consumption habits.

The implications of this worldwide process have been quite analogous to those of the process of modernization as it occurred in single countries or in a continent such as Europe in the seventeenth to nineteenth centuries: more mutual contact, interdependence, uniformity; more self-assertion and heavier claims on others; more intense organization providing opportunities to assert the rights of some groups and trample those of others; advances in technology adding new instruments of destruction and repression as well as of protest. Above all a spreading awareness, however hesitant and painful, of the commonness of human problems. It is a process that may be expected to continue for centuries, and perhaps somehow in that process all of mankind will develop a consciousness of our common rights as men and as world citizens.

It is perhaps ironic that human rights has emerged as a major item on Washington's foreign policy agenda at a time when America's power to impose its political ideals throughout the world appears to be in decline. A generation ago there was little talk in Washington of universal human rights; yet our military occupation crucially contributed to establishing liberal democracy in West Germany and Japan, and our economic policy encouraged the move toward unification among Western European democracies—whose evident prosperity in turn encouraged dramatic moves toward liberalization and democratization in such former bastions of repression as Spain, Portugal, and Greece. Today, our painful and resounding failure in Vietnam has turned Americans against foreign military intervention, the rise of OPEC has challenged our economic position, and there are gnawing doubts whether we still are the foremost strategic power; yet this is the very time when the Jackson amendment, the IT & T and Lockheed investigations, and Carter's human rights campaign have aggressively proclaimed new worldwide standards of purity of conduct. It might be argued that at a time when our military power is under a shadow, ideology can become a potent auxiliary weapon. Even more plausibly it may be argued that the current phase of debate and persuasion are as essential an American contribution to the emerging world government of the future as was the earlier phase of military hegemony.

NOTES

1. Henry Kissinger in "The Politics of Human Rights," *Trialogue,* no. 19 (Fall 1978): 3.

2. The list of signatories is, however, by no means identical with that of representative regimes or governments abiding by the rule of law. The United States is conspicuous by not having ratified any of the five documents listed.

3. Dankwart A. Rustow, *A World of Nations* (Washington: The Brookings Institution, 1967), p. 3. I have touched on other themes in the above section in the following articles: "Tyranny, Tyranny, Who's Got the Tyranny?" *International Journal of Group Tensions* 4, no. 3 (September 1974): 313–20. "Language, Nations, and Nationhood," *Les États Multilingues,* ed. J. G. Savard and R. Vigneault (Quebec: Presses de l'Université Laval, 1975), pp. 43–59, and "Transitions to Democracy," *Comparative Politics* 2, no. 3 (April 1970): 337–63.

4. Robert Michels, *Political Parties,* trans. E. and C. Paul (New York: Dover, 1959), p. 21.

5. Seymour M. Lipset and Stein Rokkan, eds., *Party Systems and Voter Alignments* (New York: Free Press, 1967), pp. 37 ff.

6. Erik H. Erikson, *Gandhi's Truth* (New York: Norton, 1969), pp. 431 ff.

Chapter 3

TAKING THE RANK WITH WHAT IS OURS: AMERICAN POLITICAL THOUGHT, FOREIGN POLICY, AND QUESTIONS OF RIGHTS

TRACY B. STRONG*

Under our present Domination of British subjects we can neither be received nor heard abroad. The custom of all courts is against us, and will be untill, by an independence, we take rank with other nations.

—Thomas Paine, *Common Sense*

The land was ours before we were the land's.

—Robert Frost, "A Gift Outright"

In the seventeenth century, when "men of the commonwealth" tried to make sense out of the chaos left by the slow and continual disintegration of an earlier world, they found it necessary to legitimate new political institutions, not in tradition, nor on divine right, nor even on power, but in the action and will of individuals. A continuing and watchful exercise by

*I should like to thank my colleagues William Taubman and Pavel Machala for their help and note a special debt to N. Gordon Levin and Paula Newberg.

33

the will became the center and foundation of the new politics, the only protection against an ever threatening chaos and corruption. These new republican politics required from their participants a constant effort; eternal vigilance was indeed the price of legitimacy. Hence, as J. G. A. Pocock has reminded us in *The Machiavellian Moment,* the republican tradition found itself continually threatened by the passage of time.[1] The virtue, indeed the *virtú*, of the founders may be unquestionable, but if human action constituted the state and made its continuance possible, then the state was always in danger of suffering from the weakness of the will of those who might compose it in the generations following its Constitution. In 1838 the young Abraham Lincoln could already warn that the example of the American Revolutionaries "must fade, is fading, has faded, with the circumstances that produced it."[2] The republican tradition emphasized the necessity of an energetic watchfulness that only would continue to preserve men in a state of freedom.

The United States clearly inherits this tradition. Its first settlers feared that should they stray but one step from the task to which God had ordained them, they would become a laughingstock to the world and a sign of human corruption.[3] Later, the American government was founded by men who were convinced that it was given to them to make nature and society come together through well-formed governance. The American nation has traditionally defined a uniquely self-conscious role for itself in the world of nations.[4]

From the beginning, part of that consciousness has been a feeling of exceptionalism, a sense that America is a place unlike any other. On the face of it, this doctrine must appear peculiar. All nations are special to those who live in them; clearly, patriotism and citizenship are not particular to America. What does distinguish America is an attribute that, once it arises in the seventeenth century, we do not find elsewhere until the twentieth century.[5] Americans have always thought that their founding was special and central to being an American. Being special, they also assume that they have a unique role to play in the world. It is worth noting, for instance, that as late as 1950 so distinguished and liberal a historian as Samuel French Bemis simply took for granted the doctrine of "manifest destiny."[6]

It makes little difference whether or not such characteristics were "real." What is important is that those who governed the country (and not only those) believed themselves and their countrymen to be special. A man as conservative as Alexander Hamilton noted in the *Federalist Papers* that "it seemed to have been given to this people" to demonstrate to the world if it were possible for men rationally to control their common life.[7] Being "special" was and is an ideological category that sat (and sits) first and foremost in the minds and actions of American men and women, including policymakers. Richard Ullmann has argued that American exceptionalism is perhaps the most dominant factor in the formulation of America's relation to other nations. "Nowhere," he notes, "has the belief in uniqueness of American institutions had more important consequences."[8]

Americans are possessed by a double genealogy. In the constant and vigilant exercise of the constitutive will, they partake of the republican tradition with its emphasis on the importance of maintaining the integrity of a state. But contrary to other nations, Americans also think their own integrity and activity to be something special and of world historical importance. For an American, not to be who one is is then not only a failure of republican virtue; it is also a failure to meet a transhistorical standard.

I

With these considerations in mind, let me turn to questions of human rights. Central to my argument is the importance of the relation of the American sense of America to the question of rights. To investigate this problem, it is necessary first to examine the interaction between the republican tradition and notions of rights.

The very idea of a republic dictates that the state exist in order to insure to individuals that which they would not be assured were there no state. Its vision is that human beings possess particular attributes, which require the presence and activity of a state to be secure.[9] Locke, for instance, found central to human beings their capacity to mix their energy with nature and to possess the results of that activity. For Locke, the state exists primarily to protect what he calls "property." We tend to call these attributes "rights," by which we mean that they are essential to what we believe human beings to be. The logic of the republican argument is that human beings are not fully human if they live in circumstances in which they are unable to exercise these attributes. Thus, the Declaration of Independence simply asserts that humans "are endowed" with certain traits, meaning that they possess them by nature, and that it is therefore unnatural to deny or be denied them.

This line of reasoning must remind us of two things. First, the purpose of the state and its only justification is to enable men to live according to those attributes that define their being. When Hobbes writes in the introduction to his *Leviathan* that "by *art* is the great Leviathan created," he is preparing his argument that obligation and entitlement derive from the creations of human action, in this case from the state. Second, and more important for our purposes here, when we engage in talk about rights in this context we are discussing what Ronald Dworkin has recently called "a trump."[10] From the strictly republican point of view, rights are in principle the reason for the founding of the state; they cannot be negotiated or balanced. Since rights are central to the definition of man in the republican tradition, they may not be subject to cost-benefit analyses or the economics of policymaking. To override a claim of right—at least, of the fundamental rights on which the state is founded—would be to question the idea of the state altogether, for the state exists merely to make possible a human life characterized by such rights. Clearly, of course, what has counted as such fundamental rights has varied from time to time and from theorist to theorist. But even in the most restricted form of this view, perhaps that of Hobbes, we find that the state may not legitimately command a person to do anything that would assuredly lead to his death: such a command would contradict the whole purpose of the state, which was to insure individual security.

In this tradition, international politics are problematic. Whereas all individuals are to have a set of rights, exercising those rights is made possible only inside a state structure. In the absence of a state of nature, Hobbes had understood the commands of nature to carry an obligation only *in foro interno*, involving no necessary observance, since he though no structure of enforcement made them feasible. International politics was a realm in which even the "trump" of rights fell, like everything else, to prosaic calculations of self-interest and security. Accordingly, Hobbes saw the realm of international politics as a constant emblem and reminder of the state of war. This realm carried no possible obligation to act on the recognition that others possessed rights. Sufficient security so as rationally to compel the observance of the rights of others could be achieved only in a state; manifestly it could not exist between states. As Hobbes, Kant, and others noted, the observance of "rights" for reasons of self-interest is not a morally secured observation. It is one thing to pursue a policy centered on rights because it happens to accord with the self-interest of a state: such is the latter-day Machiavellianism of Edmund Burke, who implored that one not go to war for profitable wrong or unprofitable right. It is quite another thing to pursue a foreign policy that centers on rights as a matter of moral duty. It is impossible to argue against this view by raising questions about the "price"—such considerations are irrelevant.[11]

To a republic, international politics necessarily appears as a realm potentially dangerous to the virtue at home. In the century after Hobbes philosophers elaborated this theme with great logic and occasionally recognition of the argument's impotence. For Rousseau, international politics made impossible that acknowledgment of others which he saw as the foundation of moral relationships. Since in the international realm the moral interests constituitive of the state often manifest themselves as self-interest, failing world government there can be no general will between the states. Were there world government, there would be no states; but, then, there could be no world government. There is no escape from this vicious circle. For Rousseau, as for others, foreign policy threatens the moral structure of the state.[12] In his *Project for the Constitution of Corsica* and in his commentary on the writings of the abbé de

Saint-Pierre he argued that the only solution to dilemmas of international politics would be not to have any.[13]

In the seventeenth-century republican tradition, rights are central to the existence of the state. The realm of international politics can therefore be interpreted as one in which the rights of individuals in other countries are important but difficult to handle. Relations between states tend to be relations that involve the purposes for which states are set up, for instance, as in Hobbes, to provide security for its citizens. A republic could not, strictly speaking, engage in actions that were contrary to the reasons for which it was founded, something Bertrand de Jouvenel calls "the law of conservative exclusion."[14] More important, even if the rights in the name of which the state is founded are more extensive than those reserved by Hobbes, the *role* of the state remains the same. Its legitimacy is still insured only by making the performance of these rights possible for its people. Should the state fail to do this, then its whole raison d'être is defeated. Hobbes, in the end, provides the correct model for the liberal state in the international realm, for such a state, even if not as centrally concerned as was Hobbes with security, is still concerned with *securing*.

The politics of republicanism has pervaded philosophical discussions of rights during the last thirty years. H. L. A. Hart, in an important article, "Are There Any Natural Rights?"[15] divides rights into two categories: those that are "specific" and pertain to particular relations between people, and those that are "general," which are held independently of any particular relationship. Following a similar structure of reasoning, Gregory Vlastos distinguishes between rights of "merit," which one has because of a particular status of attainment, and those of "worth," which, presumably, one has simply by being a human being or a person.[16] He finds correspondingly different entitlements attached to each.

The logic in this kind of understanding is extremely important. It affects any policies a republican state might undertake concerning human rights. The analysis philosophers such as Hart or Vlastos undertake reserves to the state that role which

makes it possible to translate rights of "worth" into rights that
oblige performance. Should this be achieved, then failure to
observe these rights requires a moral justification. This, too,
the Declaration recognized, "that to secure these rights, governments are instituted among men."

Several arguments have tried to defeat these views. Robert
Paul Wolff, in his monograph *In Defense of Anarchism,* re-
places the notion of a concrete right with a procedural notion
of "autonomy." Other writers in this broad vein have argued
that the whole discussion of human *rights* is misleading and in
itself dangerous. A number of writers have argued that in moral
discourse we should dispense with the notion of moral *rights*
altogether and instead speak of "morality" per se.[17] Simone
Weil writes in *The Need for Roots* that the idea of a "right" has
"a commercial flavor, essentially evocative of legal claims and
arguments. Rights are always asserted in a tone of contention,
and when this tone is adopted, it must rely on force in the
background or it will be laughed at."[18] This argument tries to
avoid a realm of discourse fatally tied to the exercise of political power. Unfortunately, the argument is merely the obverse
of the very position it tries to confute: in part, it accepts the
Hobbesian view of rights as correct. It also accepts the realm
of politics as one that rests on fear and is the brute exercise of
power. No more than the republican understanding does it
allow us to deal with an interrelation of political and human
rights.

Thus far, both houses seem plagued. The debate seems to be
between an uneasy Hobbesian republican model and an anti-
statist anarchist approach. Both approaches suffer from the
same flaw, for the model of political practice of each approach
remains unexamined. In these matters the constitutive qualities
of the particular policy are extremely important. The Hobbesian model makes it appear unnecessary to be concerned in
international politics with the *nature* of the rights that the state
exists to enforce, since in relation to other states this state must
stand in terms of securing itself. The anarchist position likewise
restricts politics only to the affairs of state and rejects even that

as illegitimate. Neither is willing to see what difference in international politics the character of a particular regime might make for rights questions.

II

I am suggesting two conceptually related ideas. First, the mode of analysis characteristic of republicanism focuses on the fact of human action rather than on its content. It thus avoids considering what difference, if any, the particular rights that constitute the legitimacy of a given state may make for that state's foreign policy. (What difference does it make that it is America that institutes a foreign policy?) Second, the dominant school of interpretation of American foreign policy has tended unconsciously to share this republican bias. This view, which has shaped both policymakers and critics for several decades, tends to misconstrue the nature of American foreign policy; its recommendations are often irrelevant, misguided, or dangerous.

The republican separation of domestic and international politics in terms of their relation to rights is fundamental to an entire generation of analysts and policymakers.[19] Such thinkers have applied the republican model categorically. For them, it is a sort of policy "category mistake" for a particular country to be concerned with other than the terms of its "interest." "Interest," however, means simply a concatenation of security with the elements that happen to constitute a particular country. In the case of America, for example, "interest" means insuring that it remains possible to be (what it means to be) an American. Other countries have different configurations of security and self. The "realistic" point of view—and the deviations it identifies as characteristic of particular policies in the history of foreign policy—implies a view of international politics as a state of war.[20]

The realists were shaped for the most part (either directly or through their teachers) by the experience of Wilson and the League of Nations; their claim was that Americans tended to confuse policymaking appropriate to relations between nations with that appropriate to moral relations.[21] The *Urwerk* here is probably Kennan's seminal lectures on American foreign policy, which divides policymakers into idealistic and realistic camps.[22] The dichotomy was not accidental, since the strong arguments were clearly on the side of those who were "realists." The general analysis claims that although moral aims may be laudable, in the conduct of foreign affairs such aims are ultimately harmful to all. For Kennan and others, Woodrow Wilson is the prime example of those who fail to realize that even if individuals are at all capable of moral action, societies are inherently self-interested. These critics point to the chaos of the 1920s and the horrors of the 1930s and 1940s in Europe as good evidence of what Wilson might have avoided had he managed to think realistically about the issue of the League.[23] In the manly clichés of this realm of moral men and immoral societies, one had best bite the (real) bullet from the beginning and get one's hands dirty.

A new look at the American experience with the Treaty of Versailles is interesting and instructive, not only for what it tells us about the nature of Wilson's foreign policy, but also for what it tells us about American foreign policy generally and the problems that typical analyses of American foreign policymaking must face. It has been argued, for instance, that an idealist-isolationist argument is already present in the foundations of the American polity and that Wilson represents one of those two styles.[24] How should we evaluate this argument?[25]

The realist's approach misconstrues what the argument in 1919 was about. One keystone of Wilson's policy was of ancient vintage in American foreign policy: he opposed the system of alliances that he thought had characterized Europe and were responsible for the Great War. More important, it was also clear to Wilson that American commercial interests were affected by the Great War. In none of this, though, did he diverge from previous American practice. He proclaims in his war message of April 2, 1917, that "neutrality was no longer feasible or desirable where the peace of the world was involved."[26] In doing so, however, he was precisely following a policy that supposedly had its roots back in George Washington. He proclaimed that American interests abroad were (in 1917) affected by the entanglements in which Europeans were getting involved. He concluded that America, in order to preserve its independence from the rest of the world, must organize the European state system so that matters such as the Great War could no longer affect the cause and course of American commerce.[27] In the fifth annual message to Congress, in which he recommends the extension of the state of war to Austro-Hungary, he makes clear that the aim is to renew the possibility of "free economic intercourse which must inevitably spring out of the partnership of a real peace."[28]

Wilson did not think he was doing anything that differed radically from traditional American foreign policy. The aims were the same: he argued that certain changes in the world situation required different American tactics. Wilson's sense of how much Europe affected American interests may have been more extensive than was that of some. This, though, is a question of judgment, not radical innovation. His attempt to link policy with American traditions was a constant theme through his tour in defense of the League. In San Diego, on September 18, 1919, he said that America in "her make-up, in her purposes, in her principles is the biggest thing in the world and she must measure up to the measure of the world."[29] There are two important parts to that statement. The first is that America is an exceptional country and has certain particular characteristics that other countries do not possess. The second is that global circumstances put America in danger of not "measuring up" to its own standards. It is not America that has changed in its nature but rather the world. America, as part of that new world, must now support the League.

What are these traditions that require such action? The idea that its traditions demanded American involvement in certain overseas questions was not only Wilson's during the debate over the treaty. On March 7, 1900, his great opponent Henry Cabot Lodge had given a speech to the U.S. Senate in which he defended in clear terms American's moral right and obligation to intervene and retain control over the Philippines. He argued there that America's historical mission was an extension of the principle of self-determination, over as much of the world as possible. During the debate over the ratification of the treaty, he returned to this theme in his insisting that the United States neither had, nor *should have* sought or received advantage from the war.[30] In an even more telling vein, in 1899 Theodore Roosevelt defended American action in the Philippines as done with "sword girt on thigh, [to] preach peace, not from ignoble motives, nor from a fear of distrust of [our] own powers but from a deep sense of moral obligation."[31] For Roosevelt, expansion was a moral imperative created by the cause of peace and by being an American. For him there was no difference between westward expansion to the Pacific and the move to the Philippines. It was not just that America was justified by virtue of the fact that we brought self-government but that the Constitution of America required it. Defending himself against Bryan's accusation of imperialism, he pointed out that "there is not a particle of difference" between the cases of westward expansion and imperialist expansion.[32]

None of this reflects the idealist-isolationist dichotomy. Rather, these men argued that the moral community that is America entitles and requires the country to demand rights for others. We see this in recent history as well. Perhaps the most terrifying and problematic aspect of the Vietnam War was that policymakers really believed that they were responding to the morally legitimate aspirations of at least a large portion of the South Vietnamese as well as to their government.[33] In the earlier case, Roosevelt and Lodge both knew that the United States might profit from expansion into the Philippines, but they did not for that reason think themselves to be motivated by the desire for profit. Here Burke's maxim not to go "to war for a profitable wrong, nor for an unprofitable right" describes accurately the thoughts of American policymakers.

What, then, was the argument between Wilson and Lodge about? Some of their views were similar. They both believed that American foreign policy could be justified only by those principles that formed America and entitled Americans to require from each other acknowledgment of certain basic rights. The justification for its foreign policy came from the

American state, the structure that made possible the transformation of general rights into specific (American) ones.

Lodge and Wilson disagreed about the possibility that a particular policy might fulfill these objectives. Lodge proclaimed his antagonism to the Treaty of Versailles in a speech to the Senate on August 12, 1919, explicitly on the grounds that America would not be able to control the actions of the other nations with whom she would be associated.[34] Wilson, on the other hand, defended American policy on the grounds that without the League America would not be able to avoid being entangled in the thicket of intra-European politics. Wilson proclaimed to Congress on February 11, 1918:

> [America] entered this war because she was made a partner, *whether she would or not,* in the sufferings and indignities inflicted by the military masters of Germany against the peace and security of mankind. . . . *It has come about in the altered world in which we now find ourselves that justice and the rights of peoples affect the whole field of international dealing as much as access to raw materials and fair and equal conditions of trade.*[35]

For Wilson, the League of Nations was precisely the instrument that would enable America to remain in control of her destiny, her principles, and her interests. Even in the Fourteen Points, he was aware that free trade was centrally important to America and that threats posed by the modern state system were real. The quarrel was not really over principles but over policy. During the course of the debate anything that looked like an argument was invoked at one point or another, to the point of obscuring the issues involved; but in retrospect, there is little reason to conclude that we were witnessing a choice between isolationism and idealism.[36]

It seems wrong, then, to analyze this important and formative moment of American diplomacy as a quarrel between two deviations from the path of realism. Contrary to the Cassandran chorus of most foreign policy analysts, it would seem that under certain circumstances a policy concern with rights, to the point of intervention into the affairs of other countries, has not only seemed an imperative of American policy but has also been linked by all its protagonists to a tradition of American policymaking. Disagreements have been about whether circumstances entail such policy. (It is true that the historical matter has complexities other than those I bring out here. Root and Beveridge each had positions that differed from those described here, the most interesting being perhaps Root's belief that Wilson was not constitutionally empowered to negotiate for anything in Paris. However, the argument here provided the enduring touchstone for a particular view of American foreign policy.)

Generally, Americans have argued that America's existence as a nation entitled it to speak out and to act in the name of those principles upon which it was founded. The rhetorical structure of annual messages of the first several presidents suggests that we have secured for ourselves the domestic benefits of free and profitable intercourse. We also face certain problems outside our borders that affect this intercourse. To pursue the former occasionally requires intervening in the latter—this was, after all, the gist of the Monroe Doctrine. In this view, Wilson's policy appears as a historically necessary extension to Europe of the Monroe Doctrine's principles. In fact, Wilson virtually said this at several points.

There has always been a strong tendency in American foreign policy to recognize in others what America claimed for itself—an assumption that being an American could not stop at one's shores but required, in certain circumstances, that interests be extended to other parts of the world. This tendency seems also to characterize those other countries that see themselves as embodying a principle derived from conscious willed choice. It is hard to imagine that an Englishman would argue that that which makes him English should also be applicable to people in other lands, and even harder for a Frenchman to believe it. But it is noticeably not hard for the Soviet Union, a country as self-willed as ours, to claim the right to intervene on behalf of various movements and revolutionary groups on the grounds that they are pursuing the same rights the USSR was

constituted to embody. The relations between the two countries are shaped in great part by their respective inabilities to
confine their senses of rights to their own borders.

There is an important truth in the doctrine of American exceptionalism. It provides the basis for understanding of the
pattern or "style" of thinking that has generally governed the
conduct of American foreign policy.[37] Debates such as those
between Lodge and Wilson are not finally about the nature of
American foreign policy but rather about the necessity and
appropriateness of a particular policy at a particular time. It is
wrong to argue that "morality" and "rights" are simply covers
for self-interest. This view reflects the incorrect belief on the
part of "realists" (and their left-wing critics) that the world of
international politics is a world in which morality can have no
play at all. Since a republican state sees itself as securing rights,
the manner in which that state secures rights is particularly
important in understanding the formulation of its foreign policy.[38]

Now, clearly there is a difference between my standing with
a fellow citizen and with a citizen of another country. It is not
a radical difference, perhaps—I do not or should not treat him
as if he were not a human being—but I do not recognize in a
foreigner qualities that I have reason to expect in a compatriot.
The important understanding enforced upon us by the republican tradition is that foreign policy is made by states and that
states are, even if not in clear ways, different from individuals.
Hence, it is important to formulate the problem of human rights
in international politics in a manner that does not leave out the
fact that we are dealing with the realm of states. The problem
is not what rights *I* should recognize and demand for another
human being but *what* rights a particular state should recognize
and require outside its borders.[39] I have made this formulation
purposively vague: it leaves unanswered the question of
whether or not one state has the right to expect from another
state the same sorts of things an individual can expect from
another individual.

The problems raised here can be brought into focus by concentrating on the issues raised by Michael Walzer in *Just and*

Unjust Wars. [40] Walzer is concerned with possible justifications for active intervention in affairs internal to another country on the behalf of dissident groups or movements inside that country. This is and must be a casuistical enterprise. Its central problem is to determine what groups are morally entitled to be recognized. He recognizes that moral claims are made real and practiced in social groups and that it is to the exercise of rights that we must properly look in international politics. His central problem is to elaborate what constitutes a group or, as he sometimes says, a "real" group. I am not sure of his answer to this, or even if he has one. But even if he does it is still not clear to me from his analysis why a particular group should be entitled to make morally obligatory demands on another group. Walzer deals with this problem—it is the problem of relating foreign policy to questions of human rights—simply by asserting that the "rights of groups are those of individuals";[41] therefore, one state is bound to treat another in the same manner that two individuals do. The analysis has much to recommend it: it recognizes that the stuff of international politics is groups in which some authority is collectively recognized. However, it does not answer the objection that moral relations between groups need not be precisely those between individuals.[42] One cannot dismiss historical boundaries, as Walzer does, on the grounds that they are "accidents" and hence not entitled to moral standing. By way of analogy, I suppose that for Walzer it would not do to treat people in a *morally* different fashion simply because of the accident of their skin color. However, the *political* world is made up of such "accidents," and the accumulation of chance over time gives us history. Human beings are who they are because of such histories; if we are to retain the notion of states as at all significant (as we must in discussing international politics), then we have to accept the centrality of such "chance."

III

I have argued four points. First, republican thought distinguishes between the rights of a citizen and general human rights. In this view, the role of the state is to insure rights; therefore, the realm of international politics is often seen as a realm of minimal rights or the absence of rights. Second, this distinction is the root of an interpretation of American foreign policy that is often characterized as "realist," but both this interpretation and the liberal paradigm on which it draws err because they both turn our attention away from the nature of the particular regime. Third, American foreign policy*makers* typically have not quarreled over the style of American foreign policy but rather over whether or not particular policies furthered that style. Fourth, it is necessary to develop an analysis that retains both the importance of the nature of the particular regime and of the fact that foreign policy occurs between states. What difference does this make for the place of human rights in foreign policy? Questions of rights reveal some of the fundamental problems and prospects of American foreign policy by demonstrating a particular confusion that affects America's behavior in international affairs. The confusion derives not only from the fact that we are a republic but from the fact that the United States is unique in many ways.

The founding of America motivated a "style" of American foreign policy that is still strong today. There are characteristic structures of thinking that lead to specific kinds of American policies—structures that themselves reflect unique qualities about the United States. Seymour Martin Lipset's claim that America is the "first new nation" has a ring of truth. America is the first country since the Enlightenment to have been explicit about what it stands for and to have made adherence to those concepts the sole criterion for membership.[43] America is the country of those who ran away from the Old World because that world would no longer have or satisfy them. It was in the New World that those who left sought to justify their leaving: legitimacy could be established only by creating and preserving a willful community of men. And so the Declaration of Independence holds it to be *self-evident* that all men are created equal. When the rebels demanded the rights of Englishmen, they did not demand them *as* Englishmen but as abstract, general human beings. Burke's suggestion that the colonists were doing nothing but what all Englishmen should have the right to do was fundamentally incorrect.

The intelligence of the Declaration is presaged in the words of the earlier Puritan settlers. Their sense of responsibility for the act of founding is overwhelming. Winthrop, for instance, after proclaiming New England to be like a City on the Hill, proceeds to the warning that the "eyes of the world are on us" and that "if we fail in their enterprise . . ." we shall be made a byword to the whole world.[44] Men and women saw themselves consciously joining a particular country. The reciprocities and obligations of that country were not shaped by past experience; rather, America was the country in which "general" rights (rights of "worth," not merit) could be acknowledged. "Give me your tired, your poor,/Your huddled masses yearning to be free" begins the tablet under the arm of the Statue of Liberty: it is the tablet of American law.

Garry Wills has recently reminded us that the Declaration of Independence invokes principles of universality and natural inevitability that cut strongly against the notion that Americans simply saw themselves defending the rights of Englishmen. These rights had the self-evidence demanded of physics.[45] According to Wills, Americans thought that the demands they had made on themselves had been there from the beginning. However, he also misdirects our attention slightly. In his analysis of the Declaration, he concentrates on the nouns, adverbs, and adjectives—they become his chapter titles. The verbs are equally important—the truths are self-evident because "we hold" them to be so. The general characteristics of human beings appear as self-evident when we *hold* them to be so. The naturalness of the physical realm depends on the volition in the act of founding.

Wills points out correctly that the founders, especially Jefferson, derived their science from the Scottish Enlightenment. Thus, they thought the rights they were claiming existed in nature. What Wills does not point out is that Jefferson and others added to this a dimension, not present in the writings of Hutcheson, that these rights had to be made concrete in the practical volition of the act of founding. The "we" that is

America acquires its pose and definition only by virtue of the act of holding truths such that they are self-evident. As Chesterton remarks: "It is the idea of making a new nation out of literally any old nation that comes along. In a word, what is unique is not America, but Americanization . . . , the process is not internationalization. It would be truer to say that it is the nationalization of the internationalized."[46]

Being an American is thus a difficult and somewhat paradoxical enterprise. On the one hand, there can be no requirement for being an American other than that of being a person. Being a Frenchman has clearly not been a matter of choice; it almost always has been a matter of birth. Americans, on the other hand, were always people who originally had come from some other place. Their tenure in this country could be justified only if they either strove for or fulfilled whatever longing and desire had brought them here. There is an analogy here to the Christian church at the end of the era of classical culture. One was an Athenian by birth, not by election; it was a sign of the decay of politics in the later Roman Empire that it began to be possible to become a Roman.[47] The power and the legitimacy of the new church rested on the fact that, in a way that neither Rome nor Athens ever could be, its members had all consciously chosen to become Christians. The legitimacy of the church rested on volition, that of the empire on space and birth. Ultimately, it was an act of political genius to found a new community on the act of choice: this, at least, was something that all individuals possessed, no matter who they were. Thus, anyone could be a Christian. As to Americans today, there was a universal or general foundation open in principle to everyone.

Choosing cannot be enough, however, for the will is weak and inconstant. No matter what arguments Hobbes and Locke might advance, one is English by birth and tradition and not English because of their arguments. In early America personal identity and volition were identical for all white males. Because the will is weak and corruptible, such identity is fragile. It constantly requires demonstrations, reminders, and proofs: Americans even have had committees to tell them what is un-American and commissions to set goals for the country.

To act as an American is to presume a view of rights as universal and general; it requires constant and vigilant exercise of those rights. It is not enough simply to recognize general rights—one must also act on them. This indicates that the quality of being American is something that is constantly in question, especially so in relation to the question of human rights in other countries. Human rights, taken generally, are all that is necessary to be an American. If one is an American, it follows that one can remain indifferent to appeals that are premised upon claims of general rights only with difficulty; were one not to acknowledge, in some manner, that those demands were legitimate, then the definition of being an American would also be threatened. In some sense, being an American means that anyone has a potentially legitimate claim on you. Reciprocally, anyone is entitled, in some sense, to make demands on Americans and America, simply by being human.

This is the double bind that a foreign policy that consciously pursues human rights issues must present to America. To be American seems to demand that any appeal concerning human rights be legitimate. In a sense, there is no distinction between any person making such an appeal and the appeals of fellow citizens. Not to draw this distinction, however, threatens the actuality of the American state itself. Should such claims be the special province of fellow citizens? A country is that which has borders, a defined and defining space; citizens within a country confront each other face to face. But in America the very existence of borders implies that the universality of its founding principles—the source of American legitimacy—is necessarily limited. Hence, as long as there is anything that is not America, being an American is potentially threatened. This conflict was at work in Wilson's efforts and in the attempt to make the world "safe" for democracy. The imperial drives that have constantly characterized American history are not actually drives to empire, certainly not in the classical nineteenth-century or Leninist senses. They are simply necessary extensions of being American.

If a foreign policy is based on human rights, it is not radically different from foreign policies that have characterized most of

American diplomatic history.[48] Considerations of human rights, and related elements of American style, have made the country both a blessing and a danger to world peace in the last 150 years. (In his later writings, St. Augustine justifies the use of power to extend the realm of love;[49] it applies fairly easily to American foreign policy.)

Foreign policy is an anxious realm for Americans, but not because it is somehow tainted. Rather, it is because the principles on which America was founded seem to require that Americans pay attention to demands from abroad. But this is a dilemma. On the one hand, it is hard to deny the legitimacy of such demands; on the other hand, it is simply impossible to deal with them all. The resulting ambivalence shows up in the earliest American history.

Washington's Farewell Address is often cited as a warning to the country not to involve itself in foreign entanglements, at least not more than it already was.[50] And so it is; but the reasons for this policy are not isolationist. For Washington, the United States was a country that "recommends itself to all." In order to remain so, in order to preserve its exemplary quality, it must steer clear of alliances with European powers. It must retain the ability to "choose peace or war, as our interest, guided by justice, shall counsel."[51] The country must maintain control of its own destiny and exercise its own volition.[52] Significantly, Washington did not think "the love of liberty" sufficient to keep America strong. It was the union of the country under the new Constitution that would embody the revolutionary spirit in a manner less susceptible to weakening.[53] This does not mean that foreign policy is bad; it is not a call for isolationism.

When Washington warned against "alliances," he meant relations between states of the sort that existed between the various American states under the Articles of Confederation.[54] Under those Articles, there was no unity; each state was left free to exercise its own will while at the same time it was bound against its will to other states. For Washington and for the Federalists in general, this was an intolerable contradiction that could be resolved only by the "more perfect union" of the

Constitution. The message of the Farewell Address is this: since there could be no unity with the states of Europe, we must avoid the sorts of entanglements that lead to the weakness, contradiction, and chaos of a situation like that prevalent at home under the Articles.[55] This is the premise of an independent foreign policy.

This should hardly be surprising. The addresses of the subsequent presidents concern the relationship between domestic prosperity and the perils posed by the absence of right and order in the international politics. John Quincy Adams evidenced such ambivalence quite dramatically in relation to the question of human rights. As secretary of state during the troubles in South and Central America in the early 1820s, he wrote to Hugh Nelson on April 28, 1823:

It has been the maxim in the policy of these United States from the time their independence was achieved to keep themselves from the political systems and contentions of Europe. To this principle it is the purpose of the President to adhere: and in the war about to commence, the attitude to be assumed and maintained by the United States will be that of neutrality. But *the experience of our national history has already shown that, however sincerely this policy was adopted and however earnestly and perserveringly it was maintained, it yielded ultimately to a course of events* by which the vileness and injustice of European powers involved the immediate interests and brought into conflict the essential rights of our own country. Two of the principle causes of wars between the nations of Europe since our revolution have indeed been the same as those in which that originated—civil liberty and national independence. To these two principles and to the cause of those who contend for them, the people of the United States can never be indifferent.[56] (italics mine)

Adams continues his admonitions with a discussion of how important it is to hold to both these "great interests." His argument is essentially the same one Wilson made almost a century later. America must be ready to intervene abroad in the name of immediate interests and of principles that are its foundation. American interest and those principles are conceptually inseparable and do not permit Americans simply to ignore the rest of the world. In foreign policy, by and large, she never has.[57]

IV

American foreign policy carries with it an internal self-doubt. It cannot ignore certain international situations, especially those concerned with rights; to do so would be to call itself into question. Yet, it has been difficult for America to deal with these issues without trying implicitly to treat others as if they were, should be, or could be Americans. Such considerations would be almost touching had there not been so many unfortunate consequences in history. Americans do not naturally distinguish between themselves as a land and themselves as an idea. What are the consequences of this confusion?

At one point in our history the consequences may have seemed acceptable. Until World War I, the pragmatic consequences of American foreign policy were not noticeably different from those of the British Empire. The American version of the "white man's burden" was to rationalize a solution to its double bind by pretending that certain kinds of people were not assimilable.[58] The Philippines were to America what India was to England. Those conquered, or rather "freed," had to be made ready for the blessings of self-determination. Henry Cabot Lodge practically echoes John Stuart Mills's *Considerations on Representative Government:*

The form of government natural to the Asiatic has always been a despotism. It is perhaps possible for an extremely clever and superior people like the Japanese with their unsurpassed capacity of imitation, to adopt Western forms of government, but whether the underlying conceptions—which are the only solid foundations of free institutions—can exist under such circumstances is yet to be proved, and all human experience is against the theory. Some of the inhabitants of the Philippines, who have had the benefit of Christianity and a measure of education, will, I have no doubt, under our fostering care, and with peace and order, assume at once a degree of self-government and advance constantly, with our aid, towards a still larger exercise of that inestimable privilege, but to abandon those islands is to leave them to anarchy, to short-lived military dictatorships, to the struggle of factions and in a very brief time, to their seizure by some great western power who will not be at all desirous to train them in the principles of freedom, as we are, but who will take them because the world is no longer large enough to permit some of its most valuable portions to lie bare and ruined, the miserable result of foolish political experiments.[59]

This passage, astonishing in its directness, says several things. First, the inhabitants of the Philippines will not be able to control themselves until they become the sort of persons that Americans are: the idea of being an American is extended to those who, for purposes of foreign policy, are not yet fully human, and therefore do not really act like Americans. Second, unless Americans show the Philippines the way, they will surely fall prey to those dangers that beset the American republic in its very earliest days—"anarchy, the stuggle for power, the play of factions." Third, the racism in the passage is an attempt to make sense of the fact that history seemed to require that this American idea-ideal be extended to those for whom these rights do not exist "naturally." To have thought or admitted that the American regime was not potentially universalizable would have shaken the semantic foundations of the country. Therefore, Lodge was forced to develop a theory that allowed one to retain the possibility of extending American rights to all men, only with a historical delay. Paternalism thus becomes easily an artificial substitute for recognizing others. (One might even go so far as to extend this notion and ascribe some of Lodge's later anxieties about the Treaty to the fact that such paternalism was clearly impossible in relation to the nations of Europe.)

If one shifts from the turn of the century to a more contemporary period, the same dynamics in American foreign policy persist, but the rationalized "solution" that paternalism provided for Lodge is no longer available. The reasons for the demise of this kind of paternalism are complex but are clearly related to the gradual triumph and spread of democratic ideals, often through the vehicle of socialism.[60] This is a historical development that threatens the foundation of republicanism, for the dynamism of history appears to undercut the centrality of volition.

The dilemma of pursuing paternalism in a changed world goes some small way to explain part of the horror of Vietnam. There is a real descriptive truth in the claim that "we were trying to make it possible for the South Vietnamese to live in freedom." The problem in pursuing such a goal arises if the people of another nation appear "incapable" or "unwilling" to exercise their rights. It is a fact that John Kennedy gave up on the Laotians on the grounds that they "didn't care" and turned in 1962 to the South Vietnamese as a people who would care—that is, who would behave as Americans "should." If, however, against all urging, another people still "refuses" to exercise their rights, then, given the power at America's disposal, it becomes natural for it to attempt to exercise those rights for them. This is part of the calamity of American policy in Vietnam: that the pursuit of rights became a Frankenstein's monster that in turn destroyed not only Americans but many Indochinese. Thus, we "destroyed the village in order to save it." What was terrible about America in this situation is that it appeared to have almost enough power to make people "free" whether they wanted to be or not.[61]

I have argued that a foreign policy that is directed toward protecting and securing human rights is not new in American foreign policy; in fact, it is part of the very stuff that gives American foreign policy whatever special characteristics it has always had. Furthermore, the pursuit of human rights goals in foreign policy tends to place the policymaker in a contradiction between that which he is obliged to acknowledge as an American and that which is possible and desirable for a state. Finally, American foreign policy can be seen historically as a series of rationalizations of this same basic tendency. To this extent, the Monroe Doctrine, the Spanish-American War, the Exclusion Acts, the debate on the League, and Vietnam are all cathexes of the same drive.

These characteristics are both attractive and dangerous. They are attractive because they insist that politics is about human beings. To that extent, international politics is not a radical break from the issues that are central to the experience of domestic politics. They are dangerous because they point out that when America engages in foreign policy it is likely to try to attain hegemony or primacy while denying that this is really what it is pursuing. If we are pursuing universal human rights, then obviously our policy must be disinterested. (This refrain goes from Monroe to Wilson to Lyndon Johnson.) Such a pursuit, however, makes it difficult to think in terms of a global political system, and of some structure of world order. There does seem to be a danger that the pursuit of the best—that is, of human rights—will possibly become the enemy of the good—that is, the achievement of some just world order.[62]

It is necessary that American foreign policy resist the desire for primacy, explicit or implicit. If it does not, any policy that attaches itself to the question of human rights is potentially dangerous, for it is precisely "rights" thinking that has in the past led Americans to try and remake the world in their own image, often with dangerous consequences. It is, however, conceivable that a rights policy divorced from drives to primacy might provide an initial impetus toward a foreign policy that has as its serious aim a more just international order. One would, I think, want to say the following. American policy should not be oriented toward individuals in other countries but rather toward other states as guarantors of rights. It is, I think, wrong to deal primarily with individual Soviet Jews or South African blacks while ignoring the Soviet Union or South Africa as states. I am not saying that one should turn a blind eye to individuals, only that they should not be the focus of a policy. There is a kind of perverse realism in much of present foreign policy that seems too often to try to alleviate the condition of particular individuals rather than to promote policies that tend to produce changes in the social fabric of a particular society.

Clearly, there are no easy answers here. But this analysis tends to indicate that the sorts of changes that should be our aim need not be *directly* related to the securing of obvious rights. The Soviet Union is, for instance, going to do little or nothing about the lot of particular Jews inside its borders. Certainly it will exact all it can for each émigré victory we "win." But it is conceivable that the Soviet Union might be induced to a relaxation of internal restraints on dissent, or of privilege. More obviously, the amount of anxiety the South African government seems to expend on the question of divestment seems to me a strong reason to initiate a paced policy by which U.S. industries would be discouraged from investing in South Africa under present conditions. This in turn might produce a situation in which American business would insist on certain changes in South African labor law, for instance that no black (or white) working for an American firm would be required to live at a great distance from his family.

The logic behind such policies is the recognition that states have a role in the securing of rights and that international relations is in the end conducted by countries. I have indicated in this chapter that American foreign policy has often manifested an anxiety that international politics is a relation of states rather than of individuals. Somehow, the acknowledgment of peer states threatens our sense of being "special." Getting over a trauma that most easily characterizes the narcissism of early adolescence can only be desirable. Adulthood has its pangs but also its rewards. After all, the aim of American foreign policy should not be to make the whole world into America but only to work in the direction that no country be constituted by an attitude toward any human being that would make our own attitude "exceptional." A world in which we were not exceptional, especially in our own view, would reach a long way toward a world in which justice would be possible.

NOTES

1. J. G. A. Pocock, *The Machiavellian Moment* (Princeton, 1975), esp. chaps. 1–3.

2. Abraham Lincoln "Address before the Young Man's Lyceum of Springfield, Illinois," *Collected Works* (New Brunswick, N.J., 1953), vol. I, p. 115.

3. This is brought out most strikingly in the last page of John Winthrop's sermon, *A Modell of Christian Charitie,* preached on board the *Arabella* shortly before landing. See the discussion in Edmund Morgan, *The Puritan Dilemma* (Boston, 1958), pp. 67–89, as well as Wilson Carey McWilliams, *The Idea of Fraternity in America* (Berkeley and Los Angeles, 1973), pp. 140–45.

4. The classic text here is Louis Hartz, *The Liberal Tradition in America* (New York, 1955), but see also G. K. Chesterton, "What I Saw in America," *The Man Who Was Chesterton,* ed. R. Bond (New York, 1960), esp. pp. 132 ff. See also Zbigniew Brzezinski's speech of December 6, 1978. See *Department of State Bulletin* for that day.

5. I refer of course to the rise of socialist countries. See Arno Mayer, *Wilson and Lenin: The Political Origin of the New Diplomacy* (New Haven, 1963). Mayer fails to appreciate that what Wilson was doing was not new to Americans.

6. Samuel French Bemis, *A Diplomatic History of the United States* (New York, 1950), pp. 215–16.

7. Publius, *Federalist Papers* (Oxford, 1948), no. 1, p. 1. See also Norman Jacobson, "Political Science and Political Education," *American Political Science Review* (September 1963): 561–69.

8. Richard Ullman, "The Foreign World and Ourselves: Washington, Wilson and the Democrats' Dilemma," *Foreign Policy* 21, (Winter 1975–76): 100.

9. See Tracy B. Strong, "The Practical Unity of Public and Private," *Humanitas* (February 1975): 85–97.

10. Ronald Dworkin, *Taking Rights Seriously* (Cambridge, Mass., 1978), pp. xi and 190–97. See Mark Twain's short story, "Was It Heaven? Was It Hell?"

11. I am not saying here that one should not examine the consequences of a particular policy. I am saying, though, that one cannot think of "rights" as somehow quantitatively commensurable with a utilitarian calculus. Hence, the "price" is irrelevant. As an example of what I think in the end wrongheaded, see Sandra Vogelgesang, "What Price Principle: U.S. Policy on Human Rights," *Foreign Affairs* 66 no. 4, pp. 819–41, which tries to make sense out of Carter's policy in terms of "politics."

12. This mirror image, interestingly, is found in proclamations of men like W. W. Rostow, to the effect that the United States was simply not "up to" the sort of policy that was required to fight the war in Vietnam correctly. Likewise, it is significant that Kissinger insisted

that secret diplomacy was necessary—not to make the tasks of diplomats easier, but to make the supposedly amoral demands of foreign policy less evident to his (moral) country; Peter Davis (director), *Hearts and Minds.*

13. See here J. J. Rousseau, "Projet de constitution pour la Corse," *Oeuvres* (Paris, 1964), vol. 3, pp. 902–39, and "Polysynodie de l'abbé de Saint-Pierre," pp. 617–34; see also the incisive commentary by Stanley Hoffman, "Rousseau and Kant on War and Peace," *The State of War* (New York, 1965).

14. Bertrand de Jouvenel, *The Pure Theory of Politics* (New Haven, 1963), pp. 109–17.

15. H. L. A. Hart, "Are There Any Natural Rights?" *Philosophical Review* (April 1955): 175–91, esp. 183 ff. See also William Nelson, "Special Rights, General Rights, and Social Justice," *Philosophy and Public Affairs* (Summer 1974): 410–21, for a sympathetic commentary, and Dworkin, *Taking Rights Seriously,* for a more hostile one.

16. Gregory Vlastos, "Justice and Equality," in *Social Justice,* ed. R. Brandt (Englewood Cliffs, N.J., 1961). The move from equality is one, if not the, important part of these lines of reasoning, themselves derived originally from Hobbes. Various solutions and questions about these problems have in fact occupied a whole generation of Hobbes scholarship, reproduced for the most part in Maurice Cranston and R. J. Peters, *Hobbes and Rousseau* (New York, 1974). The problem is to effect a linkage between the "natural" condition of man and his legal state. Only this way can rights be secured nonpositivistically. The important modern text here is probably Kurt Baier, *The Moral Point of View* (Ithaca, 1957). I do not think, however, that Baier is able to give any convincing reasons for adopting the moral point of view. It is perhaps the rather vague idea of "the sorts of human beings we are" that appears at the end of his book that has impelled Bernard Williams to develop the notion of the "human point of view" in his "The Idea of Equality," *The Problems of the Self* (Cambridge: Cambridge University Press, 1973).

17. Although he does not develop the idea, Marshall Shulman has noted that this line of thinking requires an expanded notion of interests. See his "On Learning to Live with Authoritarian Regimes," *Foreign Affairs* (January 1977).

18. Simone Weil, *The Need for Roots* (New York: Octagon, 1952), p. 18. See Robert Young, "Dispensing with Moral Rights," *Political Theory* (February 1978), and Meirlys Owens, "The Notion of Human Rights: A Reconsideration," *American Philosophical Quarterly* 6 (1969): 240–46.

19. See here the analysis in David Little, *American Foreign Policy and Moral Rhetoric* (New York: Council on Religion and International Affairs, 1969), esp. pp. 7–28.

20. This view has been best elaborated in the various writings of Raymond Aron.

21. Little, *American Foreign Policy*, pp. 14–21.

22. George Kennan, *American Foreign Policy 1900–1950* (Chicago, 1951). The views of Hans Morgenthau, summarized in the four editions of *Politics Among Nations*, are perhaps equally important. All of these thinkers owe much to Reinhold Niebuhr, on whom see W. C. McWilliams, "Reinhold Niebuhr, New Orthodoxy for an Old Liberalism," *American Political Science Review* (December 1962): 874 ff.

23. Much of the material relevant to this discussion has been conveniently gathered in N. Gordon Levin, ed., *Woodrow Wilson and the Paris Peace Conference*, 2d ed. (Lexington, Mass.: Heath and Company, 1972), with commentary in his *Woodrow Wilson and World Politics: America's Response to War and Revolution* (New York, 1968). Though the position I advance here differs considerably on the conceptual level from Levin's, I should like to say here how much I have profited from his work and his knowledge. See here also Alexander and Juliette L. George, *Woodrow Wilson and Colonel House* (New York, 1956).

24. For example, and most famously, in Felix Gilbert, *To the Farewell Address* (Princeton, 1961). But see also James H. Hutson, "Intellectual Foundations of Early American Diplomacy," *Diplomatic History* (Winter 1977): 1–34.

25. See here, for instance, Walter Lippmann, *United States Foreign Policy: Shield of the Republic* (Atlantic-Little, Brown, 1943). See against this (incorrectly, I think) Robert Divine, *The Illusion of Neutrality* (Chicago, 1962), chap 1.

26. Woodrow Wilson, *The Public Papers of Woodrow Wilson*, ed. R. S. Baker and W. Dodd (New York, 1925), vol. VI, p. 381. Also cited in Divine, *Illusion of Neutrality*.

27. See here Levin, *Woodrow Wilson*, p. 3, fn.

28. Wilson, *Public Papers*, vol. V, p. 133.

29. Ibid., p. 289. See also Wilson, "Too Proud to Fight" (May 10, 1915), in ibid., vol. III, pp. 318 and 321.

30. Henry Cabot Lodge, *Congressional Record*, August 12, 1919, p. 3784. See also Ernest May, *American Imperialism* (New York, 1968), pp. 70 ff.

31. Theodore Roosevelt, *The Writings of Theodore Roosevelt*, ed. W. Harbaugh (Indianapolis, 1967), p. 31; see also pp. 34 and 37.

32. Ibid., p. 47; but see note 58, below.

33. One of the paradoxes, not often faced, of arguments that make reference to (truly) legitimate moral appeals is that the United States might have argued during the Vietnam War that it was intervening in South Vietnam to protect the many Buddhists who were being oppressed by the Catholic regime. I am not saying that we made such an argument; certainly the scale and quality of intervention must be

related to the purpose. But, as we shall see below, the problem with moral appeals is that no one ever intervenes for an immoral reason.

34. *Congressional Record,* August 12, 1919, p. 3780.

35. Wilson, *Public Papers,* vol. VI, pp. 474 and 476 (italics mine).

36. There is something important to Levin's notion of the "missionary" in Wilson and in American foreign policy in general; however, though it may explain parts of Wilson's personal style, I do not in the end think that it explains much about his foreign policy, which, I have argued, seems based on (reasonably) well thought out political and historical considerations. The Georges have, I am afraid, taught us to make too much of Presbyterianism.

37. On the idea of "style," see Stanley Hoffmann, *Gulliver's Troubles* (New York, 1969).

38. See Rupert Emerson, "The Fate of Human Rights in the Third World," *World Politics* (1974–75): 206.

39. See here the attempt made by Peter Berger, "Are Human Rights Universal?" *Commentary* (September 19–7), esp. p. 62. The failure to make the point about states underlies Noam Chomsky and Edward S. Herman, "The United States versus Human Rights in the Third World," *Monthly Review* (July–August 1977): 22–26.

40. I should note here that though in the end I disagree with Walzer, I have (once again) learned much in trying to figure out why. Michael Walzer, *Just and Unjust Wars* (Chicago, 1978).

41. Ibid., pp. 61–69.

42. It seems to me that the central achievement of a book like Mancur Olson, *The Logic of Collective Action* (Cambridge, Mass., 1965), is to have shown that the rationality appropriate to individual decision making is not the same as, nor in fact directly commensurable with, that appropriate to collectivities.

43. See Brzezinski, speech of December 6, 1978.

44. Winthrop, *A Modell of Christian Charitie.*

45. Garry Wills, *Inventing America: Jefferson's Declaration of Independence* (New York, 1978). Wills's thesis, though, is not as novel as he would have us believe. See, for instance, McWilliams, *The Idea of Fraternity,* chaps. 7 and 9.

46. Chesterton, "What I Saw in America."

47. I draw heavily here on Sheldon S. Wolin, *Politics and Vision* (Boston, 1961), chaps. 3 and 4.

48. The case of Kissinger is troubling here, partly because there is often a contradiction between the theory (or parts of the theory) and the practice (or parts of the practice). See the discussion in Stanley Hoffmann, *Primacy or World Order* (New York: McGraw Hill, 1978), pp. 33–100.

49. "It is wonderful," he writes, "how he who entered the service

of the gospel in the first instance under the compulsion of bodily punishment, afterwards laboured more in the gospel than all they who were called by the word only; and he who was compelled by the greater influence of fear to love, displayed that perfect love which casts out fear." *Letters* (New York, 1955), vol. IV, no. 185, pp. 163–64. Augustine, however, also worried about the character of the policymaker.

50. Cf. Ullman, "The Foreign World and Ourselves."

51. George Washington, "Farewell Address," in *Messages and Papers of the Presidents,* ed. James D. Richardson (Washington, 1908), vol. I, p. 222. In a telling phrase, this will unite "security with energy" (p. 217).

52. Cf. Hutson, "Intellectual Foundations," p. 9, for a partial exception.

53. Washington, "Farewell Address," p. 215.

54. Ibid., p. 217.

55. Ibid., p. 222.

56. John Quincy Adams, *The Writings of John Quincy Adams,* ed. W. C. Ford (New York, 1913–17), vol. VII, p. 370.

57. In a similar vein, James Monroe expressed the hope that the Greeks, then in revolt against the Turks, would succeed in their contest and called for a joint U.S. and British stand on behalf of the independence of all nations. He went on to enunciate the "Monroe Doctrine"; this was hardly an "isolationist" political climate in which to articulate such an idea. See Monroe on Richardson, *Messages and Papers of the Presidents,* vol. II, p. 218; see also p. 194.

58. See here Michael Rogin, *Fathers and Children: Andrew Jackson and the Subjugation of the American Indian* (New York, 1975). This book shows, I think, that in the end Roosevelt was wrong in his parallel between westward expansion and imperialism. The Indians were never thought of as true human beings.

59. Lodge, *Congressional Record,* March 7, 1900, pp. 2621–22; see also esp. pp. 2618, 2627, and 2629.

60. See here the book by S. N. Eisenstadt and Y. Amon, *Socialism and Tradition* (Atlantic Highlands, N.J.: Humanities Press, 1975).

61. There is another element here that must go unanalyzed in this paper. During the course of this century, in part in response to the increasingly wide involvement of the United States in foreign wars (and other affairs), the nature of the American state has altered. Simply put, the executive branch (what we tellingly call the "administration") has acquired both power and inertia that seem to make it unresponsive to circumstance or opinion in all but the most extreme cases. Thus, although the American state still operates on an imperative that dates back to the foundation, the structure in which that

imperative is made policy has changed. We face perhaps what Weber called a "polar night of icy darkness and hardness," with no Augustine to worry about the quality of statesmanship. Sheldon Wolin has sought to bring this to our attention in almost all of his writing since the last chapter of *Politics and Vision* (Boston, 1961).

62. This formulation owes much to Hoffmann, *Primacy or World Order*.

Chapter 4

THEORETICAL FOUNDATIONS OF
HUMAN RIGHTS

RICHARD A. FALK*

I

In most respects, national sovereignty at the state level is stronger than ever. Such a political reality restricts the potential scope for applying rules of international law to those subject matters where governments give their consent to be bound, and are prepared to implement their consent with a high degree of compliance. The protection of human rights is in a very special category. For various reasons associated with public opinion and pride, governments are quite ready to endorse (even formally) standards of human rights despite the absence of a will to comply with these standards. Occasionally, for internal political reasons, the reverse situation pertains, such that a government is unwilling to endorse in a formal manner standards of human rights that it routinely upholds; the United States, of course, with its federalist and isolationist barriers, is the prime national instance.

At the heart of the matter is the peculiar status of enforcement in international society. Given the absence of community enforcement capabilities, the system depends on voluntary patterns of compliance that rest, in turn, on perceived self-interest. Normally governments do not agree to norms unless, at least at the moment of their creation, compliance seems as

---

* Paula Newberg has given encouragement and perceptive advice to each of several versions, always with a graceful mixture of pressure and sympathy.

though it promotes the national interest. But human rights are different, at least for many governments. In this instance, some governments have an interest in subscribing to the norms even when there is absent any attention to comply; vice versa, some have an interest in avoiding subscribing even when their intention to comply is evident. In the former case, the absence of any *real* enforcement prospects makes it feasible to give lip service to human rights, whereas in the latter case the *theoretical* possibility of enforcement inhibits certain governments from regarding human rights as binding rules of international law.

Such a situation creates the temptation to adopt a cynical view of efforts to protect human rights, a view to some qualified extent justified. However, a more subtle appreciation of the relationship between norms of law and the behavior of states in international society suggests that the protection of human rights through their formulation as norms may achieve certain limited results. What needs to be understood is the tension between normative aspiration and political constraint in relation to the protection of human rights.

To depict this tension requires an image of the overall system of world order, defined here as the main patterns and principles by which sovereign states and other actors interact with one another. One dimension of world order consists of a series of competing normative logics, each of which purports to provide an independent basis for structuring behavior in prescribed directions. A normative logic refers to a set of propositions about what ought to happen with respect to the relations among the basic actors in the world political system. In a sense, each normative logic can be thought of as an independent line of ethical or legal argument about how to relate values or societal goals to behavior, given the reality of sovereign states.

These several competing ordering logics are of greatly unequal political weight. Each logic generates a distinctive normative approach. The assessment of these distinct logics determines the relationship of human rights to the world legal order at a given period in international history. To think of human rights in the world as a whole, as distinct from some particular transgression (e.g., treatment of Indians, slavery, genocide), is a recent phenomenon and, to date, partly an American preoccupation and partly a consequence of the greater prominence achieved by human rights organizations that consider the world as a whole their proper domain of concern. Such a global focus is itself a reflection of the emergence, however weakly, of a planetary perspective based on the notion that persons, not just juristic entities like states, warrant our normative attention.

Initially we will describe these ordering logics highlighting their distinctive relevance to human rights concerns. In Section II their relative weight will be considered, as well as the "ordering mix" pertinent for human rights. It should be emphasized that the protection of human rights is dependent on the interplay of normative standards and social forces committed to their implementation. Pressure to violate human rights also reflects social forces, especially as these take shape within governmental bureaucracies at the state level. In essence, then, the protection of human rights is an outcome of struggle between opposed social forces and cannot be understood primarily as an exercise in law- creation or rational persuasion. Similarly, the ordering logics specified below are arenas of struggle as well as foundations of authority.

A. STATIST LOGIC

The predominant ordering logic since the Peace of Westphalia has been the territorial sovereign state. The government of a state has been its exclusive agent with respect to external relations. The juridical framework of relations worked out in the West has been gradually generalized to apply throughout the globe. The mainstream of international law has evolved out of the predominance of the state and of the states system. Notions of rights evolved within the context of domestic political struggles. However, from Greek, Stoic, and Christian roots came ideas of human governance associated with relations between rulers and ruled anywhere. While medieval ideas of Christian unity and natural law were alive, theorists of the emergent states system were ambivalent about such critical issues as rights of resistance, tyrannicide, and humanitarian intervention. That is, the prerogatives of the state were balanced against notions of "higher law."

Jean Bodin, writing in the sixteenth century, set forth the decisive argument in favor of centralized, secular authority, prefiguring the actual emergence of strong governments enjoying the realities of sovereign control over domestic society. The Swiss eighteenth-century jurist, Vattel, extended Bodin's views of sovereignty to the external relations of states, providing an application of statist logic to the conduct of interstate or international relations accepted as authoritative virtually until the present time. He separated natural law from positive law, placing emphasis on the requirement of governmental consent as critical to the formulation of international law obligations. Also, Vattel underscored the importance of accepting a government's own interpretation of its obligations, especially in relation to its own citizenry or to those present within its territory. External actors had no standing to complain in the absence of very specific agreements affording protection to aliens.

That is, human rights were not a fit subject for global concern unless a particular government so agreed. The positivist idea of sovereignty shielded abuses of rights committed within state territory. Some tension arose from the status of aliens abused by the territorial government, especially when the abuse was committed outside the European center of the world political system. Thus, "capitulatory regimes" and doctrines on "the diplomatic protection of aliens abroad" complemented notions of nonintervention in the colonial period. With the collapse of colonial legitimacy, ideas of granting special status to privileged aliens and the more general approach of diplomatic protection lost their influence. Powerful governments continue to maintain a residual claim to intervene to protect their nations in a situation of jeopardy, but the claim is controversial and regarded by the Third World as "colonialist" behavior. The Stanleyville Operation of 1964 in which Belgian and French paratroopers with the benefit of United States logistical support rescued a thousand or so white hostages caught up in the swirls of civil war in the Congo (later renamed Zaire) illustrates the pattern of claim and response. Third World attitudes were sharply conveyed in the subsequent Security Council debate, much to the dismay of Western diplomats who insisted on the "humanitarian" character of the mission.[1]

The pure morality of the states system is, in its essence, both anti-interventionary and anti-imperial. The main contention, which continues to attract modern champions, is that only imperial actors have, in general, the will and capabilities to do anything significant about abuses of human rights, and yet it is precisely these actors that are least trustworthy because of their own wider, selfish interests.[2] John Vincent upholds the morality of nonintervention even "in the face of outrageous conduct within the state" (as in relation to Nazi persecution of Jews or mistreatment of blacks as a result of *apartheid*). Vincent argues that there are, on balance, insufficient grounds for trust in the impartiality of the intervenor and that there are reasons to suppose that the consequences of intervention will extend beyond the correction of the perceived evil.[3] In effect, an absolute doctrine of nonintervention (at least by forcible means) is an ordering choice that acknowledges that some particular instances might justify intervention but not sufficiently to create a precedent that other potential intervenors could invoke.

This view of world legal order rests heavily on the juridical ideas of equality of states and sanctity of treaties and on the geopolitical ideology of a pure states system. It presupposes the absence of imperial actors serving as global enforcers or, put differently, of strong states with the claim of assuring compliance by weak states. This model of juridical and political equality—a world of states mutually respectful of each other's sovereign prerogatives—necessarily precludes any missionary claim to intervene for humanitarian purposes. The highest goal in such a system is the autonomy of state actors protected through maximum adherence to the norm of nonintervention.

The statist matrix of political life also means that the most substantial contributions to the realization of human rights arise from the internal dynamics of domestic politics. Far more significant than imposing human rights policies from outside is an effective commitment to their protection arising from within the body politic. Political theorists as different as Kant and

Lenin have argued that the realization of human rights is an automatic consequence of adopting the proper form of domestic government: in Kant's case, a liberal republic; in Lenin's radical socialism, as the outcome of armed struggle. That is, the achievement of human rights is a matter primarily for domestic reform; global concern is neither necessary nor effective.

Of course, there are connections between domestic political changes and external stimuli. The point, however, is that a repressive structure of governance cannot be transformed by marginal, voluntary remedial steps taken under pressure from without, of the sort associated with human rights initiatives. The maximum impact of human rights pressures absent enforcement mechanisms is to isolate a target government, perhaps denying it some of the benefits of trade and aid. There are no positive examples where such pressure has led to an abandonment of the pattern of violation or to a collapse of the governing process responsible for such abuses of human rights.

However, a domestic challenge, if it succeeds, may indeed lead to a new political arrangement untainted by human rights abridgments. For instance, the Indian electoral repudiation of Indira Gandhi's "Emergency" in 1977 was an enormous victory for the cause of civil and political liberties in a polity containing almost one fifth of the world's population. The Iranian Revolution of 1978–79 represented an extraordinary unarmed popular uprising against an extreme form of tyranny. These evolutions in national circumstances were largely achieved through the domestic play of forces, although the challenge and outcome may have been influenced to some small extent by the international endorsement of human rights. As well, the failure in the Iranian case of pro-Shah forces to intervene assured the primacy of domestic factors.

The critical political arena for human rights, then, is most often internal to sovereign states. However, to the extent that repressive regimes are sustained by outside "support" via arms and capital, then policies of governments and international financial institutions have some relationship to ongoing struggles between those who seek to promote human rights and those opposed. An important implication of this way of thinking is that noninterference with the dynamics of self-determination is the most solid external contribution foreign governments can make to the promotion of human rights. Noninterference includes, of course, refraining from covert operations intended to alter the domestic play of forces.

But what of antirepressive interference? Here, I think, the reality of hegemonial and transnational patterns of self-interest are such that likely intervenors are most often predisposed in favor of the status quo or to achieve some new configuration of control manipulated from outside. States are, by and large, oriented around selfish ends of power, wealth, and prestige; they are not reliably enough committed to human rights to be endowed with interventionary discretion, at least absent a global community mandate that would shift the ordering logic to that of supranationalist logic (see section D, below). On occasion, the pressure to intervene arises from a domestic constituency that identifies closely with the victims of repression. Here, the effective motivation to intervene on behalf of human rights arises out of domestic politics, and grounds for suspicion may not exist.

And what of counterinterventionary moves designed to neutralize the intervention of others? The interdependence of international political life means that to stay out while others go in can amount to a form of "intervention." As a consequence, an exemption from nonintervention norms enjoys wide backing in international society. The dictates of statist logic suggest that if one state intervenes in a given country, then counterintervention of a proportional character is an appropriate and permissible response. Of course, such relations are imprecise, and each side is interested in prevailing rather than neutralizing its adversary. Nevertheless, these considerations play into an assessment of what must be done to allow the domestic arena to operate as effectively as possible to uphold human rights in light of statist logic.

B. HEGEMONIAL LOGIC

Juridical equality has been up against the geopolitical reality of gross inequality since the inception of the states system. As a consequence, some polities have been much more penetrated than others. The colonial system, assimilated into world legal order with different degrees of formality in the nineteenth century, upheld imperial patterns of control. These patterns were justified by the colonizers, as had the conquest of the New World some centuries earlier, by humanitarian, civilizing claims, and were formalized in such legal doctrines as state responsibility, diplomatic protection, and extraterritoriality. These humanitarian rationalizations and their doctrinal embodiment have been totally discredited during the decolonizing period, losing by now their earlier status of claims of legal and moral right. Both international law and morality rest to some extent on a consensus among actors; if that consensus is eroded or shattered, then the norms it had earlier supported are weakened or destroyed. The hegemonial relationship persists in informal and covert patterns, although it is everywhere renounced as a valid ordering logic, except possibly in the form of support for humanitarian intervention undertaken by states.[4] Nevertheless, when the United States explicitly proclaims a human rights diplomacy that it will implement as a general element of its foreign policy, this entails an implicitly hegemonial attitude toward the internal affairs of certain foreign countries. These are possibly self-serving in the sense of promoting material and strategic interests (e.g., toward Indochina), possibly genuinely humanitarian. The hegemonial element arises to the extent that human rights are promoted by interventionary means, through diplomatic pressure, withholding aid or credits, giving aid and comfort to dissident elements, and even by military operations. Of course, unintended consequences occur. The promotion of human rights by the Carter administration was never intended to overlook strategic considerations by undermining or alienating governments allied to the United States; in fact, however, the evidence suggests that opposition groups in such countries as Iran, South Korea, and Tunisia were emboldened by Carter's encouragement of human rights in foreign societies. Indeed, Mehdi Bazargan has confirmed, unwittingly, Henry Kissinger's attack on Carter's human rights diplomacy as a factor in the collapse of the shah's regime in Iran early in 1979. If such a result had been anticipated, it seems assured that the Carter administration would have refrained from its posture of human rights support.

The hegemonial outlook is not a reciprocal tolerance of the sort appropriate to contractual relations among equals in the statist framework. On occasion, it may involve some efforts to bargain concessions in human rights for economic assets with foreign states (Soviet Union) of equivalent power; the effectiveness and side benefits (and costs) of "linkage" geopolitics is controversial and should be considered a special instance of statist behavior rather than an exercise in hegemony. Hegemonial logic is an acknowledgment of the structuring role of power in a political system lacking an established governing process. In this regard, it is international relations as explained by Thomas Hobbes. In essence, there is no such thing as equality in international life on the level of states, no matter how much equality on the level of persons is achieved.

Hegemonial claims may be promoted by regional or even subregional actors, possessing relatively greater power within their relative domain and possibly motivated, in part at least, by human rights concerns. It seems evident, for instance, that both the Vietnamese-backed invasion of Cambodia and the Tanzanian-backed invasion of Uganda in 1979 were motivated (and tolerated, if not endorsed) but *not* legitimated as such because the target regimes were guilty of such flagrant, extreme abuses of elemental human rights. In effect, there is an ordering logic relevant to human rights that is associated with the capacity and will of governments or groups of governments to intervene in foreign societies to insist on political adjustments of a fairly fundamental character. The principal locus of this hegemonial capacity and disposition is in the leading global states that take a definite interest in events in all regions of the world. Exceptional circumstances of abuse and relative capability to act, as we suggest above, may create a much more geographically limited conception of hegemonial role in certain settings, as between neighboring small countries.

The normative underpinning for the hegemonial logic is connected with "leadership," supposing some implicit correlation between power and virtue that gives powerful states a mandate to impose their will on weaker states and that, on balance, this works out positively. Such a hegemonial process may obtain the acquiescence, tacit approval, and/or cooperation of other like-minded states. This kind of support, even if limited to the absence of censure for violating nonintervention norms, operates to confer a weak form of legitimation on *certain* hegemonial claims based on human rights abuses. Usually, the hegemonial features are omitted from any argument in justification. Instead, the claim is made that the projected action can overcome societal evil elsewhere: a given government adopts a policy to promote the well-being of others. India made such a claim to justify intervening to promote the secession of Bangladesh from Pakistan in 1971. Here, the element of geopolitical ambition—splitting asunder Pakistan, a traditional enemy—coincided with liberating the people of East Pakistan from the abuses of their human rights that reached genocidal proportions. The United States, given its political traditions, is peculiarly prone to suppose that its exertions of influence on other societies are selfless undertakings for the benefit of foreign peoples. Throughout the cold war, interventionary diplomacy of all forms was justified in large part by U.S. policymakers as a commitment to "freedom" (by which was meant, as it became increasingly clear in the Vietnam era, merely that the regime was noncommunist or non-Marxist, no matter how otherwise repressive of elemental human rights it might be). A human rights rationale was used as one rallying cry to engender support for waging a geopolitical struggle, the goals of which were quite unrelated to human rights.

On the other side of the struggle, the Soviet pattern of response amounted to an ideological mirror image of the Western crusade. The Soviet conception of "freedom" has been associated with nothing more substantive than the pro-Soviet orientation of a foreign government; the Chinese People's Republic has deliberately fused geopolitical affinity and political virtue to the greatest degree by their tendency to give moral endorsements to virtually *any* regime that adopts an anti-Soviet stand, even if it is also extremely anticommunist (e.g., Chinese positive response to Pinochet's access to power in Chile or to the Shah's rule in Iran).

It is one thing to believe that the spread of a certain ideological orientation toward governance has human rights benefits. It is plausible for democrats (or republicans) to believe that liberty for the citizenry and checks on governmental power will produce a polity respectful of human rights. It is also plausible for socialists to believe that a polity governed by the working classes will produce a polity respectful of human rights. In both empirical instances, such beliefs have proven naive, given repressive tendencies operative *within* each ideological frame. It is complex and controversial whether the repressive features of communist or capitalist societies inheres in the orientation toward governance. It would seem evident that the protection of basic human rights for most sectors of the population has been achieved in some advanced industrial countries with noncommunist governments in the North (i.e., among the OECD membership). Very few states in the South have been able to realize political and civil rights, although it has been argued by Jorge Dominguez that Third World capitalist countries have a generally better record when it comes to political and social rights, whereas socialist countries do better with respect to economic rights.[5]

The more elusive case for hegemonial claims arises in relation to building up a defense against international aggression. Here, the argument is that the overriding normative issue is maintaining a context for national self-determination in the face of a serious threat posed by an expanding imperial actor. As such, weaker countries are faced with an either/or prospect and would serve the cause of domestic political virtue by accepting a subordinate relationship to the more benign of the rival imperial actors. Such was the diplomatic posture of the United States in the first phases of the cold war, dramatized by John Foster Dulles's contentions that nonalignment by Third World governments was "immoral." Such a hegemonial logic vindicates for *its* constituency the overthrow of Dubček in Czechoslovakia, Allende in Chile, or Mossadegh in Iran, as well as support for their far more repressive successor regimes. Of course, the more severe repression that arises after the hegemonial intervention is never acknowledged by the intervening government(s). Hence, the contradiction between the liberating claim and the oppressive reality is never confronted. It is inevitable that the intertwining of hegemonial logic and statist behavior would produce these patterns of behavior. In one central respect, "hegemonial logic" is nothing more than an exemption for the strong from the constraints of "statist logic." Its "justifications" based on benevolent motivation have not been validated by patterns of Great Power practice throughout history and seem flawed by the difficulty of separating out the pursuit of interests at the expense of a weaker, foreign society and the promotion of its well-being. In this regard, a case could be made to strip away the normative pretensions that "cover" the exercise of power in international relations with figleaf claims of moral and legal purpose.

The Third World stress from the outset has been on the primacy of nonintervention as a stance, at least with respect to "legitimate" regimes (i.e., noncolonial, nonracist). The disintegration of colonialism together with the postindependence interventions of the superpowers in Africa and Asia have strengthened, at least temporarily, the antihegemonial posture. Also, the greater political self-consciousness of the Third World on a world level since the early 1960s, both in its own arenas and in the United Nations, has deprived the United States of global support for hegemonial geopolitics.

In some Third World settings, a regime in power may solicit new varieties of hegemonial intervention to sustain its control in the face of rising domestic opposition or declining governing capacity. Nonstate actors, especially international economic institutions such as the International Monetary Fund, are playing increasingly important roles in this respect. Mobutu's regime in Zaire has virtually turned over the internal administration of economic policy to IMF guidelines and guidance in 1978, thereby impairing Zaire's political independence. The IMF operates as an instrument for the diplomacy of the noncommunist leading states in the North. As a consequence of this nonstate hegemony there is a penetration of national sovereignty, including the subordination of the dependent states to outside hegemonial forces, comparable in certain respects to what occurred during the colonial period. Of course, there is a real dilemma here. At times the only sovereign option is to alienate normal prerogatives so as to promote national goals. The idea of intervention by invitation is at one level self-contradictory. At another level it reflects the hierarchical structure of the world political economy that coerces weaker states to compromise their independence so as to avoid internal dissolution.

At what point a regime loses "legitimacy" under statist logic by inviting intervention is partly a factual question (extent, quality, purpose, and popularity of prior intervention by others) and partly a theoretical question (extent of governmental authority to alienate sovereign right of self-determination as an exercise of political independence, as when the country in question is faced with economic collapse, civil insurrection, or external attack). One element here is assuredly the genuineness of the invitation to outsiders that depends, in part, upon the perceived autonomy of the established government. From an international law perspective, if a foreign power is engaged on one side of a self-determination struggle this weakens, in general, inhibitions on intervention by others. In fact, since at least the time of John Stuart Mill, prior intervention generates a formal case for counterintervention so as to restore balance, facilitating the dynamic of self-determination. In other words, to the extent that overlapping and antagonistic hegemonial claims exist and are tied to contradictory images of the political preconditions for human rights, then the adoption of hegemonial logic by two or more international actors has the effect of escalating and internationalizing political struggles in the modern world, causing additional loss of life and devastation. The Indochina war between 1946 and 1975 illustrated this destructive pattern. In this light, the statist stress on nonintervention seems normatively more beneficial in most circumstances than the hegemonial stress on benevolent intervention. This priority is a historical judgment. It rests upon an assessment of the imperial motivations and practices of leading governments, as well as on the tendency of ideological adversity to incite competitive patterns of intervention and justification carried out at the expense of weaker politics. It is relevant to note that most of the fighting and dying since World War II has been done along the Third World periphery of the world political system. That is, "peace" is preserved at the core, even among bitter antagonists, because war is too costly in such arenas when the stakes are high, as they are in the nuclear age. The political space outside the core (in the North) is where contending power positions and capabilities (including new weaponry) can be tested at "acceptable risk" to the hegemonial actors, even if "unacceptable costs" result for weak states. Such considerations form part of a critique of the role of hegemonial logic under present international circumstances. In an altered global setting one can imagine a more positive view of hegemonial logic, especially if imperial policies and relationships no longer existed and a global consensus on human rights justifications was shared by the potential range of hegemonial actors. Even then, however, claims of hegemonial intervention would be suspicious, given the record of the past, especially if executed as a matter of unilateral decision.

C. NATURALIST LOGIC

Far less consequential in its behavioral impact than either statist or hegemonial logic, is the naturalist notion that certain rights inhere in human nature and should be respected by all organized societies. Here, the basis of human rights is prior to politics; the absence of consent by a sovereign authority to a given rule or standard is not necessarily an acceptable excuse for nonobservance. To the extent that human rights rest on an inherent, universal, minimum morality, their status is both prior to, and independent of, their formal acceptance by a government. To the extent that a legal imperative is asserted, then most jurists require some form of acceptance of norms by the government in question to occur, although the process can be an implied one, as through the formation of customary international law, or it could be entrusted, in part, to transnational and supranational lawmaking and law-declaring processes. In part, the naturalist case is an appeal to the conscience of the rulers, or more broadly, as a spring of action to the conscience. Hence, every political actor is responsible, including leaders and private citizens. Each can also serve as a claimant of human rights or as agent of their enforcement. Human rights, imposing responsibility on all, amounts to a plea that all actors become "political" to the extent of struggling on behalf of certain agreed decencies. This is also the essential ground for claiming that some human rights are universally valid (whereas others are contingent on time, place, ideology, and volition).

Whereas statist logic accords primacy to jurisdictional principles, naturalist logic accords primacy to normative standards. Ideally, the state machinery would use its power to act within the guidelines of natural rights. The main difficulty with naturalist logic relates to the vagueness of the norms and ambiguity of the mandate. Those with power lay down what often appear as self-serving interpretations of what natural law requires, usually on the basis of nonnaturalist goals that rest on statist or hegemonial analysis. In this regard, disembodied naturalism ("that which is right") is disregarded by policymakers and leaders as sentimental and moralistic. At the other extreme, a naturalist justification for controversial behavior may provide a government with a normative rationalization for what appears from an impartial perspective to be an imperial adventure.

In recent years, claims by outside governments to topple regimes in Uganda and Cambodia implicitly raised an extreme naturalist case for intervention, although under circumstances where segments of world public opinion regarded the intervenors (Tanzania in the first instance, Vietnam in the latter) with extreme suspicion. In effect, the naturalist contention was that these regimes in place were so shockingly bad by objective moral standards that the only moral question for outsiders was whether it is possible to intervene effectively. Significantly, Vietnam's role in "liberating" Cambodia was not phrased by its leaders in Hanoi in naturalist/humanitarian terms but rather as a matter of statist prerogatives to uphold its own sovereign status. Tanzania's role in toppling Amin's regime was more directly justified along naturalist lines, although it also rested on a self-defense rationale. It was only because Amin's barbaric practices caused such widespread outrage that Tanzania's violation of Uganda's sovereign rights was tolerated by its African neighbors; as it was, despite Amin, there was a reluctance in the Organization of African Unity to endorse Tanzania's invasion. In Third World settings, especially Africa, the noninterventionist features of statist logic are generally given precedence over naturalist claims because a fear persists that such claims could generate warfare and new regional patterns of imperial abuse reinforced by a renewal of hegemonial logic.

Given the sensitivity about hegemonial behavior, with good reason one might add, it is desirable that any interventionary mission, however grave the alleged violations of rights, enjoys wide community support. The difficulty of achieving such support even in extreme cases suggests the vitality of statist logic or, put differently, the political weakness of naturalist logic standing on its own. If a course of action dictated by naturalist logic also coincides with the perceived implications of other logics (especially statist and hegemonial), then an improved prospect for effective action exists. In such an instance, however, motives are clouded, and cynical observers (often accurately) attribute the real motive to practical influences and dismiss the naturalist argument as window dressing. This either/or style of analysis misses the instances where naturalist considerations exert some influence but not necessarily *sufficient* or *decisive* influence that might have been sufficient on its own to explain an interventionary act.

Naturalist logic does have a bearing on public opinion and may inhibit some repressive policies. It may provide the most effective case on which to build popular support for taking human rights seriously. In addition, the influence of naturalist logic may express itself in relation to the normal desire that most rulers and ruling groups have to be regarded with respect, if not esteem. With transnational groups active in publicizing gross violations of human rights, there seems to be some incentive to avoid censure even when no government or international institution is prepared to object strenuously to a pattern of violation in a particular foreign society.

A final aspect of naturalist logic is its attractive doctrine that all persons, not only citizens, should be protected against state abuse. As such, the particular politics associated with the serious promotion of human rights contributes to the formulation of a movement for global reform in which the central objective is the well-being of people rather than the sanctity of juristic persons called states.

Governing by naturalistic logic is up against a variety of constraints, especially to the extent that the existing national systems of political order lose legitimacy in the eyes of the masses. Given the dynamics of power and economic scarcity, there is a persistent need to coerce and mystify to protect the rich and deter the poor. The bureaucratic character of the modern state also renders naturalistic logic less relevant to the decisional process. Political leadership in many complex organizational settings is heavily influenced, if not dominated, by a variety of competing pressure groups representing different parts of the government—so-called bureaucratic politics. Under these conditions a government will more readily use the rhetoric of high ideals while ignoring them in practice. Public policy is set by reference to a pragmatic calculus, shaped partly by pressure, partly by perceptions of interest. The spirit of doing right by doing good cannot prevail in such an atmosphere. Yet there is a subsidiary trend, exemplified by the notion of war crimes as prosecuted at Nuremberg and Tokyo in 1945, that failures to uphold minimum rights are criminal acts even if committed by the highest public officials acting in the course of their bureaucratic duty. Although the Nuremberg judgment was set in a framework of positive law, its validity rested more on the public consensus that Axis leaders, especially Nazis, had acted in defiance of naturalist logic. Its validity has been repeatedly challenged as a mere exercise of "victors' justice," especially given the allegedly "criminal" character of Allied reliance on atomic attacks against Hiroshima and Nagasaki in circumstances of dubious military necessity.

Naturalistic logic remains, however, the underpinning of human rights, validating their claims in a more fundamental way than the fact of whether an agreement to uphold certain rights exists is binding by way of treaty commitment. There is in all societal spheres an active moral force that is sensitive to patterns of abuse deemed contrary to nature; such patterns are perceived as wrong, as justifying resistance, opposition, and even outside financial and military assistance. The various forms of support given by outsiders to those engaged in the struggle against apartheid in South Africa draws on this naturalist logic. There is a core sense of decency and fairness that gives human rights their motive power in the popular imagination, despite an understanding that the influence of these norms on governmental policy often tends to be at most honorific, minimal. It is this potency attached to moral claims that produces various forms and enthusiasms for populism, including shouts of "power to the people," "take it to the people," and so forth.

D. SUPRANATIONALIST LOGIC

Here, we move to a different kind of logic, based on the inability to deal with questions of human rights by reference to the relations among and within sovereign states. The creation of a supranational logic as an act of will by national governments complements the traditional language of diplomacy by a metalanguage of supranationalism. Whereas the lines of argument arising from statist, hegemonial, and naturalist logic are based on the *horizontal* ordering of separate states, supranational logic aspires to *vertical* ordering from above.

A weak sense of supranational community is operative at both the regional and global level and has been given increasing institutional expressions in recent decades. This sense is conventionally associated with expression of collective action by governments representing states in permanent international organizations. The League of Nations and the United Nations are the most prominent examples of such organizations; their shortcomings rarely lead even their critics to propose a world without such a central global actor. Globalist logic also characterizes various groupings of governments sharing a common position (Third World, OECD) or goal (nuclear suppliers, OPEC). Also, regional logic is operative to a limited and uneven extent in different parts of the world, with an impressive record of achievement and growth in Western Europe.

The regional context is very uneven and complex. The European record since World War II stands out in the human rights framework. The European Convention on Human Rights and European Court of Human Rights give human rights a solid institutional foundation; several of the participating governments have accepted compulsory jurisdiction of disputes about compliance, granting individuals competence to submit human rights complaints about abuses by even their own governments. This innovation has practical and theoretical importance, acknowledging formally that nationals as well as aliens are victimized by human rights abuse and giving all victims of abuse a procedural basis for securing relief. Of course, the relatively secure protection of human rights by governments in the region makes this acceptance of supranationalist review less of a threat to statist logic than might be supposed. That is, the assurance of human rights by the availability of third-party, supranational procedures is not a threat if *generally* redundant in relation to national policy. Nevertheless, it represents a breakthrough.

Recent positive achievements by the Organization of American States include issuing reports on systematic patterns of human rights violations occurring within particular states in the Western Hemisphere; espcially useful have been reports on abuse in Chile since 1973.[6] Elsewhere regional developments have proceeded less far, although in Africa and in the Middle East organizational frameworks exist, and some attention has been given to organizing responses to violations of human rights, but on a selective basis, generally limited to regional outcasts not permitted to participate as normal regional members. Here, the distinction between regional aggression and enforcement may grow blurred. We need to have recourse to criteria of naturalist logic to assess whether such regional interventionary diplomacy seems to possess an authentic justification in human rights. Even if such a justification exists, it remains necessary to question whether the encroachment of statist logic is a positive contribution to the overall quality of world order at the current stage of international relations. These questions can be considered concretely with respect to Cuba since Castro in relation to the OAS, Israel in relation to the Arab League, and South Africa in relation to the OAU.

With respect to human rights, the main global arena of supranationalist logic is the General Assembly of the United Nations. In its initial decade, dominated by the United States, the General Assembly was principally a bearer of Western hegemonial logic. Since then, it has become increasingly a bearer of both statist and naturalist logic, as both an arena dominated by governments concerned with the protection of state sovereignty and at the same time being a forum in which the principal normative concerns of world public opinion are given expression. As such, it transmits contradictory signals, exhibiting strong rhetoric, selective moral perception, and finally, expressing a political will that is constrained by the overall calculus of statist and hegemonial interests. As such, the escalating line of UN response to South African apartheid is indicative of the furthest reach of its activist stance based on a virtually global consensus on the level of rhetoric. Such results are deceptive. No implementing action has been taken despite the years of condemnation and the many calls directed at the South African government demanding the abandonment of apartheid. Some states, especially the United States and Great Britain, have strong economic and geopolitical interests in South African stability. These countries, together with others, are glad to condemn apartheid, even as they act behind the scenes in various ways to assure the stability of the government in Pretoria that acts in defiance of the demands issuing out of the United Nations. Of course, many of these governments ardent in their condemnation of South Africa, have their own closets full of skeletons, yet their collocations of interests allow them to oppose apartheid without inhibition. That is, such opposition generally is more informative about interest patterns than suggestive of degrees of attachment to human rights. Hegemonial divisions and statist anxieties stymied efforts to fashion a response in the United Nations to reported mass atrocities in Cambodia after 1975 and in Uganda during Amin's rule. Such passivity in the United Nations, given the grave circumstances in these two countries, which are only two especially visible examples of many, discloses the inability to deal evenhandedly at the supranational level with the broad array of international human rights concerns. Less visible instances of mass atrocity, including the policies of Indonesia toward the people of East Timor or the internal policies of Equatorial Guineau, also tell us something about the selective perception of human rights violations in the world today.

An aspect of this limitation on supranationalist logic arises from the inability of the United Nations to escape from its womb shaped by hegemonial and statist logic. The activities of the United Nations are deeply constrained by the *will* of hegemonial actors, especially the two superpowers, and by deference to a statist conception of the *structure* of world order. These constraints are manifest in the lack of financial independence or sanctioning authority and capabilities. The United Nations lacks financial independence or sanctioning capabilities. The structures of authority in the United Nations represent a compromise between statist and hegemonial logic. Superpower veto rights in the Security Council alongside the Charter pledge to prohibit intervention in the domestic jurisdiction of member states is expressive of the formal extent to which the United Nations is derivative from and dependent upon other stronger ordering logics. Some activity by the General Assembly suggests the opposite potentiality, namely, the inability of formal constraints alone to prevent the United Nations from playing an active norm-related role where a consensus of governments exists (as was the case with respect to demands for a new international economic order). Whether perceived as the conscience of the world or an unconstitutional encroachment on statist prerogatives, the reality of the General Assembly's role in certain human rights contexts is undeniable, principally by establishing a climate of concern about particular patterns of abuse that encourages sanctions or even interventions.

In addition, the rhetoric of the Secretariat of the United Nations creates a weak independent sense of global identity that arises from some identification with longer-range planetary concerns. The Secretary-General, perhaps even more than the Pope, speaks as a voice of conscience that is oriented around the morality of the whole human species, rather than on behalf of a particular segment. Although constrained by practical inhibitions, the secretary general is expected to be a voice of globalistic logic, reinforced by the content of naturalist logic. By way of contrast, the pope is expected to speak as an interpreter of naturalist logic whose voice is entitled to great respect by non-Catholics, especially when reinforced by supranational logic (i.e., on issues of war and peace as opposed to distinctively Catholic positions as on birth control).

The Secretary-General does not now possess an important voice. He is not expected to challenge successfully the main policies of the superpowers, except in very marginal ways, and the effort to mount such challenges is more likely to weaken the United Nations than inhibit a hegemonial actor like the Soviet Union or the United States. Dag Hammarskjöld challenged Soviet policy as related to the Congo struggle in the early 1960s and was eventually rebuffed, and U Thant's criticism of American policy in Indochina caused a hostile reaction in Washington but no shift in policy.

More generally, the United Nations can, at best, provide a global frame for statist logic. Efforts to hold world conferences under United Nations auspices on such global issues as oceans, environment, population, food, human settlement, and disarmament have mainly served as vehicles for statist propaganda. Only governmental representatives participate in a formal way. With the exception of the law-of-the-sea negotiations where a serious if difficult bargaining process has been under way, the outcomes of such UN spectacles are rhetorical flashes in the pan. It is true that the technical and political preparations for such a conference is a learning experience for the delegations and their support groups, perhaps influencing national policy. For instance, there is no question that environmental protection by states throughout the world was encouraged by the UN Stockholm Conference on the Human Environment in 1972 even though its supranational initiatives of a normative and institutional character have been of only minor significance. Another virtue of global conferences of this sort is that they provide a dramatic context for nongovernmental, populist groups that would otherwise lack the resources to organize a global presence or gain access to the media.

Despite the spread of repressive tactics of governance, it is significant that the United Nations has never sponsored a global conference on human rights. Indeed, governmental pressure a few years ago led UNESCO to withdraw from Amnesty International even the right to use its facilities to discuss the worldwide practice of torture, after Amnesty International published evidence that more than sixty members of the United Nations practiced torture. It is no wonder disaffiliation by the UN occurred; it is some wonder that some slight affiliation was contemplated. However, sustained public pressure on behalf of particular human rights—in this instance, prohibition of torture—has resulted over the years in a series of increasingly strong condemnations of torture in the form of General Assembly resolutions.

What the UN does in the human rights area is to set standards and generate norms, as well as put pressure on a few politically isolated states whose abuses are serious (e.g., Chile, Israel) although by no means the worst, if severity of abuse were the principal criterion for agenda attention. In this regard, the UN role is restricted and arbitrary, and its impact is quite limited even where its concern is great (e.g., southern Africa). This appraisal may underestimate the United Nations contribution by way of formulating an authoritative framework for human rights in the form of a series of instruments, including the Universal Declaration of Human Rights (1948), the International Covenant on Economic, Social, and Cultural Rights (1966), and the International Convention on the Elimination of All Forms of Racial Discrimination (1966); in addition, the International Labour Organization has generated a series of conventions pertaining to work and workers' rights. Also, the Commission on Human Rights attached to the UN Economic and Social Council issues reports on a variety of human rights situations around the world that enjoy respect for their accuracy and exert some influence.

The Charter of the United Nations also sets forth a compromise between dominant logics, although it seems oriented around a more globalist set of goals, especially war prevention. The Charter could support a political shift in the direction of a more cooperative, centrally guided world legal order, but as matters stand, the potentiality of the Charter is totally dependent for realization upon governments of sovereign states. As such, it is not realistic to expect an expanded role for supranationalist logic until there is a significant shift in outlook by several leading governmental participants as a result of domestic cultural revolution or international ecological or security trauma. Something has to shake down the power-oriented, territorially based morality of statist logic before a more autonomous type of globalist logic can gain influence. Unless (and until) this happens the United Nations is present mainly as the chrysalis for a different set of world order solutions and as a supplemental instrument of convenience when normal statist modes break down or are stymied. Because its procedures can be manipulated by tides of opinion, outcomes in the United Nations may appear arbitrary or even contrary to the dictates of naturalist logic. To the extent this happens it undermines the slight additional weight accorded to the supranational logic by virtue of its status as a metalogic. Indeed, such a deterioration in the perception of the United Nations leads to a reinforcement of statist logic and, for powerful states, to a strengthening of hegemonial logic.

E. TRANSNATIONAL LOGIC

A variety of ordering activities in world society occur across national boundaries, reflecting neither statist territoriality nor the universalist sweep of globalist logic. In essence, the distinctive transnational aspect is the nongovernmental initiation of a stimulus in one state so as to have an impact elsewhere. The growing significance of a transnational perspective reflects the increasing interdependence of international life combined with the persisting weakness of global institutions. It is a halfway house that responds to global needs yet accepts the territoriality of power and authority. Transnational order as a logic is intermediate between the horizontal language of statism and hegemony and the vertical language of supranationalism.[7] It often bases its claims on an alleged universality of outlook detached from other ordering logics, yet transnational actors are situated within sovereign states and subject to their control, except to the extent that some transnational economic actors can overwhelm the statist capabilities of weak states either on their own or through the support of hegemonial actors.

The identity of transnational actors is formally nongovernmental, although in certain settings links with some governments exist. The multinational corporation, the modern successor to the royal chartering of trading companies, is the most formidable and salient instance of a transnational actor. There is a dazzling array of transnational actors in all those sectors of modern life where activity is of concern to more than one territorial polity and where the multistate concern cannot be effectively represented by the direct cooperation of governments.

The transnational and nongovernmental context of human rights is obvious. Interventionary obstacles restrict what governments or intergovernmental institutions will do, and geopolitical considerations may insulate some polities from human rights criticism or make their leaders reject such criticism as politically motivated. Therefore, it is not surprising that nongovernmental organizations devoted to the promotion of human rights across borders have emerged in recent years. Amnesty International, International League for Human Rights, and the International Commission of Jurists are among the most significant transnational actors whose special concern is the human rights field. By issuing reports, applying informal pressure on foreign officials, and keeping in touch with victims of human rights abuse, these organizations exert an important, if selective influence. Of course, statism intrudes as a constraint. Access to facts can be seriously curtailed by governments eager to avoid adverse publicity. No enforcement or sanctioning processes are directly available, although the impartial disclosures by these transnational actors may create a climate in some countries that builds pressure for more coercive stands on human rights in official arenas. The various moves against racism in southern Africa reflect this interactive process.

Transnational actors in the human rights area are private associations that depend for their existence on voluntary contributions of money. Their stature is partly a reflection of the quality of their work, their freedom from partisan causes, and their commitment to widely shared values. Hence, their influence results from having an impact on public opinion in all relevant arenas.

These initiatives focus on civil and political rights that have been globally and nationally endorsed through their embodiment in the Universal Declaration, the main global and regional human rights covenants, as well as in national constitutions and statutes. As a consequence, even many repressive governments are technically committed to these norms and may be marginally vulnerable to arguments from within or without stating that the call for human rights is nothing more than the call for domestic law enforcement. The process of internationalizing is complex and variable, normally emanating from initial national acceptance and implementation, moving into international arenas only when national efforts are frustrated.

Within the wider conception of human rights, as extending to every person the right to the basic necessities of life, transnational groups associated especially with religious and educational organizations have been important. The World Council of Churches, the National Council of Churches, the Third World Forum, and the World Order Models Projects are examples of transnational actors seeking to generate support for humane patterns of governance that center on the full realization of human rights. Some of these groups take an active stand that is political in character; for instance, church organizations that give funds to liberation groups engaged in armed struggle, especially those in southern Africa.

In terms of ordering logics, normative transnationality is

fragile and vulnerable, depending for its very formal existence on statist indulgence and voluntary private financing. And yet, given "the space" available in democratic polities, these transnational initiatives are relatively well established, enjoying a large measure of autonomy, and able to maintain contact with oppositional groups in many repressive societies. Awarding Amnesty International the Nobel Peace Prize in 1972 confirmed, in one sense, the contribution and prominence of the transnational approach to the promotion of human rights.

F. POPULIST LOGIC

The weakest, potentially most subversive, of ordering logics is that of "the people," taken in Rousseau's sense of being the ultimate residue of sovereign rights. Governments, institutions of any character, are derivative, and corrupting to the extent that they substitute various particular interests for the promotion of general interests. All political institutions are imperfectly representative, whatever their claim. And yet governments, especially, have at their disposal overwhelming capabilities to resist all challenges except occasionally those that arise from revolutionary groups that seek themselves to take over control of state power.

At the margins of power are a growing number of individuals and loosely organized groups that distrust the capacity, *in general*, of any government to uphold basic human well-being, including individual and group rights. These individuals and groups deny governmental and intergovernmental claims to possess a monopoly of legitimated authority. Often in the context of human rights these groups react to the failure of governments to follow through on their own promises such as contained in the Nuremberg principles or the Helsinki accords. Positive and diverse populist initiatives include the Bertrand Russell War Crimes Tribunal (originally organized in response to the Vietnam war, more recently perpetuated as a commission of inquiry into the denial of human rights in Latin America and West Germany, and now carried forward in a proposed permanent form by the Lelio Basso Foundation); the proclamation at Algiers on July 4, 1976, of the Universal Declaration of the Rights of Peoples that supplements conventional international law with a series of claims based on the inalienable rights of peoples; and aspects of the counterconferences at major UN conclaves on global policy issues. This is the perspective of planetary citizens, who try to emphasize the degree to which supranationalist activity needs to be strengthened by agitational activity; usually, these individuals and groups are able to work in countries that already tolerate some opposition activity.

At this stage, populist initiatives are significant mainly as thorns in the side of certain state and imperial actors. In human rights contexts, this means mobilizing public awareness about certain categories of abuse. It is a moral logic based on declaring what is right, as such drawing its inspiration from naturalist logic.

The populist approach is distinguished from the transnationalist approach by its rejection of statist legitimacy. Transnational actors tend to accept the legitimacy of the overall world order system, seeking to induce governments to do what they are obliged to do with respect to specific claims of right. Populist actors insist that statist prerogatives are derived from popular sovereignty and fully accountable to it, that their thrust is more radical, and that often their attacks on abuses of human rights rest more upon fundamental indictments of repressive structures of governance (e.g., imperialism, fascism). Of course, the interaction of logics is evident here. Some transnational actors have arisen as a consequence of populist pressure and adopt as their goal a populist program of action. Environment groups, especially those with an antinuclear focus, such as Friends of the Earth, are illustrative of this admixture of populism and transnationalism. Other forms of populism become coopted by a statist logic, operating virtually as an adjunct to governmental authority and accepting as a constraint the consent of the territorial sovereign—for instance, the International Committee of the Red Cross has assumed this basic character. Still other types of populism essentially act as pressure groups on behalf of supranationalist logic as is the case with the United World Federalists, or perhaps the United Nations Association.

In effect, populism is a protean logic that can either act independently or to reinforce the thrust of any of the other logics in a wide variety of respects. It can also act to oppose other logics, as is the case of the interaction between revolutionary populism, with its antecedents in movements associated with philosophical anarchism, and statism.

Conceived of as a logic, then, populism like supranationalism is operative at a different level of social organization. Supranationalism provides a metalanguage or metalogic in relation to the various logics associated with statism. Populism provides a kind of sublanguage, taking its stance that is "below" the state, in the special sense that moral and political legitimacy depends upon the sentiments of the people, at least in the more limited sense of "the citizenry."

II

The present system of world order is evolving in ways significant for the protection of human rights. To grasp this process of evolution it is helpful to distinguish among the six principal ordering logics that together comprise what we mean by the present world order system. Figure 4.1 conveys an impressionistic sense of the changing relative importance of these ordering logics since World War II, projecting trends speculatively into the near future of 1985.

In the specific setting of human rights, the relative importance of these logics is somewhat different than in relation to the overall character of world order. For one thing, imperial geopolitics is not very frequently motivated to accord dependent societies protection of human rights, but in its quest for control over foreign societies may exert a consistently negative impact. Even here no easy conclusions are possible. Uganda under British rule achieved a better record of compliance with human rights than during the period of Idi Amin's reign. It seems possible, however, to generalize to the extent of suggest-

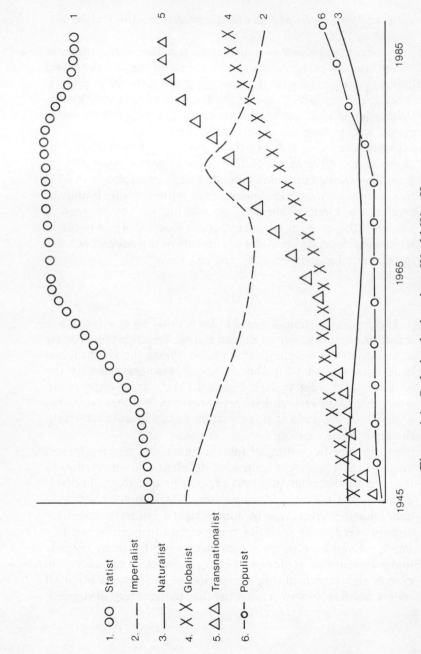

Figure 4.1. Ordering logics since World War II.

1. OO   Statist
2. —|—   Imperialist
3. ——   Naturalist
4. X X   Globalist
5. △△   Transnationalist
6. —o—   Populist

ing that political independence is a necessary but not sufficient condition for the realization of human rights in the contemporary world. Why, it might be asked? Because explicit colonial rule runs so contrary to popular aspiration and to legitimate political arrangements (as defined by international consensus, manifest in General Assembly resolutions) that severe forms of repression are required to sustain stability. The colonial hold-outs in southern Africa reinforce this line of reasoning.

Figure 4.2 tries in rough terms to suggest the relative significance of the six ordering logics for the protection of human rights. Note, especially, that this indication of relative importance should not be confused with degrees of effectiveness. That is, the world order system as a whole has a poor record with respect to the promotion of human rights. The basic mixture of statism and imperial geopolitics that dominates international politics is not conducive to the promotion of minimum human rights, especially given patterns of gross inequality, ethnic animosities, high population growth, and mass poverty that are characterisitc for such a large part of the planet. In effect, state power is typically exercised on behalf of a privileged minority of the total society, while the majority population of most national societies endures misery of various types and is repressed to the extent that its representatives challenge as unacceptable the patterns of benefits and burdens prevailing in a particular polity. This primary domestic hierarchy is reinforced by imperial geopolitics, creating and shaping relationships of mutual benefit between the hegemonial elites of dominant governments and their counterparts in dependent, weaker states. In effect, then, the basic structuring of power is statist-imperialist in a manner that entails only very modest opportunities for the external promotion of human rights.[8] Neither the incentives nor the capabilities exist given the present character of world order, except in aberrational circumstances where a target polity can be isolated from geopolitical support. Given this limited possibility, the instances of international enforcement may seem arbitrary in the sense that they do not necessarily concentrate on the most serious violations. At the same time, to date, these target polities are genuine and gross viola-

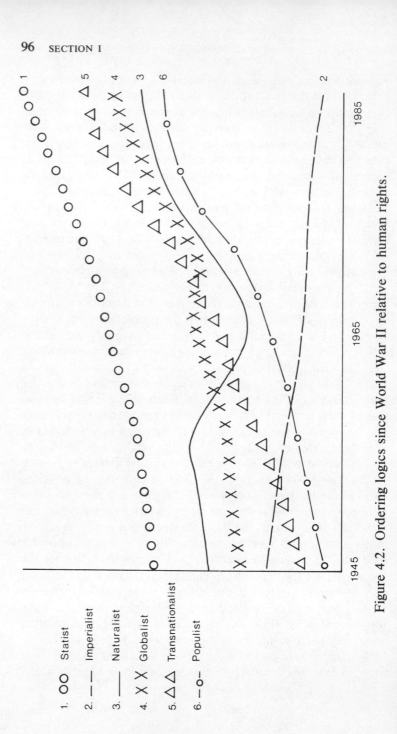

Figure 4.2. Ordering logics since World War II relative to human rights.

tors of minimum standards of human rights—for example, Rhodesia, South Africa—and therefore may be "victimized" by being "selected" but not because they are "innocent." The institutional focus on violations is, as a practical matter, limited to a focus on vulnerable violators.

This skeptical assessment of world order capacity can be expressed differently. A given system of political order can be evaluated by reference to its capacity to realize particular world order values. Again, such an evaluation is somewhat subjective as we lack "hard" agreed indicators as well as relevant, comprehensive, and reliable data. Nevertheless, the crude quality of a particular system of word order can be expressed by its relative value realization for a given array: peace, economic well-being, human rights, environmental quality, and humane governance viewed as a cumulative assessment of the other four value dimensions. The idea of appraisal is a matter of past record, present assessment, and future prospects. Figures 4.3–4.5 offer a judgment about value attainment and expectations, based on a hypothetical scale of 100 as an acceptable minimum. These are crude simplifications of reality designed only to be suggestive in relation to prior analysis of ordering logics. To be more useful, it would be necessary to justify the scaling of value attainments by some objective method and to correlate the emphasis on values with each of the six ordering logics.

These figures summarize a developmental view of the world order system, its deficiencies and its prospects.[9] Figure 4.5 selects one scenario of the future, perhaps an optimistic one, that anticipates significant progress with respect to satisfying the basic economic needs of people on the planet, but accompanied by further deterioration along the other value dimensions. The reasoning behind this view is based on the priority accorded to economic production and distribution, partly expressed by a continuing trend toward various forms of socialist organization at the state level and by a refusal in such circumstances to allow much "space" for dissent or competitive politics. The countries in the South will be faced by a fundamental challenge to expand production and employment to keep pace

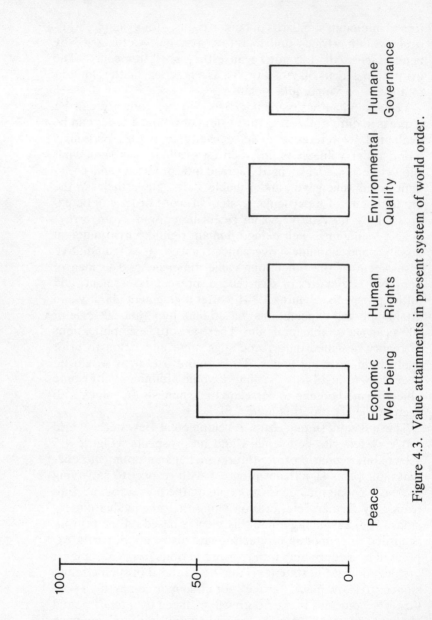

Figure 4.3. Value attainments in present system of world order.

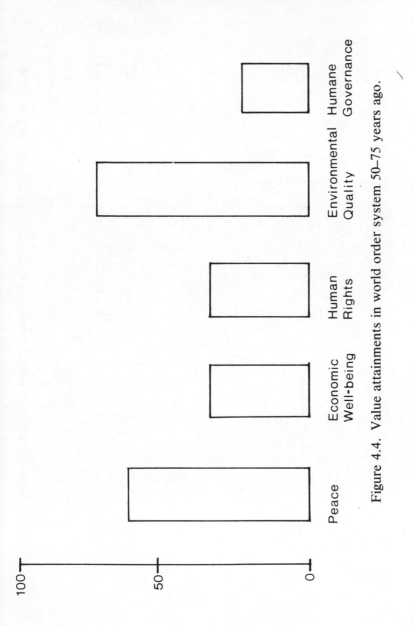

Figure 4.4. Value attainments in world order system 50–75 years ago.

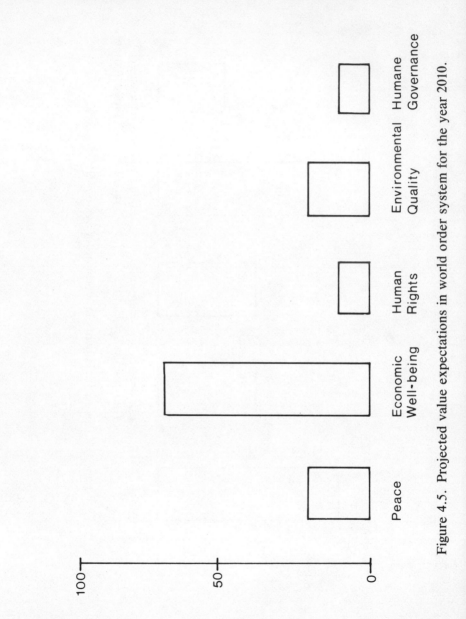

Figure 4.5. Projected value expectations in world order system for the year 2010.

with a growing population and work force. The countries in the North will be confronted by increasingly costly tradeoffs between health and affluence, as well as by a decline in relative economic power that may result in a falling standard of living on the average.

This view of the future is structural in the sense that it attributes a strong constraining influence on the overall value-realizing potential (including nonviolence, equity and environmental quality, as well as human rights) to the framework of states as reinforced primarily by imperial geopolitics, more recently augmented by a complex network of transnational social, economic, and cultural forces. The overall point is that the present world order system does not appear to have a very satisfactory value-realizing capacity. This deficiency is mainly a consequence of its organizational fragmentation in a setting of high-technology weaponry, rapid population growth, the pervasive inequalities correlated with racial patterns of domination, and a governing process on the state level that is overwhelmingly dependent on coercion to secure the compliance of distinct national populations with the imperatives of minimum order. In such a political framework, the promotion of human rights across boundaries is sporadic and arbitrary, depending above all else on the occasional convergence of geopolitical goals with the promotion of human rights.

For instance, the promotion of human rights by the United States in the early years of the Carter presidency reinforced the domestic process of moral recovery from Vietnam and Watergate and served to expose the relative deficiencies of Soviet society. By resetting the global moral agenda around rights, the Carter initiative also diverted attention from and eroded the morale of Third World advocacy of a new international economic order. Such a result was not, in all probability, a planned side effect of the human rights diplomacy; however, since many of the flagrant abuses of human rights were in Third World countries, the effect of the focus was to deprive the Third World of much of its moral advantage—vis-à-vis the world economic system. As such, United States human rights diplomacy initially served the practical ends of American foreign policy, although in a generally controversial and non-sustainable way. Positive relations with the Soviet Union seemed obstructed, and worse, by linking superpower relations to human rights. Besides, it was questionable whether the rhetoric of concern about foreign abuses of human rights was being translated into improved patterns of observance. Causal calculations of impact are notoriously difficult to make, especially as official elites of target polities will never acknowledge the reforming influence of outside criticism on their patterns of governance. Thus, the increased rates of Jewish emigration and the release of prominent Soviet dissidents in April 1979 are recently being hailed as a belated tribute to the trade linkages of the Jackson-Vanik legislation and to Carter's human rights diplomacy. Other analysts with equivalent plausibility consider the apparent Soviet policy shift to be part of an effort to establish a political climate in the United States that will enhance prospects of the ratification of the SALT II treaty. Such an illustration suggests the complexity that is present here. At issue is the effectiveness of a reward-incentive-punishment policy under a variety of conditions and with respect to diverse sets of actors.

Another kind of alleged impact of human rights diplomacy eroded the grip of repressive friendly governments on their populations, alienating present leaders and stimulating the opposition to act more boldly. We have here primarily an interaction between statist and populist logics as ordering processes. The assumption in the modern world is a decisive shift in the balance of forces within the state to the mechanisms of government. And yet popular movements from below are under certain circumstances capable of mobilizing sufficient support to overthrow even a brutal, ruthless tyranny. Part of the motivating energy in such a context is the conviction of the people and their leaders that they have been denied certain rights that are worth fighting, and even dying, to secure. In effect, populist logic is reinforced in a repressive national setting by naturalist logic. It may be further reinforced by transnational and supranational logics as well, to the extent that such actors help identify and censure the pattern of human rights abuse. Even hegemonial support for human rights of the sort associated with President Carter's advocacy contributes, even if unintentionally, to the outcome of a struggle against repression in a foreign society.

The struggle between the Shah's government and the Khomeini movement is a spectacular instance of this dynamic. Leaders of the Iranian Revolution, as well as such critics of the human rights diplomacy as Henry Kissinger, share the judgment that the movement against the shah was tangibly helped by Carter's general posture of support for human rights.[10] Relevant here is not only the reality of the causal link but the evident unwillingness of the Carter leadership to acknowledge that adverse political consequences in geopolitical terms might follow, or seem to some observers to follow, on occasion from a genuine commitment to human rights as an element of American foreign policy. The prevailing assumption, borne out by the declining importance of human rights as an operational element of U.S. foreign policy since the start of 1978, is that geopolitics takes clear priority over human rights. Given the actualities of the world, including the play of domestic political forces, reconciliation is not generally sustainable over time. In addition, adverse domestic consequences are perceived to follow for a politician who sacrifices tangible national interests for the sake of such intangible goals as the promotion of foreign policy. And indeed it may be that this domestic backlash is a more powerful inhibitor on the promotion of human rights by American political leaders than are the supposed adverse overseas consequences as measured by rising tensions or weakened alliances. Experience is so limited, however, that other factors should be considered—for instance, perhaps the perceived failure of Carter's human rights policy was a matter of insufficient persistence and patience, of an outmoded calculus of gains and losses in foreign policy, of an inadequate public campaign to build popular support.

On the record to date even the verbal endorsement of human rights by the Carter administration, with relatively little effort at follow-through, has proved nonsustainable, at least for now. In effect, unless human rights can be successfully combined with geopolitics, as it might be by concentrating on violations in the Soviet sphere during periods of East-West tension, it seems like an inappropriate emphasis in the current world order system. This is the point of Kissinger's critique. Foreign policy is concerned with the promotion of national interests, as related to the power, security, wealth, and prestige of a state. Human rights do not fit into such an outlook, except under special, limited pragmatic circumstances. At most, however, this assessment suggests that statist and hegemonial logics seem organized around the pursuit of ends that rarely include a serious commitment of national resources to the promotion of human rights.

Given systematic reliance on repressive methods of rule by the great majority of states, any international body such as the United Nations that depends on overwhelming levels of membership support to take any kind of action is bound to have its role confined, at best, to "special cases." By a special case is meant one that seems to present a human rights issue that has features restricting its applicability to the situation pertaining in one or two states, either because of the character of the violation (genocide) or the identity of the violator as a pariah state. In contrast is the instance of an abuse such as torture that is attributable to a large proportion of states or terrorism, which enjoys tacit support under certain circumstances. General condemnation is possible, but in such a form as to assure no systematic consideration of the range of violations or preconditions. If spectacular abuses of human rights occur that offend a major state, a vague rhetorical posture might be adopted by one or more of the political organs of the United Nations, but without more substantive action. It is not clear whether such rhetoric, without action, is at all productive.

In these respects, apartheid is the perfect special case, while torture is an apt illustration of a general systemic condition too sensitive to examine. In a specific instance—for example, Chile, where its occurrence could be associated with the consequences of the CIA's intervention against Allende—this may change, but the reasons are less important for their human rights effects than their intentions, such as chastising the

United States in the UN. In addition, the United Nations as a global arena is not accorded independent capabilities to alter behavior at the state level and rarely has such capabilities delegated to it. The United Nations is barred by the domestic jurisdiction provision in its own Charter from more than symbolic and verbal initiatives. Such initiatives can significantly shift the balance of legitimacy by, for instance, vindicating support for armed struggle against racism; but they can also engender frustration, expose weakness, and create a mood of futility by having repeated resolutions calling for change lead to no consequence more substantive than a subsequent resolution.

The main conclusion, at once obvious and fundamental, is that the cause of human rights in the present world system is overwhelmingly dependent on the normative orientation of the governing process at the state level. Some pressures can be brought from outside on this process; for example, impartial transnational organizations, whose motives are harder to discredit, can do this in certain situations, especially where the leadership in the target polity wants to avoid having an international reputation as repressive, and when the abuse can be corrected without weakening its hold over the society. Yet this pressure can be only marginal, perhaps leading to some cosmetic changes in judicial procedures, in improved conditions of confinement, or possibly even release for prominent prisoners of conscience. Nevertheless, the governing orientation of states is primarily shaped by internal factors, especially by attitudes of domestic leaders relating to the retention of power and maintenance of domestic order, what has been called "the rulers' imperative."

These world order limits on the promotion of human rights seem firm, at least in the next decade. If one considers the present historical period to be one of "transition," however, a new political frame of reference that involves some drastic changes in the state, regional, and supranational levels of organization provides a different perspective. There is disagreement about the depths of transition. Some consider "the crisis of world order" to be one of simply adjusting to the passing of

American primacy that helped organize international relations after World War II. Such adjustments involving a more pluralistic, complex variant of world order involve neither structural change nor normative shifts in emphasis.

A second, more fundamental view of transition suggests that the interdependent character of security, economic, and ecological life requires greater capabilities for management, perhaps even central guidance. Here, too, the functional shift toward central guidance does not imply any reduction in the internal political autonomy of state actors. Perhaps over time a more integrated world system would begin to translate awareness about the abuses of human rights into a more formidable role for the supranational ordering logic at the expense of both statist and hegemonial logic. This move toward "the management of interdependence" is sometimes described as a "moderate" (as compared with the present and past) world order system in which cooperative aspects of relations between state actors are augmented while competitive aspects are diminished. It may be that the attainment of moderation would encourage gentler modes of governance, resting on more consent and less coercion. Such a development is feasible if the relationship between economic and demographic growth can be reconciled with improved life circumstances for most inhabitants of most polities in the world.

A third, even deeper view of transition exists. Its time horizon is a matter of decades. It views the crisis of world order to involve the disintegration of the state system as it emerged from European regional politics in the middle of the seventeenth century, often conveniently associated with the Peace of Westphalia concluded in 1648, at the end of the Thirty Years' War. From this perspective a new world order system is emergent that will combine an organizational framework suitable for a planetary polity with appropriate new beliefs, values, and myths. The essence of such a system, if it is to achieve transition, is the attainment of political stability on a planetary scale. This could take either of two principal forms, with a range of interim possibilities. It could be a centralized tyranny that imposed its will on the various peoples of the world. It could also be a relatively decentralized form of central guidance (combining the growth of functional activities by international institutions with the deconcentration of power at the state level) that was premised on a symbiotic link between leadership and the consent of the peoples of the world. A precondition for such voluntarism is that the system operated to stabilize international boundaries and to satisfy the basic needs of all peoples, thereby combining the stability important to leaders with the equity sought by the poor. The idea of "equity" covers a range of substantive arrangements proceeding from a minimalist commitment to assure satisfaction of basic material needs as a matter of right for everyone to a maximalist commitment to a just polity that achieved substantial equality among its inhabitants, as well as equality among such collectives as sovereign states. Nonutopian conceptions of equity could not do more than reach a compromise between a basic-needs approach and the achievement of genuine equality.

In the negative variant of the poststatal system, human rights will be denied in more systematic and flagrant ways than is currently the case. In terms of ordering logics, the supranational (or conceivably the hegemonial logic via world conquest, condominium, or oligopoly) logic would be greatly expanded at the expense of both statist and populist logic, the latter for these purposes being already trivial. Supranational logic would assume a hierarchical relationship of repressive superiority that would extend to the strict control of even regional and subregional expressions of supranational logic. In the positive variant, the essence of world order will be the progressive realization of human rights by means of a combined strengthening of populist and global logic, mainly at the expense of statist logic.

In this conjectural spirit it is worth noticing the following aspect. The protection of human rights in a given world order system is not rigidly the exclusive preserve of any one of the ordering logics. It all depends on the value base that animates a given political actor at any level of social organization. As racist and religious militants' movements have demonstrated, repressive intolerance can rise from below (via populist logic) as well as imposed from above (via statist logic). Similarly, holders of effective power may, under certain circumstances, act to remove human rights abuses within their own polity (e.g., civil rights in the United States).

From a formal point of view, a balance among ordering logics is important as "a check" against tendencies to abuse authority. The present world order system, confronted by an indidious mixture of inequality, misery, and scarcity, is most profoundly obstructured by the unbalanced domination of ordering logic by the sovereign state. Yet supplanting the state by a centralizing mutation is unlikely to diminish its repressive features for very long. Besides, the state helps to neutralize certain adverse features of the hegemonial logic. Strengthening weak states and weakening strong states seems like a reasonable short-term approach to the role of the state in the world system. It is for this reason that the positive direction of global reform, at this historical stage, seems to require a simultaneous stengthening of supranational (global and regional), naturalist, transnational, and populist logics at the expense of the statist and hegemonial logics.

In one respect, strengthening the progressive potential of naturalist logic may be the most important emphasis at this point in the transition process.[11] It helps to orient other ordering logics around emergent values, building a normative foundation and social consensus that will help create the sort of community sentiments needed if a beneficial form of world order is to be brought into being some time early in the twenty-first century.

NOTES

1. For an analysis of the Stanleyville Operation along these lines, see Richard A. Falk, *Legal Order in a Violent World* (Princeton: Princeton University Press, 1968), pp. 324–35.

2. See, e.g., Hedley Bull, "The Grotian Conception of International Society," in *Diplomatic Investigations*, ed. Herbert Butterfield and Martin Wight (London: Allen and Unwin, 1966), pp. 51–73; Peter F. Butler, "Legitimacy in a States–System: Vattel's Law of Nations," in *The Reason of States*, ed. Michael Donelan (London: Allen and

Unwin, 1978), pp. 45–63; and R. J. Vincent, *Nonintervention and International Order* (Princeton: Princeton University Press, 1974).

3. R. J. Vincent, "Western Conceptions of a Universal Moral Order," in *Moral Claims in World Affairs,* ed. Ralph Pettmann (New York: St. Martin's, 1979), pp. 52–78, esp. pp. 68–72.

4. See Ian Brownlie, "Humanitarian Intervention," and Richard B. Lillich, "Humanitarian Intervention: A Reply to Dr. Brownlie and a Plea for Constructive Alternatives," in *Law and Civil War in the Modern World,* ed. J. N. Moore (Baltimore: Johns Hopkins University Press, 1974).

5. See Dominguez, "Assessing Human Rights Conditions," in *Enhancing Global Human Rights,* Jorge I. Dominguez et al. (New York: McGraw-Hill, 1979), pp. 21–116; see also Richard A. Falk, "Comparative Protection of Human Rights in Capitalist and Socialist Third World Countries," *Universal Human Rights,* vol. I, No. 2, April–June, 1979.

6. A more comprehensive framework for the protection of human rights has been embodied in the American Convention on Human Rights, which includes provision for an Inter-American judicial procedure. The treaty is in force despite the absence of the U.S. ratification. Yet it remains to be seen whether it influences the behavior of the many authoritarian governments within the region.

7. For an imaginative, persuasive presentation of this conception of normative ordering, understood as the central feature of the international legal order, see Gidon Gottlieb, "The Nature of International Law: Toward a Second Concept of Law," in *The Future of the International Legal Order,* ed. Cyril E. Black and Richard A. Falk (Princeton: Princeton University Press, 1972), vol. IV, pp. 331–83.

8. Falk, "Responding to Severe Violations," in Dominguez et al., *Enhancing Global Human Rights,* pp. 207–57.

9. For a more detailed view, see Richard A. Falk, *A Study of Future Worlds* (New York: Free Press, 1975).

10. For example, see interview with Henry Kissinger, *Trialogue,* no. 19 (Fall 1978).

11. Note, of course, that naturalist logic, on behalf of a particular dogma or ideology, can operate in a very regressive manner with regard to what we conceive to be human rights.

SECTION II

The following four chapters examine the role of governmental and nongovernmental institutions (and in some cases, informal social configurations) that handle concerns with implications in the field of human rights. Richard Barnet as well as Graciela Chichilnisky and H. S. D. Cole look at the ways that economic policies—pursued in both the private and the public sectors—affect relations among nations and, subsidiarily, relations between these policies and institutions on the one hand and the individuals affected by them on the other. The essay on basic needs and economic distribution employs a methodology that is an interesting offshoot of Falk's earlier essay: exploring alternative scenarios (perspectives, situations, methodologies) of international relations in order to assess which assumptions are best used to further a particular goal—in this case, the promotion and protection of rights and the equalization of economic resources. Barnet's paper looks at one piece of this puzzle by analyzing the multifaceted role private corporations play in international food production. Both essays are concerned with the dimensions of policy that play public and private interests against one another, and both conclude that the place of the individual and of individual rights is extremely difficult to locate among conflicting priorities of larger entities.

Joseph Elder, examining land tenure policies and rural development in South Asia, takes a slightly different tack by concentrating on the interplay between development problems and social forces. His interest is in the ways that different sources of legitimacy for political or social understanding help or hinder

111

political progress, particularly in the area of rights, as traditionally defined by the modern nation-state. His endeavor is
taken up, with a different emphasis and tone, by Stephen
Young, who contrasts these modern values and value structures with ancient sources of rightness in Southeast Asia. His
thesis—that there are functional equivalents to rights as western society has defined them firmly located in other political
and social traditions—supports some of Elder's arguments.
The two essays together form an interesting discourse into
some standard but very problematic issues at the core of social
theory.

Chapter 5

HUMAN RIGHTS AND BASIC NEEDS IN A NORTH-SOUTH CONTEXT

GRACIELA CHICHILNISKY*
AND
H. S. D. COLE*

INTRODUCTION

Since 1976, Western international development communities have begun to think anew about human rights. This trend has at least two independent sources. First, the U.S. government has tried to incorporate a concern for human rights into its foreign policy, in both legislation and executive pronouncement. Because some American actions in this area have involved using trade and aid relationships as levers to persuade other governments to respect rights, the consequences abroad are as much a part of general international problems as they are specifically human rights concerns. In fact, those laws that concern the allocation, modification, or discontinuation of economic collaboration on the basis of compliance with international standards of human rights sometimes pair this concern with stipulations about satisfying basic needs.[1] However, the

---

*The authors are codirectors of a UNITAR study on technology, domestic distribution and North-South relations. We draw here on contributions of many of the researchers for that study. In addition, we are especially indebted to the work and criticism of Ian Miles and Paula R. Newberg.

issues of rights and needs may be alternately complementary and contradictory, and their relationship requires clarification.

Second, and less directly, this new concern with human rights follows a certain decline in the moral appeal of socialism and communism in the Western cultural community. In the adversarial ideological contests of the cold war—roughly, from the end of World War II to the signing of SALT I—capitalism was often not accepted as legitimate and had little appeal for the idealistic struggles of the 1960s. In the 1970s, political limitations have changed this kind of thinking. The Western banner of human rights has appeared, therefore, at a point when the United States is trying to recapture moral leadership in an international ideological vacuum of sorts.

Another, related change has occurred in the area of scholarly research. After a period when the accepted standard of intellectual excellence was equated with so-called objective or non-value-oriented research, a more recent crisis of belief in quantified science has prompted more value-oriented work.[2] It is increasingly clear that values need not conflict with the quality of thinking. Research on human rights and basic needs is therefore acceptable now, and the growing literature in the area is witness to this change in attitude. Although we refer to human rights and basic needs in the title of this essay, we join this subject with some reluctance. In part, this is because we do not necessarily share the definitions of rights and needs that are used or assumed by U.S. policymakers or analysts.[3] In addition, we believe that the reasons that the United States has for promoting human rights policies are not always solely humanitarian. Pronouncements and action are also geared toward establishing legitimacy for the North in the current North-South debate. By focusing on human rights issues as defined by the North, the countries of the South tend to be identified as the main violators. This, in an international context, questions the legitimacy of the demands made by the South for equal treatment in global economic and political affairs. Criticism based on "moral principles" undermines the position of the South in such crucial areas as international negotiations on oil prices or export-import commodity arrangements, which are carried out in monopolistic competitive markets and in the eye of the public opinion. Furthermore, questions of human rights must be asked and answered in an interdependent environment, across regions and across nations. Before one accepts too readily the implicit links between U.S. foreign policy—particularly economic policy—and a stated concern for human rights, it is necessary to reexamine the assumptions that underlie these views of the world and test their legitimacy.

There are many ways to grant legitimacy to a political or moral argument. Conventional economic thinking, which is an essential foundation for Northern policies, is given legitimacy in part by its presentation as a formal quantified analysis. Mathematical economics thus provides an apparently rigorous basis for policy. By contrast, most other perspectives or world views have been mostly represented in less formal quantified terms.[4] This is due not only to their greater stress on overtly "political" factors (which are usually perceived as less readily quantifiable) but also to the relative magnitude of the research institutions of the North and the South that produce quantified research. Such institutions are not univocal, but they have in general biases that are apparent in the emphasis and characteristics of their research.

In this study we shall treat human rights together with basic needs in one perspective or set of values that we consider consistent with the interests of a large majority of people in the South. Furthermore, we shall argue that in order to consider these questions properly, a purely domestic or national perspective only distorts the problem.

We will demonstrate the contrast between the liberal perspective and its alternatives and the degree of legitimacy that each receives in the following two ways. First, we offer a brief summary of the mainstream liberal analysis of current global problems and its critique as provided by the representatives of the Southern countries and certain analysts in the North. Then we proceed to alternative scenarios, and discuss the implications of these perspectives for North-South economic policies and for the place of human rights in these policies.

In the North there is a basic insensitivity to the importance and implications of current world crises. Liberal solutions require very little restructuring for the world economic order. This complacent view is now prevalent—and fundamental unanswered questions about current Northern international economic policy are not being asked. Some of these questions are especially important if we view trade and cooperation policies in conjunction with attempts to improve human rights. Although we will concentrate on aspects of economic policy, we will stress the connections with more general sociopolitical questions and try to identify and clarify some of these.

The views just discussed are almost exclusively reflected in massive "global" mathematical models, which are, in a sense, legitimizing agents for economic policies in the North-South debate. These represent the most complex, if not the most sophisticated forms of centralizing, simplifying, and concentrating the arguments and nexus of power in the Northern institutions. These models are currently constructed by national governments, international agencies (such as the World Bank and the United Nations), transnational firms, and university-sponsored research. Because in general these models are based on the same assumptions the liberal perspective uses, they are incapable of exploring adequately many unanswered questions or providing a satisfactory basis for stimulating alternative policies. This is even true of those international economic transfers so central to current Northern policy. To illustrate this we will refer to a growing body of work that, although it uses conventional tools of economics, challenges them on their own terms. By this we do not mean that trade and cooperation policies fail because they are distorted by nonmarket forces; rather, these policies, even through a perfectly operating market, may have an impact contrary to that which can be expected from conventional economic thinking.

This analysis of economic policies is particularly relevant for the issue of human rights. Because of the close links between international economic policy and domestic political structures in both the North and the South, attempts to implement inadequate economic policies may lead to symmetrical changes in political structures that make improvements in human rights almost impossible. Aid and trade policies are often assumed to be an integral part of a general increase in welfare and equity; however, under certain circumstances they can produce an effect diametrically opposed to those intended, thereby reinforcing and perpetrating economic and political inequalities with a concomitant loss of basic human rights.

SCENARIO ANALYSIS OF CURRENT PROBLEM AREAS AND FUTURE DIRECTIONS OF REORGANIZATION OF THE INTERNATIONAL SYSTEM

The world economy today differs from that of the 1950s and 1960s. We believe that the present state of the world economy reflects a process of significant restructuring of international relations and national economic systems. There are, however, many ways to diagnose current problems. In the Northern liberal perspective the problems of inflation, poverty, regional inequalities, underused capacity, and unresolved issues of international organization form a series of only loosely connected crises—the energy crisis, the debt crisis, the monetary system crisis, and issues related to the environment and population growth. In other perspectives these phenomena are often intimately linked: they are all aspects of a structural crisis of world order.

Current uncertainty over future directions is not restricted to economic processes alone; political and social affairs are also changing between and within countries. This restructuring is important in the study of North-South relations because: (1) it may imply a break with the pattern of world development between 1950 and 1970 to such an extent that both theory and empirical material derived from this period is less relevant to present and future developments; (2) at times of such flux, there seems to be more potential for major discontinuities in existing patterns of North-South relations; for example, increasing competition among Northern countries may improve the bargaining position of the South; (3) whether or not (and how) previous patterns of growth are reestablished is vitally important to the future course of world development.

Whereas all interest groups concerned with present events and with long-term development questions share a common set of concerns, they have different priorities and see different mechanisms for change. In particular, the degree of linking in the world economy and of the political institutions required to bring about the change they propose varies considerably. The contrasting proposals for change that different actors put forward reflect their interests and are therefore often confusing: in part because these interests and proposals are rarely spelled out in detail; in part because they are rendered ambiguous or even contradictory by the divergent meanings given to terms such as "new international economic order," "collective self-reliance," and "basic needs", and in part because policy proposals are usually attempts to compromise conflicting interests.

To analyze future world development, we can use at least two different approaches to scenario analysis. On the one hand, we can study the main actors, interest groups and institutions that have, or may have, sufficient political and economic power to influence or shape this future. On the other hand, we can study the major perspectives that correspond roughly to groups classified by a combination of their outlooks and prognoses, especially with respect to structural change and normative concerns.[5]

Our methodology combines these two approaches and seeks to explicate the theoretical assumptions that underpin different forecasts. For instance, in this study we develop scenarios focused on two distinct sets of issues—first, the current world recession and strategies for overcoming it; second the situation of the South within the world economy. In developing these scenarios we take into account distinct "perspectives" representing the contrasting positions in the debate of major actors.

With respect to the set of problems discussed above, contrasting perspectives derived from different actors within and between the North and the South are considered. The rationale behind developing this procedure is not that we believe that the two sets of issues can be separated for analytic or policy purposes—clearly they cannot—nor that we believe that different theoretical stances are all equally valid, but rather for the following reasons:

- 1 By systematically treating different approaches to the world system and its problems, we can depict a set of strategies that are presently being proposed and identify a range of important issues for further analysis; likewise, we can develop our evaluations of these different strategies.

- 2 We identify the interests associated with particular approaches, the possible coalitions or contradictions among these interests and their possible relative power, and thus consider the extent to which they may be realized as well as the extent to which the policies and scenarios derived from them might be implemented. This depends also on the adequacy and internal consistency of the approach as well as on the support it receives.

- 3 We can define our own theoretical perspectives and prescriptions relative to those of others; thus, we expose our own assumptions and analyses to critical scrutiny and raise crucial questions that may be addressed to the modeling and case studies. The compromise between ''seeking the truth'' and self-interest is a difficult one to create. We hope this method limits self-interestedness.

It is important to provide perspectives that differ from the dominant perspectives of development that represent primarily the interests of Northern actors. Using scenario analysis therefore permits us to be as explicit as possible about the implications of preferences and targets, to clarify and demark policy issues and constraints, and to identify the long-run implications of social and economic policy.

The perspectives on existing crises and future directions of development are obviously affected, first by whether the analysis is based on the viewpoint of the developed or the developing societies and second, by the underlying world view (i.e., ideological and theoretical foundation) upon which the analysis is based. For example, in relation to their North or South orientation, very different emphasis is put on the relative roles of the North and the South in their respective past and future development. In general, the Northern views pay remarkably little attention to the situation of the South: Southern countries are seen in these perspectives largely as a source of raw materials, as an export market, and/or as a potential economic competitor. Conversely, Southern perspectives generally emphasize the responsibility of the North and of Northern-oriented actors such as transnational firms in explaining the present Southern economic situation, although they differ markedly in their analysis of what the future of North-South economic relations might be.

A. NORTHERN PERSPECTIVES

Liberalization: Perspective 1. Several international organizations (often dominated by the United States) such as the Organization for Economic Cooperation and Development (OECD) and the Trilateral Commission hold fundamentally similar diagnoses of world system problems. Their current differences, although minor, may yet emerge, especially if they are forced to compete for scarce resources, markets, or political support.

According to this perspective, the world economic system is fundamentally healthy and capable of providing sustained increases in welfare. The fact that the world economic system did not achieve its potential in recent years is attributed to an unusual sequence of events external to the North (in particular, the oil crisis) and to policy errors. This perspective rejects the view that market-oriented systems and democratic political institutions have failed. Schematically, the diagnosis of this perspective is shown in Figure 5.1.

The prescriptions for revitalizing growth that emerge from this perspective vary. Broadly speaking, they can be sum-

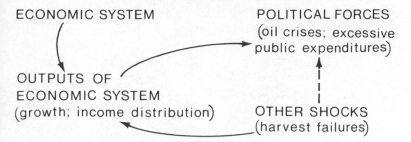

Figure 5.1. Schematic basis of the northern liberal perspective.

marized as follows. Nations should accept the common norms of the competitive market with budget setting restricted monetary growth and efficient public expenditure, and there should be some attention to medium-term planning. The goals are full employment and price stability: to insure the latter in the medium and long term, it may be necessary to endure relatively high levels of unemployment in the short term.

Some form of international cooperation is required. Nations in a position to do so should initiate world recovery. To facilitate this, short-term exchange-rate fluctuations should be removed, including barriers to Southern imports (including manufacturers). "Buffer" stocks should be set up to insure a steady supply of raw materials. Terms-of-trade shifts may occur in favor of some resource-exporting developed and developing countries. The South will experience significant growth through trade with the North and through investment by transnational firms (with adequate guidelines). The North is seen as regaining much of its previous rapid growth, although in the long term demand for goods and services may diminish. The prescriptive component of this perspective therefore may be summarized schematically, as shown in Figure 5.2.

There are two main critiques of the Northern liberal perspective. One can be related to certain elements of the OECD and to certain national governments in the North. In this critique, "exogenous" factors are incorporated into the system, technological change plays an important role, and this is linked to a much longer term cyclical behavior pattern and sometimes to a continual absence of equilibrium. Thus, current unemploy-

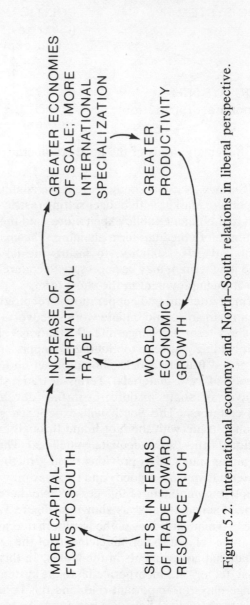

Figure 5.2. International economy and North–South relations in liberal perspective.

ment, inflation, domestic conflict, international rivalry, and protectionism in the North are related to issues of industrial restructuring, technical change, and political uncertainty. With transnational investment and increased manufacturing capacity in the South, this suggests sustained high levels of unemployment. Economic problems are likely to exacerbate political problems nationally and internationally. From this perspective, therefore, the Northern liberal view is overly complacent.

The second critique to the Northern liberal perspective is based on an analytic approach to the world system that centers on the North. This represents a more fundamental break with the two previous approaches in terms of political strategy, although many elements of economic analysis overlap with the interventionist perspective. Similar to the preceding critique, the current world crisis is considered to be more than a temporary phenomenon. However, it differs from that critique in arguing that state activities alone will not overcome the crises and imbalances fundamental to capitalism. The rate of profit is particularly important here: it is proposed that it must decline and that as it declines, real wages and employment are pushed down. This leads to a confrontation between capital and labor that can produce authoritarianism and international conflict. In contrast to Northern perspectives, the Southern perspectives concentrate on the present situation in the South as the starting point of analysis.

B. SOUTHERN PERSPECTIVES

New International Economic Order: Perspective 2. The New International Economic Order (NIEO) perspective corresponds to that advanced in such "Southern-oriented" organizations as the Group of 77 and the United Nations Conference on Trade and Development (UNCTAD). The view presented here is constructed primarily from arguments proposed by the South during the 1970s. These include the Lima Declaration (1975) adopted by the United Nations Industrial Development Organization (UNIDO) Conference, and the position of the

Group of 77 at the seventh special session of the United
Nations General Assembly. The many alternative statements
of the NIEO represent compromises between different interests and theoretical perspectives; many disagreements
are masked by their common concerns with certain initial measures. The NIEO approach draws fairly heavily upon analyses
developed by, among others, the Economic Commission for
Latin America (ECLA) group.

This perspective assumes that the basic problem the South
faces is the nature of its economic links with the North: the
functioning of the world market is biased against the South. It
asserts that despite political pronouncements, Northern policies are based on self-interest. Because the activities of North-
based transnationals operate against the host countries, the
South's earnings are both low and unstable. This position is
summarized in Figure 5.3.

Rather than concentrating on diagnosing the development of
the world economic events of the 1970s, this approach tries to
tackle the protracted crises of the Third World. On the whole,
the perspective accepts the idea that economic growth in the
North is beneficial to the South and therefore argues for
increased North-South trade. However, it argues that
preferential terms of trade for the South and a reduction of the
debt burden must be negotiated and that flows of advanced
technical skills and development assistance should increase.
Fixed targets, such as those of the Lima Declaration, should be
set, and the activities of transnationals should be controlled to
achieve them.

The growth paths within the countries of the South would
resemble those previously followed by the North. This requires
rapid economic growth, a diversified industrial base (with
emphasis on heavy industry), and the development of new
growth centers. The expansion of the industrial work force and
the acquisition of requisite skills are of first importance; relatively less attention is devoted to the rural sector. In all sectors,
indigenous appropriate technologies should be developed. Between the countries of the South there would be increased
trade and exchange of information.

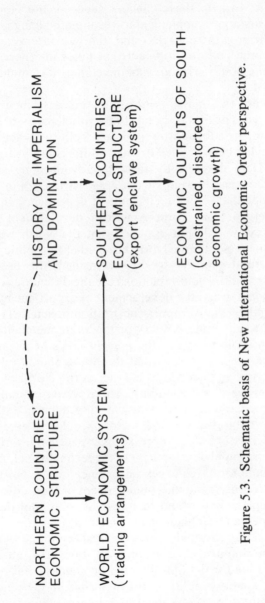

Figure 5.3. Schematic basis of New International Economic Order perspective.

In order to help these changes succeed, the North would have to undergo complementary economic changes: reduced long-term growth; material- and energy-conserving policies: and research and development that takes into account problems of the South. This view of development is summarized in Figure 5.4.

There are two major critiques of this described Southern perspective. The first responds to the problems associated with earlier import-substitution policies: collective self-reliance. This term has been applied in widely different ways by different groups. Here it refers to positions advanced by social and economic research groups from Asia, Africa, Latin America, and Europe that draw on elements of dependency theory that first emerged from Latin American development thinking.

In this view it is not assumed that the North will change relative to the South: the North has neither the political will nor the structural capacity to do so. Instead, the predominant qualities of North-South relations are the difficulties caused by transnational firms, the development of export enclaves in the South, and previous import substitution policies. These have all failed to eliminate poverty or moderate inequalities in the South. In some respects, the present crisis helps the South.

This perspective argues that the South should take advantage of crisis and economic conflict in the North by "delinking" from the world economy. There would be major reductions in economic and political dependence rather than complete autarchy. Several factors would be essential: improved terms of trade; more stringent regulation of transnational firms; rapid development of the technological, industrial, and agricultural bases to lessen reliance on the North. Coalitions of Southern nations—independent of their different political complexions—would therefore have to pool their otherwise inadequate technological, financial, human, and natural resources. More formally, international economic associations would be important, and planned Southern intraregional specialization for the South would be equally vital.

Some domestic political restructuring may be necessary, although these may well meet with internal objections. These

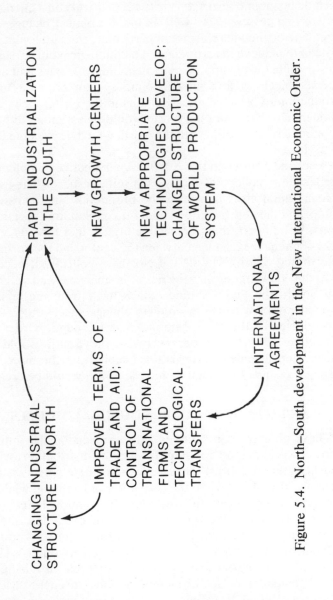

Figure 5.4. North–South development in the New International Economic Order.

include economic restructuring (with political consequences of indeterminate scope) as well as initial political changes that stimulate economic reforms. In particular, state intervention is crucial to achieve investment and technological objectives and to stimulate locally appropriate technological styles and active social objectives and an economic system oriented to the production of basic goods. Again, as in the NEIO view, complementary changes in the North would be essential, although economic reintegration with the North would be possible in the long run.

A second critique to this Southern perspective complements the Northern collectivist analysis in some respects. They share a focus upon class relations, the production and transfer of value, and the contradictions built into exploitative social relations. In addition, this perspective argues that there is a process of unequal exchange between the center and the periphery (North and South). Unlike the Northern collectivist perspective, this view argues that the nexus of change is and will be in the South; the South should detach itself from the crisis of capitalism in the North in order to change successfully. With the policies of the New International Economic Order and collective self-reliance perspectives, the South would not escape dependence on international capital. Furthermore, patterns of unequal exchange within the South would be created.

A CRITIQUE OF CURRENT GLOBAL MODELS

These different perspectives help us question the implications of world market behavior for income distributions within and between countries. These questions arise when assumptions are shared and when they are not. For example, while the Northern liberal view and the New International Economic Order both emphasize the importance of expanded international trade between North and South for fostering world development, they derive different policy prescriptions. These views also emphasize the importance of trade in raising the living standards of lower-income groups through "trickle-down" and other transfers. (By "trickle-down" we mean a process whereby, as the rich increase their wealth, the demand for goods and services produced by the poor increases, and so raises the latter's wealth.) Some perspectives dispute that perceived serious malfunctioning of world markets as they currently operate can be overcome. Others argue that the outcomes of the operation of certain unregulated markets are themselves often detrimental to the interests of developing nations and to low-income groups in the North and the South. These issues are fundamental to questions of basic needs. We will argue below that these questions cannot be satisfactorily explored using the global models embedded in Northern economic thinking because these models exclude entirely questions of income distribution within countries and implicitly assume that present tendencies will continue.

One model does propose a Southern view: the Bariloche model. However, the alternatives proposed by the Bariloche model do not study the market behavior and its effects on distribution. Instead, the model emphasizes global development under egalitarian distribution of basic consumption goods within each economic region.

Current global models in the main ignore the effects of the operation of domestic and international markets on distribution and furthermore provide only an oversimplified account of the role of technology. Those models, which do deal with questions of domestic income distribution, do not simultaneously take account of the operation of the world market. A more detailed critique of selected national and global models is given below and summarized in Tables 5.1 and 5.2.

As summarized in Tables 5.1 and 5.2, these models, as well as those used in present studies at the World Bank and at the UN, have a number of shortcomings. In particular, their treatments of income distribution, technical change, and social and political factors are inadequate. Essentially, existing models analyze capital accumulation in which GNP growth rates are the product of investment and improvements through time in capital productivity. Similarly, estimated levels of employment and unemployment are based on limiting assumptions about labor productivity, investment, and population growth. Both of

TABLE 5.1

A Summary Comparison of Selected Single-Region Models with Issues Dealt with in the Present Study

STUDY	FOCUS OF STUDY	ASSUMPTIONS ABOUT TECHNOLOGY	ASSUMPTIONS ABOUT TRADE	ASSUMPTIONS ABOUT DISTRIBUTION	ASSUMPTIONS ABOUT MARKET	NUMBER OF PRODUCTION SECTORS
Ahuwalia and Chenery (1974)	A simple growth model for a segmented economy to demonstrate distribution under technological and institutional dualism	Harrod-Domar or Loontief fixed coefficients assuming capital is always a constraint with no technical change	Not considered	3 income groups determined by ownership and physical assets and wage differentials	Prices and wages given exogenously with profits as residuals	4
Foxley (1975)	An optimising multisectoral model of the effects of redistribution on production and employment in Chile	Fixed coefficient with no technical change	Foreign sector treated through fixed input-output components	Only redistribution between 2 consumption classes and changes in employment levels considered	Prices, wages not considered. Rate of profit determined by technology	15
Adelman and Robinson (1973, 1976)	A nonlinear dynamic macroeconomic model of Korea to explore income factors affecting income distribution in the short and medium term	Cobb-Douglas production function with capital-labor substitution. Experimental rates of technical change	Imports fixed exogenously and export targets set	15 consumer categories and 6 skill groups and 6 wage rates for firms and sectors	Prices and wages determined endogenously. Employment, etc., determined through market via profit maximization	29 (with 4 firm sizes)

Table 5.1 (Continued)

Rodgers, Wery and Hopkins (1976)	A long-run simulation model (BACHUE) of employment and demographic factors in the Philippines with most economic variables exogenous, e.g., output, investment and, trade	Fixed technology via input-output tables	Imports and exports given by input-output table subject to balance-of-payments constraints	Distribution between labor classes depends on employment characteristics of technology	Prices given exogenously with wages derived from separate labor markets for urban/rural and skilled/unskilled	(24)
Taylor and Lyhy (1978)	A multisectoral general equilibrium model of Brazil	Constant elasticity of substitution production function for skill types and aggregate capital. Pure labor-saving technical change	Trade levels given exogenously through input-output tables	6 skill categories and entrepreneurs income given by wage, profit rate, and employment	Prices and wages determined endogenously. Fixed differentials between sectoral rates of profit	25

TABLE 5.2

A Summary Comparison of Selected Global Models with Issues Dealt with in the Present Study

Study	Relation of Social and Political Variables to the Model	Assumptions about Technology	Assumptions about Trade	Domestic Distribution	Number of Regions	Assumptions about Market Behaviour	Perspectives Generally Supported by the Study
Limits to Growth (System Dynamics) (Meadows 1972)	A "holistic" approach with variables and sub models dealing with selected sociological phenomena	Based on historical NS experience with anticipated future diminishing returns to investment	Not considered but implicit continuation of past trends	Not considered but implicit continuation of past trends	1	Prices increasing as resources become depleted. No other explicit market assumptions	World stagnation scenario
World Integrated Model (Hierarchical Systems Theory) (Mesarovic of Pestel 1974)	"Political judgments are introduced as exogenous policy variables	Fixed capital-output ratios calibrated to give model internal consistency for base year	Exports and imports are a fixed share of total world trade per region	Not considered but implicit continuation of past trends	10	Constant prices supply and investment bound to available consumption	World stagnation scenario plus elements of northern liberal and NIEO
Fundacion Bariloche (Herrera 1976)	A conceptual model describes social and political aspects of the society	Cobb Douglas production functions with exponential change parameters used to calibrate model over 1960-70 period. Optimization is used to allocate capital and labor inputs.	Imports and exports are a fixed share of gross output	Egalitarian distribution of basic goods	4	Constant prices except for land	Collective self-reliance plus unequal exchange

Table 5.2 (Continued)

UN Input-Output (Carter 1976)	Almost no discussion of social and political factors, although it is claimed that the model can be used to analyze a wide range of scenarios	Technical coefficients assumed to depend on per capita regional income. Largely based on U.S. experiences	Experts fixed share of total world exports, imports a fixed proportion of regional consumption of the good importers	Not considered but implicit continuation of past trends	15	Prices of raw materials and pollution abatement increase with growth	Northern liberal plus Internationalist NIEO
RIO (Tinbergen 1976)	Mainly discussion of transnational political and economic institutions and desirable human goals	Qualitative sector by sector analysis of major transnational issues	Discussion of trade. Different strategies for different issues including international division of labor, cartel formation and collective self-reliance	Need for more North-South equalization up to half of present inequalities, qualitative considerations only	Not applicable	Qualitative discussions only	Internationalist NIEO plus some aspects of collective self-reliance
The Great Debate (Freeman and Jahoda, 1978)	Analysis of economic development "profiles" based on competing social theories. A construction of corresponding "images of the future"	No macroeconomic parameters assumed. Specified industries and technologies considered in relation to economic profiles	Alternative explanations of change in domestic and international distribution hypothesized semi-quantitative considerations only	From 2 to 8 depending on issues		Critique of different assumptions and implications derived from them	Northern structuralist

these assumptions are important for the analytical results of the models.

Equally important, assumptions about trade and aid are important to the development strategies devised on the basis of the models' results. Their assumptions limit the range of available policies. For instance, they bias the design of policies toward unrealistically optimistic levels of investment and rates of technical change while disregarding other important variables. Even if the targets set for the models could be met—which would mean doubling per capita income levels in the poorest countries by the year 2000—and even if the assumptions about investment and technical change were reasonable, the living standards of the poorest would still be well below minimum needs without domestic redistribution. In fact, with the exception of the Bariloche model, which assumes a perfectly egalitarian distribution of basic consumption goods, global models do not account for income redistribution.

A consideration of income distribution is necessary for a better understanding of economic relations. Without significant income redistribution, moreover, there is no possible way to achieve human rights on an equal basis for all people. Domestic and world markets, and many social and political relationships among different world actors link income distribution with trade and growth. In a period of structural change, a model that does not include these factors can play only a limited role in understanding and forecasting major trends and planning for normative goals in the world economy.

In general, one must accept limitations in the construction of models appropriate to the study of the complex issues discussed here. However, certain characteristics of present models compound these problems. In particular, their high level of disaggregation leads to demands for data that cannot be realized and inflexibility of the relationships. All this adds to their unreliability.

For the majority of current global modeling studies, even if the results were reliable, it would not be possible to draw detailed policy conclusions from the models at the level of existing administrative institutions. There are also many technical limitations in the model with regard to data and methods of calibration and projection. For instance, the data usually used are necessarily based on outdated national accounts and input-output tables and are quite unsatisfactory for the policy-oriented objectives to the models. Often it appears that parametric fitting is designed to give "plausible" projections and that what is plausible is largely a function of the modeler's personal and ideological predispositions, although this is rarely stated. A clear underlying theory is usually absent from the studies, and they often become exercises in mere projection. In view of the above, detailed quantitative projection over a long time span is of doubtful value. Results are at best schematic or illustrative of possible tendencies.

All that is required is that the choice of aggregation should be such that the main qualitative results obtained would not differ if greater detail were added. More detailed phenomena have then to be deduced from an "enlightened interpretation" of the results of the aggregated model. Since a major criticism of existing large multisectoral models is that insufficient sensitivity testing is carried out and that the models inevitably contain somewhat arbitrary assumptions, it is important to show how the results depend on the assumed structure of the model and the relative magnitudes and details of the relationships. Apart from questions of clarity, the advantage of retaining a simple model is that a relatively large number of scenarios and alternative assumptions may be tested.

AN ALTERNATIVE MODEL FOR THE
STUDY OF BASIC NEEDS, AID, AND TRADE

We will now reexamine the questions of basic needs, trade, and aid within an alternative global model that we now call the North-South model.[6] This model, derived from our own normative assumptions, studies income distribution within and between countries of the North and South as mediated through market behavior and its effects. It emphasizes the importance of productivity and consumption in basic-goods sectors (such as agricultural products) for production and distribution in the economy as a whole. It also considers the role of technology in determining, through market operation, income distribution within and between the countries of the North and South.

The North-South model has two regions, the North and the South. Each one produces and exchanges three types of goods in domestic and international markets: basic consumption goods, luxury goods, and capital goods. There are three income groups: two skill/income labor groups in each region and non-wage earners. These income groups are differentiated not only by their earning patterns but also by their consumption patterns.[7]

TRADE, NORTH-SOUTH DISTRIBUTION, AND DOMESTIC DISTRIBUTION IN THE NORTH-SOUTH MODEL

It is assumed that the South trades with the North and that these two regions have different technologies and elasticities of supply for factors of production (labor and capital). The South has abundant labor supply and significant dualism in the production of goods. If the economy of the South attempts to increase growth by increasing the exports of the basic consumption good (which is produced in a relatively labor intensive way) while maintaining the level of domestic investment demand, the domestic price of the exportable good (capital or luxury goods) and the purchasing power of wages will decrease in domestic investment demand further growth.

The results discussed above pose doubts about the general reliance on export-led growth to help bring about development in the South. (See Perspectives 1 and 2 above.) The results discussed here apply only to certain economies and trade policies. The results indicate a need for a careful appraisal of case studies on the advantages of increased trade, with a focus on the conditions studied in the model (dualism, high availability of labor, specialization). If the general conditions in which the results are obtained are satisfied, then increased trade of basic-goods exports by the South is not favorable to NIEO goals. This is also true of the South exports goods that are not basic consumption goods but that divert resources away from the production of basic goods domestically.

These results point to the fact that the growth of the South cannot in general be based on the highly elastic cheap labor provided by extreme mass poverty. Such elastic labor supply will, in the long run, seriously deteriorate the terms of trade for the exporter, even though in the short run total revenues for exports accruing to a small elite could be increased.

We can summarize two important points here. First, it seems necessary not only to protect local production (i.e., import substitution or infant industry) but to protect domestic markets within the South in order to prevent deterioration of terms of trade between North and South. Better income distribution within the South—which implies larger domestic markets and are accompanied by lower rates of population growth (which may be accomplished by satisfying basic needs)—can reverse the current deterioration in terms of trade.

Second, the results of the North-South model indicate a far-reaching relationship between the North-South terms of trade *and* the distribution of wealth within the South. The North cannot evade a certain amount of responsibility for Southern distributions (as happens in Perspective 1). On the other hand, in contrast to Perspective 2, the South cannot separate its demands for better terms of trade with the North from its need to improve its domestic distributions. Although the results of the North-South model are not necessarily valid for all countries, they are general enough to question the view that the growth of the North is *necessarily* beneficial to growth in the South through the mediations of increased international trade.

There are conditions under which aid policies favor more equal development between the North and the South. There are also conditions under which NIEO recommendations, including North-South terms of trade, may be consistent with transfer policies. Many analysts have argued that the transfer targets from the North to the South sponsored by NIEO and interventionist perspectives are unrealistic, particularly in view of the problems facing the economies of the North.[8] It is true that, if the transfers were of the proportions they have been historically, their impact would at best not be significant. However, there is another question: If dramatically increased aid targets were obtainable, would they be consistent overall with other goals, such as equalizing North-South welfare and improving North-South terms of trade? These problems are especially important because these perspectives rely on trade for development of the South.

The North-South model demonstrates that, in general, aid and betterment of North-South terms-of-trade policies may be in conflict. Aid may also help the donor more than it helps the receiver. This is indicated by studying international and domestic markets in the form of significant real transfers of luxury or investment goods (or armaments) from the endowments of the high-income groups in the North to the South. Under certain conditions this turns the terms of trade *against* the exportables of the South. Such deterioration of the South's terms of trade may be sufficiently high that, after the transfer takes place, the North is strictly better off. It has somewhat fewer resources but is much more valuable in market terms; therefore, it has more real wealth, whereas the South has less real wealth.

When the North-South model is used to study the effects of aid, the economy of the North is disaggregated into two income groups: the rich and the poor. A transfer of real resources, consisting of luxury or investment goods (or armaments) from the high-income group in the North to the South, would be a most favorable equality-promoting transfer, since it is the rich and not the poor in the North who are assumed to give from their initial resources. Nevertheless, if low-income groups in the North and South initially have few goods transferred, the market mechanism turns terms of trade against the South. Thus, exports from the South increase, and prices for these exports decrease. In addition, real consumption in the South decreases, and real consumption in the North increases as a whole.

If a different aid policy is used in which the high-income group in the North transfers basic consumption goods to the South, the results differ. Under the same conditions as above, the outcome through the market adjustments that follows the transfer is either: (1) the real wealth of the South increases after the transfer of basic goods, but the real wealth of the poor in the North decreases and the welfare differential between poor and rich in the North increases, or (2) the welfare of the South decreases after the transfer of basic goods, and the North-South welfare differentials increase.

These results indicate that it may not be possible to achieve the goal of decreasing overall inequalities. It may not even be consistent with aid in the form of real transfers of either basic or nonbasic goods. In particular, there may be a contradiction between the interests of low-income groups in the North and in the South. This contradicts certain critiques of the liberal Northern perspective from the left. The question then becomes: Are the conditions under which aid would help decrease overall inequalities likely to exist? Or one may ask if it is more likely that: (1) the existing conditions preclude the effective use of aid as a means of equalizing incomes; (2) the existing political and economic forces can always manipulate the relevant parameters to bring about the conditions that would turn aid to the advantage of the donor. These issues obviously require case studies that focus on the values of the parameters studied here, especially to avoid negative outcomes. Furthermore, if the situation is such that we are within the set that produces negative outcomes of aid, part of an aid policy should be to attempt to change those conditions. Our study points to the likelihood that in many cases both questions do not generally have favorable answers for those who support aid policies. This would also be consistent with the collective self-reliance perspective and the findings of the Bariloche study.

CONCLUSIONS

Our central thesis is that liberal economic policies put forward by Northern institutions are inconsistent with the stated Northern concern for improving levels of human well-being and human rights. It may be argued that if their advocated economic policies have the economic effects for which they argue, then they would have some merit. But in a particular set of circumstances that are also those most likely to foster a lack of human rights—that is, a low overall level and wide inequality in economic well-being—those economic policies contradict their implied economic objectives and therefore also contradict human rights concerns. A gap exists between explicit policies and expressed concerns with human rights issues. Assumptions about aid and trade, in particular, have been brought into question in this paper. They are detrimental in certain circumstances to the economic and social interests of the lowest-income groups in both the North and the South. Northern liberal policies therefore need reappraising.

A concern with human rights in Southern countries often does not coincide with the economic self-interest of the Northern countries. This means that linking human rights directly to economic policy by the current U.S. administration may be self-contradictory. It may be true that, in the case of a few nations that have a somewhat dependent economic situation with the United States, such as Latin America, making the release of political prisoners a prior requirement for new trade agreements might work in these countries in the short run. However, U.S. economic policies and trade policies have much larger impact than these few political strategies. Current economic policy reinforces the political actors within developing societies who are responsible for violating human rights—authoritarian governments of several political complexions and the elite groups with which they are allied. At the same time, these policies damage the interests of the lower-income groups within those societies. Thus, linking economic policy to human rights requirements may seem to succeed in the short run; in the long run, the situations may be far worse.

NOTES

1. Section 116 of the Foreign Assistance Act of 1961, as amended in 1976, as well as Sections 701 and 703 of the 1977 Authorization Act for the International Financial Institutions use language concerning basic needs and needy people.

2. Literature in the social studies, particularly in the philosophy of science and the sociology of knowledge, has been concerned about debates of this kind for many years. The issues include both discussions about values themselves and discussions about the ways values are used, consciously and not, in methodological presuppositions for analytical work. Among recent writings in science, history, and politics are: Paul Feyerabend "Against Method" in M. Radner and S. Winokur, ed., *Analyses of Theories and Methods of Physics and Psychology* (Minneapolis: University of Minnesota Press, 1970); Thomas S. Kuhn, *The Structure of Scientific Revolutions,* 2nd ed. (Chicago: University of Chicago Press, 1970) and *The Essential Tension: Selected Studies in Scientific Tradition and Change* (Chicago: University of Chicago Press, 1977); Barry Barnes, *Scientific Knowledge and Social Theory* (London: Routledge and Kegan Paul, 1974); Karl R. Popper, *Conjectures and Refutations,* (New York: Harper and Row, 1963), *The Logic of Scientific Discovery,* (New York: Harper and Row, 1958), Marshall Sahlins, *Culture and Practical Reason,* (Chicago: University of Chicago Press, 1976).

3. The term "basic needs" and its current wide acceptance in the international development community can be traced to the work of the Bariloche model, to which one of the authors was a major contributor. See *Catastrophe or New Society? A Latin American World Model,* Fundación Bariloche (Buenos Aires), and the International Development Research Centre (Ottawa), 1976 (IDRC-064e). A discussion of current U.S. policy analyzed in the United States can be found in remarks by Albert Fishlow and Oscar Schachter, "Basic Human Needs: The International Law Connection," *Proceedings of the 72d Annual Meeting,* American Society of International Law, Washington, D.C., April 27–28, 1978, pp. 225–32. See also Robert E. Asher, *Development Assistance in the Seventies: Alternatives for the United States* (Washington: The Brookings Institution, 1970).

4. See *Catastrophe or New Society?* and Graciela Chichilnisky, "Development Patterns and the International Order," *Journal of International Affairs* 31, no. 2 (1977): 275–304.

5. For instance, see Christopher Freeman and Marie Jahoda, eds., *World Futures: The Great Debate* (London: Martin Robertson, 1978), and H. S. D. Cole, Ian Miles, and Jay Gershuny, "Scenarios of World Development," *Futures* (1978).

6. The preliminary findings of the UNITAR project (Project on the Future, 1978) are presented in a progress report entitled *Technology, Domestic Distribution and North-South Relations.*

7. John Clark, H. S. D. Cole, Henry Lucas, "Calibration and Solutions of a Macro-Model of North-South Relations," *Applied Mathematical Modelling* (forthcoming).

8. For example, see the computations of North-South transfers that would be necessary to bring the North-South wealth inequality ratio

to 6: 1 by the year 2000, instead of the present 13: 1 ratio, in Wassily Leontief et al., *The Future of the World Economy* (New York: Oxford University Press, 1977), and Graciela Chichilnisky, ''Basic Needs in the North-South Debate: Imperatives and Distortions'' (Harvard Institute for International Development, August 1978).

Chapter 6

HUMAN RIGHTS IMPLICATIONS OF CORPORATE FOOD POLICIES

RICHARD J. BARNET

I

In what sense is having food a right? The idea that being human entitles one to the minimum calories to support life and health has appeared in one form or another in a variety of documents that purport to express a global consensus. The United Nations Covenants on Human Rights drafted at the end of World War II explicitly promise access to food: nutrition is the most basic economic right. Anyone who is denied food, therefore, is by definition being treated as less than human. More recently the language of "basic needs" has been incorporated into national and international declarations. A "need" as basic as food does not allow even for controversy; people cannot survive without it and individual survival is the precondition, obviously, for society. The "basic-needs" strategy is often cast in the language of rights. Whether access to food is truly a "right" in a traditional legal sense depends upon whether the claim is enforceable. When the promise of food is merely rhetorical, the reality of hunger dramatizes the absence of the right.

The rhetoric of "basic needs" is controversial, not because it embraces access to food, but because it leaves other things out. Thus the Cocoyac Declaration of 1975 declared:

Development should not be limited to the satisfaction of basic needs. There are other needs, other goals, and other

143

values. Development includes freedom of expression and impression, the right to give and receive ideas and stimulus. There is a deep social need to participate in shaping the basis of one's own existence, and to make some contribution to the fashioning of the world's future. Above all, development includes the right to work, by which we mean not simply having a job but finding self-realization in work, the right not to be alienated through production processes that use human beings simply as tools.[1]

The right to food has been traditionally enforced by revolution. The French Revolution, the Russian Revolution, and in our day food riots in Egypt and Poland all attest to the fact that governments that are callous to the hunger of the people lose legitimacy and may lose power. By the same token, leaders clinging to office try to demonstrate a commitment to overcoming hunger. Thus, a few years ago, the new Polish leaders subsidized bread prices, and after the Cairo food riots President Sadat imported 100,000 tons of wheat as food aid from the United States.

The existence of starvation offends the most elementary notions of justice. Most people today believe that the state has the responsibility to create a society in which people do not starve. But even in societies dedicated to extreme forms of rugged individualism and the anticollectivist ethic, hunger confuses the issues. How can the familiar rhetoric of capitalism with its emphasis on "equality of opportunity" be relevant in a society such as Chile, for example, where malnutrition handicaps millions of children at birth? The mental retardation and dullness that characterizes the huge global population deprived of sufficient calories in the early years of development makes class divisions permanent. Individuals impaired at birth are robbed of "equal opportunity" to compete. Without basic mental equipment, no amount of hard work can enable them to surmount the misery of poverty. There are powerful reasons to assert the right to food as a basic human right with special clarity in the closing years of the twentieth century. It is not only that the absolute number of hungry people is increasing and that the increasingly internationalized food system is significantly widening the gap between the well fed and the underfed all over the world. Even more significant is the fact that the world is losing traditional mechanisms for articulating and enforcing the right to food without replacing them with new modes of allocation.

Who eats in the modern world is much related to who works. It has not always been quite so true as it is today. In traditional societies obligations to feed the aged, children, relatives, village elders, and others not directly engaged in food production were the foundation of the common life. Most of the world's population was engaged in some form of agriculture, which helped to assure access to food sufficient at least for subsistence. Global trends in the world food system are clear: fewer and fewer people are raising the world's food. Millions of people formerly in subsistence agriculture are being uprooted from their land and are physically separated from their traditional food supply. Land in poor countries, once used for self-agriculture, is now being used for export crops. Typically, high-technology agriculture, spearheaded usually by the multinational food conglomerates, the fertilizer and seed companies, the farm machinery manufacturers, the grain traders, and the food packagers and processors move in, and the people who once were subsistence farmers move out, usually to the city. Thus, those who were "self-employed," to use the familiar terminology, enter the job market and the money economy. Separated from their land, they must now buy the food they once raised themselves. However, hundreds of millions cannot find work and hence have no money to provide themselves or their families adequate calories. Even among those who still farm, the cash requirements for "inputs," especially seeds, fertilizers, and machinery, are now so high that they must sell what they once retained for family consumption. Even the millions who work to provide food for others do not eat adequately themselves.[2]

The pace of social and economic transformation across the planet is undermining the three traditional impulses for protecting human life. One is religious—the obligation to respect individual souls—which is derived from a duty to a supreme being or supernatural source. Despite revivals of religious sentiment in our time, particularly the new Islamic movements, the world is becoming increasingly secularized, and the religious injunction to provide "daily bread" has lost much of its force.

The second impulse is social. In traditional societies people look after one another because there is a high degree of mutual dependence. One cares for the children in part because one expects to be cared for by them in old age. But the breakdown of communities dedicated to caring for all members, especially the family and the village, is happening everywhere. One characteristic of industrialized society has been the separation of families as wage earners scatter to find work. As a consequence, the old are more likely to be abandoned and working mothers are to care for their children. The physical characteristics of urban life no longer provide an easy setting to maintain communities or extended families; the result is the isolation, inwardness, and self-absorbtion of modern men and women that three generations of sociologists have explored.

The third impulse for valuing human life is economic. It is in society's interest that workers be fed enough to keep them fit for their tasks. How strong the economic interest in feeding the productive population is depends greatly on the state of the labor market. As Karl Polanyi has shown in *The Great Transformation*, there has been an economic interest in restricting benevolence when, as in the case of the Speenhamland reforms in England, the welfare system destroyed the incentive to work. Workers, "fearfully handicapped by hunger," as Engels put it, were not in a position to reject drudgery and debasing work nor to bargain over wages and working conditions. With automation and higher wages the condition of workers improved, but the need for additions to the work force declined. Now the slowdown of the world economy—which appears to be a structural, not a temporary phenomenon—and the labor-saving strategies of corporations—automation and production shifts to ever lower wage areas of the world—are creating a new reality. More and more of the world's population is becoming irrelevant to the productive process, either as producers or as significant consumers. In particular, the work force in the Third World is increasing so much faster than work opportunities that in many places most of those who seek work will not find it. In a time of austerity, disguised subsidies for makework jobs are less available. The "underemployed"—the street hawkers and odd-job people who may work all day without earning a living wage—cannot possibly maintain an adequate calorie level, particularly in a time of inflation.

Marx talked of the "reserve army of the unemployed" as a necessary capitalist instrument for "disciplining" the labor force. The hungry crowds at the factory door tended to make the people properly appreciate their opportunities. As the system prospered, a strong interest developed for keeping the reserve army alive, and healthy and reasonably content. But the reserve army of the unemployable has now become unmanageably large—not only in the Third World but increasingly in certain pockets in industrial countries as well. Thus, the purely economic interest in feeding large numbers of formerly potential members of the work force has become much weaker. The number of mouths to feed has so exceeded the number of jobs and potential jobs that the idea of "surplus population" has reappeared in various forms. "Triage" and the "lifeboat ethic" are responses to contemporary reality: that existing food production and distribution systems cannot feed large numbers of people now and cannot hope to feed them in the near future. The world is therefore forced to choose who is to survive and who is to be abandoned.

If the world food situation is seen in these terms, human rights problems are immediately obvious. Who is to decide who is invited into the lifeboat and who is to be shoved out? By what definition does a city or a country or a region become a "basket case" on which further food is not to be wasted? If human starvation can be accepted as a cruel necessity of life for the unfortunate born in a "basket-case" country, or a food-deprived region, then the concept of human rights has no meaning for hundreds of millions of people.

If "food power" is not to become a threat or a weapon to be

used against people on the edge of starvation, then the notion of secure access to food must be vigorously reasserted as a right that attaches to all men and women at birth. Such a right is not rooted in historical tradition; entitlement to food has never been recognized as an unconditional right by which the rhetoric of UN documents is actually implemented, except perhaps in some socialist countries. The reasons for making such a right universal are now pragmatic and moral. Unless such clear norms are created and supported by an overwhelming international consensus, the politics of scarcity will dictate "triage" strategies that will keep the world in a permanent state of grotesque and dangerous conflict. Unless the impulse to respect human life is nurtured by a powerful political consensus and supported by legal institutions, the trend toward debasing and devaluing human life will reach a point at which the concept of human rights will lose all meaning.

II

If secure access to food is recognized as a right, then it is necessary to examine trends in the organization of the world food system to determine whether they provide a political and economic climate within which such a right can be realized. Although it is true that most food is still grown locally, international trade in food is assuming ever greater importance. Increasingly, the worldwide food production and distribution system is coming under the control of a relatively small number of multinational corporations. Five grain companies effectively control the world traffic in wheat, corn, barley, and soy. Two farm machinery companies control 60 percent of the farm machinery market in the United States and also have a decisive role in the world market. A small number of grain and chemical companies now control the world seed market. U.S. seed company sales abroad went up 38 percent in the first three years of the decade.[3] The new seeds, which in some places have dramatically increased yields, require large amounts of chemical fertilizers, which the same companies supply. These "wonder seeds" of the Green Revolution now play a major role in the agriculture of some of the poorest countries of the world. In Pakistan, for example, in less than ten years the area planted with the new seeds grew from 50,000 to more than 32 million acres.[4] Finally, retail processed food is also largely controlled by a few multinational companies. The distribution of such products is having profound effects on dietary habits all over the world, especially in poor countries where malnutrition is a severe problem. Multinational corporations play a crucial role in the food production and distribution system; the impact of that role on world hunger, and the human rights implications of alternative corporate strategies are therefore extremely important to discuss and assess.

The obvious must be stated at the outset. As powerful and important as they are, multinational corporations are not the only factor in the world food system. Local landowners, local governments, peasants, and local consumers have their own interests, prejudices, and traditions, and these are important in determining who eats and who does not. The food system is a chain linking producers, distributors, and consumers, and many of the decisions about what people eat are beyond the control of corporations. But some of the most crucial decisions are direct consequences of their strategies and their power. As the world food system becomes increasingly internationalized and increasingly integrated, the role of the global food producers, processors, and distributors increases.

At the production end of the chain, corporations have had several major effects. First, high-technology agriculture has led to increasing concentration of land, increasing dependence upon imported inputs such as seeds and fertilizers, and increasing use of cash crops to maintain the economies of underdeveloped countries. As land becomes more valuable, marginal farmers must sell and either work as sharecroppers or go to the city. In addition, mechanized agriculture requires increased credit. Obviously, wealthier farmers are preferred risks for loans to buy imported seeds and fertilizers. Thus, the gap between the rich and the poor increases within the country. Numerous studies in Mexico, Taiwan, China, and elsewhere show that where land is more equitably shared, production increases because the incentive to produce rises. Where the poor farmer is less able to control what he grows because these decisions are made by the moneylender or the owner of the land, he is less able to provide for himself and his family. When he leaves the land and goes to the city, he is cut off from his traditional food supply. He is now in the money economy, but without a job he has no money for food. All over the Third World the influx of former farmers from the countryside far exceeds the number of available urban jobs.

Second, the mechanization of agriculture has sharply reduced employment possibilities in the countryside. In the Punjab, for example, which has been a center of the Green Revolution, the amount of human labor needed in the fields has fallen by 50 percent. According to Donald K. Freebairn, "the introduction of mechanical harvesting will eventually result in an overall decrease of about 90 million man-days of employment in the Punjab, most of it for day laborers." According to K. C. Abercrombie's study, "Agricultural Employment in Latin America," 2.5 million jobs in agriculture were lost in 1972 in that part of the world, and the trend is continuing.[5]

A third important consequence of multinational activity in the food system is a shift in total agriculture in Third World countries to cash crops. With the rise in agribusiness, cash cropping has increased dramatically. The principal cash crops—coffee, tea, bananas, cotton—grew more than twice as fast from the mid-1950s to the mid-1960s as the entire agricultural economy in underdeveloped countries. Coffee production in Africa has increased more than 400 percent in the last twenty years. Because export crops are profitable subsistence crops have increasingly been replaced by cash crops for export. Land that was used for growing black beans, the staple of the poor in Brazil, has been converted to soybeans for cattle feed. Black beans then must be imported, and the price is prohibitive for the poor. There are similar examples from all over the Third World. Iran, which used to be agriculturally self-sufficient, was importing $800 million of food in the last years of the Shah; much of this food came from U.S. grain companies, while agricultural land in Iran was used for export operations controlled by multinational firms.

The high-technology-export crop model is rational and beneficial for some but irrational and even catastrophic for much larger numbers. Foreign sales of U.S. seed and fertilizer companies are nonetheless highly profitable. Mechanization helps the richer peasants to "get rid of tenants and to keep for themselves whatever portion of the harvest (a third to a half) used to fall due to the tenants."[6] Consumers of coffee, tea, bananas, and strawberries around the world benefit from increased production, and the owners (usually foreign) derive large profits. However, the export of luxuries undermines the incentive and the capability of Third World countries to provide basic nutrition for their people. Scarce land, credit, water, and technology are preempted for the export market.

Dr. Ernest Feder, formerly of the Food and Agriculture Organization, investigated the strawberry industry in Mexico. Lappé and Collins in their book *Food First* summarize his findings:

> Dr. Feder's research makes clear that, first of all we should not speak of the Mexican strawberry industry located in Mexico. Officially, Mexican growers produce the berries and even own some of the processing facilities. The real control, however, remains with the American investors and food wholesalers. Using production contracts and credit facilities, these American firms make all the important decisions: the quantity, quality, types, and prices of inputs; how and when the crop will be cultivated; the marketing processes, including prices for the producers; the transportation and the distribution; and the returns on capital investments. U.S. marketing control is so powerful that despite efforts by the Mexican government to develop markets in Europe, all Mexican strawberries pass through American exporters even when ultimately retailed in a third country such as Canada or France.[7]

Such contract farming attached to multinational export operations is increasingly the rule in the Third World. The contract farmers are an exploited underclass that have now become indispensable to the integrated world food system. In Guatemala, according to Ray Goldberg of the Harvard Business School, 70 percent of the cucumber pickers are children under fifteen. The "sorting and grading for export was done, in one operation, by 27 women who were paid $.80 a day."[8]

Rich and generally well fed countries are now importing more and more of their food from poor countries with a high rate of malnutrition. Most of the food is nonessential—cocoa, coffee, tea, bananas, or sugar. Poor countries, on the other hand, import staples from the United States—chiefly wheat, corn, and rice. This division of labor and trade contributes directly to hunger in poor countries because the producers of the export crops are paid so little—the farmer in Ghana gets about 16 percent of the export price of his cocoa beans—that they cannot afford to pay for imported wheat or rice in sufficient quantities.

Contract farming in vegetable products is one example of agricultural operations in one part of the world serving the interests of people living in another. The huge increase in beef production is another example. To feed cattle, grain is converted from a relatively inexpensive source of calories into an extremely expensive, wasteful, and energy-consuming product that is beyond the reach of all except an international meat-eating elite. There has been a dramatic increase in the numbers of that elite, in Europe, Japan, and the Soviet Union, particularly, but it is a small fraction of humankind. In Colombia, as Robert Ledogar has shown, Ralston Purina set up a remarkably efficient chicken-and-egg operation that was integrated with its feedmills. The problem is that land once used to grow staples for the poor is now used to grow feed for chickens that only the middle class can afford. A quarter of the population must work a week or more to buy a dozen eggs.

Thus, there is growing evidence from all over the world that food strategies that are highly profitable for the multinationals actually increase maldistribution of food and increase hunger. Many observers conclude that the bottom 20 to 60 percent of the population in various Third World "food-deficient countries," which are increasingly integrated with the global food economy in the ways described, have less adequate and less nutritious diets than did their parents and grandparents. The reasons transcend the operations of the multinationals, but the conclusion is inescapable that these strategies are central to the unfavorable effects of the global transformation of the world food distribution system.

The ideology that supports the global strategies of the food multinationals is comparative advantage. According to theory, specialization and increasing trade presumably are the keys to enriching all participants. But this is ideology, not science: the integrated world agriculture system operates to overfeed a few and underfeed the many. Equally important, dependence upon exporting food makes poor countries extremely insecure, for they depend upon a world market they cannot control. Although production has increased dramatically for tea, coffee, cocoa, sugar, and similar commodities, prices have fallen in real terms and, when compared with imported agricultural inputs and manufactured goods, disastrously so. Short-term price rises as in sugar and coffee bring a reaction because there are many competitive sources of supply. The fluctuation in agricultural exports is a direct cause of hunger in poor countries dependent upon cash crops. Susan George describes some recent fluctuations:

> The value of Brazil's sugar exports to the U.S. drops from $100 million to zero. The Philippines, on the other hand, export over 800,000 pounds of sugar to the U.S. in 1975 and nearly three times that much in 1976. Guinea's cocoa exports to the U.S. fall from nearly two million pounds to nothing and Chad's from over five million to nothing; while Liberia and "other West Africa" make up part of the difference by jumping from zero to over four million pounds. Mexico's cotton exports to the U.S. are halved, while India's increase by 400% and Pakistan's drop by 90%. For long fibre cotton, Egyptian exports are multiplied by four and Sudan's by fourteen but Israel's are reduced ninefold. Peruvian cotton exports meanwhile move up from zero to nearly eight million pounds.[9]

Were the rhetoric of basic needs and right to food to be translated into practical policies, explicit choices would have to be made by governments and corporations, and benchmarks of progress would be quite different from those that operate today. The criteria of success for agribusiness is efficiency as defined in narrow economic terms. There is no doubt that more food is being produced than ever before, that there have been dramatic increases in yields, that a growing middle class around the world is eating better, and that agricultural exports play a crucial role in the U.S. balance of payments. But the human costs of developing such a world food system are ignored or minimized. Sometimes it is argued that the starvation of millions of landless peasants and urban unemployed is a temporary phenomenon, but all the indications are that the food-distribution problem is worsening. The resource waste that characterizes the food system—it is not uncommon to spend 200 calories of energy to produce one calorie of food—is assumed to be necessary and even progressive. Creating a global food market expands the horizons of profit, but it does not get food to the people who most need it at the cheapest cost in resources (fossil fuels, minerals, and water).

Unless the goal of feeding everyone is made an operational priority of all governments, eliminating mass hunger is not possible. Where governments do adopt a priority of providing a minimum calorie and protein level for everyone before luxury foods are imported or good exports are emphasized, malnutrition can be substantially overcome. A comparison of Cuba with its neighbors and China with other Asian societies with teeming populations suggests that eliminating hunger is a matter of political choice.

What is the responsibility of corporations in the making of these political choices? What are the responsibilities of governments? To what extent is it fair to charge corporations with being violators of human rights? To what extent is it fair to expect corporations to be aware of the consequences of their operations and to be held responsible for them?

Let us take three different cases that recur in one form or another all over the world. The first is where a corporation leases a large area where local crops are raised, mechanizes production, and then converts them to high-price export crops, leaving the surrounding population without secure access to food or adequate income. In such a situation corporate intervention would cause an increase in hunger directly and inevitably unless the former subsistence farmers were employed under conditions that would provide them the income to buy the calories and proteins needed for life and health. The farmers turned employees would have to be paid on a scale commensurate with the cost of imported food and other necessities of life. If they are to be integrated into the world economy, sufficient jobs would have to be created and the farmers' wages would have to be indexed in some way to world prices, for the money they received for their product would now determine whether they eat. A corporation that is not willing to pay on such a scale is commiting a clear violation of human rights. It need not depend upon any government for legislation or change of policy. It has the power itself to implement the right to food for its workers. All it needs to do is to forgo the profit margins afforded by exploitation just as it has had to forgo them in the industrial world with the rise of the labor movement, the social democratic ethic, and social legislation. An international agency with the power to index prices, to monitor such corporations, and to report to the public on exploitation of agriculture workers could play an important role in helping to eliminate hunger.

The second case concerns the direct impact of corporations on consumers. The multinational corporation is having as profound a social effect on those underdeveloped societies where the hunger problem is concentrated by changing consumption habits and tastes as it has by changing the organization of food production. In *Global Reach,* some of the research on the effects of advertising and promotion campaigns were summarized:

"The food industry in developing countries has been a disaster . . . a minus influence," says Derrick B. Jelliffe, a leading nutrition expert. Companies are using advertising to take what Berg calls "blatant advantage of nutrition consciousness." J. K. Roy's studies in West Bengal show that poor families under the influence of advertising are buying patent baby foods "at exorbitant rates" although they could buy local cow's milk at much lower cost. They had been persuaded (falsely) that the packaged food has "extraordinary food value." In the Caribbean, Berg reports, nurses are employed by companies to get the names of new mothers at the hospital and then to "race to the women's homes to give free samples and related advertising."

In his studies of changing dietary habits in rural Mexican villages, Joaquin Cravioto finds that the two products which peasants want and buy the moment they come into contact with the advertising message are white bread and soft drinks. Bread becomes a substitute for tortillas. Depending upon how enriched it is, there may be some gain in protein and vitamins, but a loss in calcium. But the most important impact of this shift in eating habits in poor villages is that it takes a much greater share of the virtually nonexistent family food budget. Coca-Cola, nutritionally speaking, is a way of consuming imported sugar at a high price. People like the taste, but its popularity, as Albert Stridsberg points out, is due to the advertising campaigns of the global giants. "It has long been known that in the poorest regions of Mexico," he notes with satisfaction, "where soft drinks play a functional role in the diet, it is the international brands—Coke and Pepsi—not local off-brands, which dominate. Likewise, a Palestinian refugee urchin, shining shoes in Beirut, saves his piastres for a real Coca-Cola, at twice the price of a local cola."[10]

Clearly, the Coca-Cola Company cannot be held responsible if a farmer starves his children so that he can guzzle Cokes. However, whether a local government that permits or encourages the importation of expensive sugar when its people are starving should be immune from a human rights indictment is

another matter. Until governments, including the U.S. government, develop policies for policing and shaping the integrated
world food system in ways that will eliminate rather than increase hunger, it is naive to expect corporations to take the
lead. But to avoid a nutrition crisis of catastrophic proportions
in the 1980s requires governments to develop such policies
and to set a framework within which the human rights consequences of a broad range of corporate strategies can be
assessed.

There are some situations where the lethal consequences of
corporate promotion strategies are so clear that persisting in
these strategies constitutes a clear violation of human rights.
The infant formula case is a classic illustration. Nestlé and
other integrated food companies have for many years been
promoting infant formula in Third World countries by advertising and using hired nurses to visit maternity wards and to
advise mothers on the benefits of infant formula. Not only is
formula obviously more expensive than breast-feeding, but
warm climates, lack of refrigerators, and above all the contami-
nated water with which the formula is mixed mean that it is a
life-threatening product. The babies die of diarrhea. The evidence of these effects has been available for several years. The
companies have issued statements that deny the effects and
claim that they have desisted in the promotion campaign, but
there is evidence that this is not the case. A campaign to publi-
cize the matter has been undertaken by a group under the
auspices of the National Council of Churches. Investigating
such charges and preparing indictments against specific companies should be the responsibility of an international agency;
equally important, such information should be available for use
in the United Nations, particularly when specific cases warrant
condemnation by the General Assembly.

A third case where corporations have a profound effect on
world hunger is in research. Research choices have crucial
consequences. Certain products can be developed that, it can
be safely predicted, will increase hunger. Others can open up
the possibilities of feeding millions who otherwise might go
hungry. Whereas investment for research in the food business

is among the lowest of major industries, a significant emphasis has been on the development of substitutes for primary agricultural commodities for commercial products. A big shift from sugar to fructose made from corn oil in response to the sudden high price of sugar in 1974 took place in the industrialized countries. Since then per capita sugar consumption in the United States is down about 10 percent, and consumption of fructose corn syrup, which is twice as sweet as sugar, has almost doubled. (It is used principally in soft drinks, jams, confectionary, and bakery products that take about three quarters of all the sugar consumed in the United States.) The consequence has been the depression of the world sugar market; world sugar reserves now stand at about 30 percent of annual consumption. Continued depressed prices mean, of course, that real wages of sugar workers in poor exporting countries fall. The process is compounded by the imposition of import quotas to protect the failing domestic sugar industry in the United States.

Other synthetic products have been developed that also undercut the economies of poor countries and aggravate hunger among their populations. The jute and cotton economies have been seriously undermined by the development of plastics for clothes, bags, and carpet backings. Experiments with synthetic chocolate and coffee are under way. Other new products are now being developed that substitute for commodities on which poor countries depend, including guayule, an important potential source of synthetic rubber, and crambe, a grain that grows in the U.S. Midwest that can be used as a substitute for imported rapeseed oil in food industry processes. Some research on the wing bean, a potential new food crop, is going forward, but the food companies emphasize new products to feed animals rather than people.

We have seen how technological innovations associated with the Green Revolution had the paradoxical effect of increasing hunger in certain places while it increased the food supply. Other research-and-development decisions are having similar effects. Research choices are made by corporations in accordance with their goals, which are increasing profits, assuring

long-term access to basic commodities needed for the manufactured items on which high profits are realized, and increasing
their share of the world market for such items. These goals
frequently conflict with the goal of increasing the world food
supply and food access for the hungriest people. Large farm
interests have succeeded in minimizing federal funds for research on new crops; there is little interest in developing technology that could help feed the hungriest because these people,
without government subsidies, do not constitute a market. In
times of austerity food aid declines; what remains is geared to
the promotion of new markets for existing agricultural products, not developing new products to increase the access of
poor people to food. As a consequence, according to a *Business Week* report, fewer than 20 out of 350,000 plant species are
cultivated today as food and fiber crops.

If a hunger crisis is to be avoided, decisions about what to
grow and where ought to be vested in institutions with an
incentive to feed the hungry. The failure to develop food sup-
plies for the hungry is not something for which corporations
can now be held responsible. Their inaction is not the same
problem as producing products that are inherently dangerous
because they are either impure or mislabeled or because the
cultural context in which they are consumed will cause predictable harm. But the international community has the responsibility to increase food access by making available appropriate
technology where it exists and encouraging its development
where it does not exist so that food self-sufficiency can increase.

A world food plan to achieve these goals is essential. Failure
to mobilize energy and political support for restructuring the
world food production and distribution system over the next
decade is failure to meet the most basic of basic needs: this is
a clear violation of human rights. There are practical steps to
alleviate hunger that governments can initiate and corporations, working with new ground rules, can help to implement.
If these steps are not taken, one must conclude that corporations and governments are complicit in what the Latin American bishops at Medallín called "institutional violence."

Whether a death sentence is pronounced in a board room, an economic ministry, or the headquarters of the secret police, whether in innocence or by neglect or by design, the effects are the same.

NOTES

1. Quoted in Richard Falk, "Comparative Protection of Human Rights in Capitalist and Socialist Third World Countries," paper prepared for the American Political Science Association, September 1978, p. 8.

2. See Robert J. Ledogan, *Hungry for Profits* (New York: IDOC, 1976), pp. 94–98; Andrew Pease, "Technology and Peasant Production: Reflections on a Global Study," *Development and Change* 8 (1977); K. N. Raj, "La Mécanisation de l'agriculture en Inde et en Sri Lanka," *Revue International de travail* (Geneva: International Labor Office, October 1972); K. C. Abercrombie, "Agricultural Employment in Latin America," *International Labor Review* (July 1972); and Susan George, *Feeding the Few* (Washington, D.C.: Institute for Policy Studies, 1978).

3. George, *Feeding the Few*, p. 37.

4. Pease, "Technology and Peasant Production," p. 140.

5. As quoted in George, *Feeding the Few*, p. 40.

6. Raj, "La Mécanisation de l'agriculture en Inde et en Sri Lanka." Raj quotes from S. R. Bose, "The Green Revolution and Agricultural Employment under Conditions of Rapid Population Growth." (manuscript)

7. Frances M. Lappé and Joseph Collins, *Food First*, (New York: Houghton Mifflin, 1977), p. 257.

8. Ray A. Goldberg, *Agribusiness Management for Developing Countries—Latin America*, (Cambridge, Mass.: Ballinger, 1974), p. 178.

9. George, *Feeding the Few*, pp. 10–11.

10. Richard J. Barnet and Ronald E. Muller, *Global Reach* (New York: Simon and Schuster, 1975), pp. 183–84.

Chapter 7

SOCIAL JUSTICE AND POLITICAL EQUALITY: LAND TENURE POLICIES AND RURAL DEVELOPMENT IN SOUTH ASIA

JOSEPH W. ELDER

CURRENT OBSERVATIONS OF SOCIAL JUSTICE AND POLITICAL EQUALITY IN SOUTH ASIA[1]

When national independence came to the countries of South Asia in the decades following World War II, there was widespread hope that rapid economic growth and the reduction of long-standing inequalities would come in the wake of independence. Leaders enshrined these hopes in national constitutions, the preambles of development programs, postindependence textbooks, and countless speeches. Implicit in many of these statements was the suggestion that an empirical relationship exists between political "equality" (often defined specifically to include national independence, universal franchise, and basic civil liberties) and economic "equality" (often defined diffusely to include some sort of equitable distribution of goods and services throughout the population). Given the predominant role of agriculture in the economies of these countries, leaders suggested that land reforms, extension services, and new agricultural technologies in the context of political independence could bring widespread prosperity and equality to the majority of their populations.

When the Asian Development Bank opened for business in

1966, it commissioned a task force to survey its member countries and determine the current status and future prospects of their agricultural sectors. The task force's ensuing report[2] concluded on a cautiously optimistic note: scientific technologies (such as high-yielding seeds and chemical fertilizers) accompanied by infrastructural supports (including irrigation systems, local credit, transport, and storage facilities) and external financial assistance might enable many Asian countries to become self-sufficient in food grains and even to export modest amounts of foreign-exchange-earning agricultural surpluses.

Severe food shortages and the continued widespread existence of rural poverty and underemployment in Asia in the early 1970s suggested that the cautious optimism of the Asian Development Bank's first report had not been warranted. Six years after publishing its first report, the Bank commissioned a task force to reassess the state of agriculture in Asia. Its second report was more sobering than its first:

> For the region as a whole, food production growth has barely kept pace with population growth, and in some countries, despite the introduction of the new food grain technology, per capita cereal production actually fell during the past decade. . . . Food consumption patterns have changed little during the last ten years . . . the bulk of the population does not consume the minimum dietary requirements for normal health. . . . The majority of households . . . lack even the purchasing power to obtain an adequate diet . . . the underemployed labor force in the rural economy is large and growing larger . . . in most areas . . . real wages have either remained static over the past decade or have declined. The rapid growth of the landless labor force has maintained a downward pressure on real wages. . . . Rural poverty is thus particularly widespread . . . and there is a general consensus that the problem has worsened considerably in the past decade. The basic problem is one of restricted access to productive resources and profitable employment opportunities.[3]

According to World Bank figures, the South Asian growth rate between 1950 and 1975 (in recent per annum) was 1.7 percent—the lowest of any region in the world (contrasted with 2.4 percent for Africa, 2.6 percent for Latin America, 3.2 percent for the developed countries, 3.9 percent for East Asia, and 5.2 percent for the Middle East). Within South Asia, the most densely populated countries showed the slowest growth rate: Bangladesh (−0.6 percent), India (1.5 percent), and Pakistan (3.2 percent).[4]

As if the slow growth rate and low level of food production in South Asia were not enough to generate concern, what growth rate there was often seemed to benefit the rich rather than the poor. Thus, according to the Asian Development Bank's second report: "There is some evidence of increasing inequality of rural incomes [in South Asia during the past decade]."[5] In India, for example, between 1964–65 and 1970–71 the proportion of total rural income earned by the *highest* 20 percent of the rural population *rose* from 44.6 to 46.6 percent, while the proportion earned by the *lowest* 20 percent *dropped* from 7.5 to 6.4 percent.[6] During approximately this same period, the proportion of uneconomically small farms (0–1 hectare) in India increased from 39.8 to 50.5 percent.[7]. Perhaps most pessimistic of all was the report's prediction that by 1985 for the Asian region as a whole there would be domestic food grain deficits of between 21 and 46 million metric tons.

An International Labor Organization study published in 1977 generally corroborated the findings of the Asian Development Bank. This study found evidence for increasing rural poverty in seven South and Southeast Asian nations. For example, between 1957 and 1970 the proportion of rural people beneath the poverty line in Malaysia increased from 30.0 to 36.5 percent. In the Philippines the poorest 20 percent of the population became poorer. And in Bangladesh over 80 percent of the population suffered a decrease in real income. The ILO attributed this increasing impoverishment to "unequal ownership of land and other productive assets, allocative mechanisms which discriminate in favor of the owners of wealth, and the pattern of investment and technical change which is biased against labor."[8] Additional recent reports indicate that 33 percent of the rural population in Bangladesh and 30 percent of the rural population in India own *no* land.[9] Furthermore, concentrated among the 30 percent rural landless in India are a disproportionately large number of scheduled caste scheduled tribe members ("ex-untouchables").[10]

What have been the responses of the Asian Development Bank, the International Labor Organization, USAID, and other similar agencies to these disturbing findings from rural South Asia? Typically the responses have included distress, feelings of helplessness, and expressions of concern but few "realistic" recommendations.[11] One reason it has been difficult to do much more than express distress has been the fact that, from the perspectives of most such organizations and agencies, what has happened in South Asia is "just"—that is, "fair" within recognized "frameworks of legitimacy." Aside from occasional blatantly illegal and/or corrupt moves on the part of the wealthy sectors of South Asian countries, most of the increasing concentrations of wealth have come about through the legitimate mechanism of the market operating within constitutionally established frameworks protecting private property. How can the Asian Development Bank, the International Labor Organization, the World Bank, or the American public generally be too critical when increasing economic equalities in South Asian countries are both legal and, to a certain extent, predictable?

Some of the public pronouncements made during the past decade, however, seem to reflect uneasiness about a concept of justice that concludes that increasing economic inequalities in South Asia are just.[12] Several books published in the West in the early 1970s focused attention on the distributive aspects of development programs, implying that some concern for economic equality needed to be incorporated into development programs.[13] The uneasiness about a concept of justice that did not include some concern for economic equality was reflected in the U.S. Congress' 1973 Foreign Assistance Act, which instructed AID to direct its attention and resources specifically to the rural poor in developing countries.[14] Similarly, the Asian Development Bank and the International Labor Organization studies describe the need to pursue policies that will reduce economic inequalities, and thereby implicitly reduce injustices, in developing countries. Even if these various activities reflect feelings that increasing economic inequality is *not* just according to some as yet unspecified framework of legitimacy, one is hard-pressed to identify the structure or conceive of the implementation mechanism for such a framework of legitimacy.

EQUALITY, JUSTICE, AND LANDHOLDING POLICIES IN PRE-TWENTIETH-CENTURY SOUTH ASIA

The current paradox—that increasing economic inequality is just—may be a result of a unique convergence of Western values regarding equality and justice. To what extent do the nations of South Asia subscribe to these same Western notions of equality and justice, and to what extent do they share the same sense of paradox?

The classical Hindu law texts stressed hierarchy and inequality. The majority of the creation stories, the *dharma* texts dealing with correct conduct (such as the *Laws of Manu*), and the *artha* texts dealing with the acquisition of economic wealth and political power (e.g., the *Arthashastra*) enunciated principles of legitimate hierarchy and legitimate inequality. In principle, the *varna* (rank) into which one was born determined one's political standing and rights. If a high-ranking Brahman and a low-ranking Shudra committed the same crime, the Brahman might be let off with a reprimand, whereas the Shudra might be required to pay a heavy fine, suffer imprisonment, or be executed. Political inequality was just because it was in the cosmic order of things for people to exist within a hierarchical structure.

Historical and anthropological data from South Asia also provide evidence of hierarchy and social, economic, and po-

litical inequality. Anthropologists such as H. N. C. Stevenson
and Louis Dumont have seen the principle of hierarchy as one
of the major defining characteristics of South Asian society,
and they have defined two separate South Asian hierarchies—one sacred and the other secular.[15] Other anthropologists such as McKim Marriott and Ronald B. Inden have
suggested that South Asians have characteristically viewed
their own hierarchical world monistically and have *not* distinguished between separate sacred and secular hierarchies.[16]
Regardless of the outcome of this dispute, it is probably safe to
say that concepts of a just hierarchy coupled with just inequality have characterized dominant groups throughout much of
South Asian history. Periodically, countergroups and movements that have opposed these concepts of hierarchy and inequality and have stressed political, social, or religious equality have appeared in South Asia. These have included the
Buddhists and Jains, members of *bhakti* (devotional) cults,
"outsiders" such as Muslims and Christians, and certain tribal
groups in remote and upland areas. Despite the important roles
such groups have played at different times and places in South
Asian history, their views of equality and justice have in time
been overwhelmed by those of the dominant Hindu groups.

Landholding patterns in South Asia have typically reflected
the dominant South Asian views of hierarchy through multiple
prisms of differences and legitimate inequalities. In the typical
village context, different kinship groups held different "claims
to the fruits of the land." Thus, certain families might have the
right to farm a certain piece of land and retain a portion of the
harvest for themselves (provided they shared some of their
harvest with such village servants as the sweepers and the
priests). Other families might have the rights to graze their
cattle on that land after each harvest. Still other families might
have the rights to collect firewood from trees growing on that
land, to pick any edible greens growing on the edges of that
land, or to be hired as occasional laborers on that land. Furthermore, different "claims to the fruits of the land" were
transmitted through different channels—some by the families

themselves, some by caste councils, some by local rulers or members of prominent families. Within this context, questions of who actually "owned" the land (in the Western sense of land "ownership") could hardly be answered.

The British discovered the complexities of these "claims to the fruits of the land" when the East India Company began to acquire the rights of *diwan* (tax collection) in increasingly large sectors of South Asia during the eighteenth and nineteenth centuries. A few indigenous categories of landed persons, such as the *inam*-holders who had received tax-free title to certain lands from local rulers, approached Britain's notions of legitimate "landowners." But on the whole it was difficult for the British to superimpose their concepts of "landownership" over South Asian rural notions of "claims to the fruits of the land."[17]

Gradually, the British managed officially to superimpose their concepts of "ownership" (as filtered through indigenous intermediaries) throughout the territories they controlled.[18] The usual British techniques was to take the "colloidal suspension" of landed relations extant in a given locality at some arbitrary point in time and to declare that *that* "colloidal suspension" was from thenceforth onward the fixed, official landholding pattern. Given the fact that the "suspension" at any one place and time was apt *not* to be the "suspension" at another place and time, the British discovered that their efforts at establishing landholding patterns were never fully consistent, satisfactory, or complete. As a result, the British continually improvised, declaring "temporary" settlements in some places and "permanent" settlements in other places, and adopting a wide range of different tax-collecting systems, including *zamindari* (taxes-from-tax-collectors), *ryotwari* (taxes-from-cultivators), and *mahalwari* (taxes-from-village sectors).

The multiple systems of landholding that evolved in the eighteenth and nineteenth centuries by the British in South Asia reflected multiple frameworks of legitimacy and hence multiple concepts of justice. During this period in South Asia, "landholding" as the British now defined it became a major base of political power, since it almost inevitably implied control over people. To this extent, political and economic frameworks of legitimacy overlapped in practice, if not in principle.

EQUALITY, JUSTICE, AND LANDHOLDING POLICIES IN TWENTIETH-CENTURY SOUTH ASIA

In the early 1800s a few South Asians such as Ram Mohun Roy began to advocate steps toward universal franchise and political equality for South Asians. Over the succeeding decades new South Asian voices called for equal access with the British to administrative examinations, civil service positions, and memberships on boards of local districts and municipalities. The Indian National Congress, founded in 1885, provided a more formal vehicle for those South Asians seeking greater political equality with the British. In the early decades of the twentieth century, with leadership from figures like Tilak, Gandhi, and the Ali brothers, increasing proportions of South Asian populations supported concepts of political equality and demands for political independence from the British. Gandhi, because of his special sensitivities to the plight of South Asia's untouchables, began to insist that claims for *political* equality with the British were hollow if they were not coupled with *social* equality for the untouchables. In 1921 Gandhi wrote that *swaraj* (self-rule) "is a meaningless term if we desire to keep a fifth of India under perpetual subjection. . . . Inhuman ourselves, we may not plead before the Throne for deliverance from the inhumanity of others."[19]

Similarly, Gandhi believed that a nonviolent system of government was impossible if a wide gulf existed between "the rich and the hungry millions." In 1946 he wrote:

> The contrast between the rich and the poor today is a painful sight. The poor villagers are exploited . . . by their own countrymen—the city-dwellers. They produce the food and go hungry. . . . Everyone must have a balanced diet, a decent house to live in, facilities for the education of one's children and adequate medical relief.[20]

His approach to the problem of unequal income was twofold: (1) equal distribution—each individual should receive enough to supply all his or her natural needs and no more, and (2) trusteeship—each individual with superfluous wealth should consider himself or herself a trustee of that wealth to use it for the benefit of those nearby. Looking toward the independent India of the future, Gandhi in his practical trusteeship formula said:

Just as it is proposed to fix a decent minimum living wage, even so a limit should be fixed for the maximum income that would be allowed to any person in society. The difference between such minimum and maximum incomes should be reasonable and equitable and variable from time to time so much so that the tendency would be towards obliteration of the difference.[21]

Except for a few radical figures such as Mahatma Gandhi, the nonviolent activist, and M. N. Roy, the Marxist humanist, there was little discussion in preindependence South Asia of *economic* equality. Certainly, economic equality was not coupled in any intrinsic way with political equality. The leaders of South Asia's newly emerging nations adopted, in effect, the same separation between political equality and social and economic justice as did their British and American mentors.

The formally adopted constitutions of newly independent South Asian nations typically confirmed their citizens' rights of private property and prohibited the expropriation of their private property (such as land) without compensation. The general concepts of landholding in South Asia continued to be dominated by frameworks of legitimacy combining earlier British revenue demands and court-established laws of inheritance operating within current market economies. Even with later constitutional amendments, the rights of private property remained intact, as did the principles of compensation for private property.[22]

LAND REFORMS AND RURAL DEVELOPMENT
PROGRAMS IN POSTINDEPENDENCE
SOUTH ASIA

The countries of South Asia have gone their various ways since achieving political equality as independent nations. Nevertheless, all of them have engaged in some measures of land reform within the limits of their constitutions. These reforms have included such measures as:

1. Abolishing taxing intermediaries between landholders and the state.
2. Establishing ceilings on the total size of permissible landholdings to any one citizen, and the acquisition of "surplus" lands above the ceilings.
3. Redistributing "surplus" lands to the landless.
4. Protecting tenants and small subholders.
5. Consolidating scattered small landholdings.
6. Prohibiting land fragmentation by barring the sale of plots of land below a certain size.
7. Resettling on formerly uncultivated lands.[23]

Why have South Asian nations enacted these various land reforms? The reasons have typically been complex. Preindependence commitments to land reform have come back to haunt postindependence political leaders. National elites have felt embarrassed by criticisms from abroad about the gross inequities in their rural areas. Landless groups have brought actual or potential pressure on candidates and officials. Parties and persons in office have often recognized the political price they may have to pay for legislative inaction. Generally, the principles undergirding land reform legislation have been those of some diffuse sort of economic justice as identified by Westernized elites and sought by some landless or near landless groups or their champions—"land to the tiller," "the reduction of gross economic inequities in the countryside," and so forth. Some of the few land resettlement programs in South Asia have experimented directly with principles of economic equality such that each qualifying farm family has re-

ceived identical amounts of land, credit, and technical assistance.[24] But such consciously egalitarian projects represent
only a tiny portion of the land reform programs in South Asia.

When one takes an overall historical look at South Asian
land reforms, one is struck by the fact that their net effects
(with few exceptions) consistently seem to have benefited the
wealthier sectors of the rural population at the expense of the
poorer sectors of that population. As the figures from the Asian
Development Bank indicate, the proportions of the rural populations in South Asia with no land (or with land under one
hectare) have increased, as have the proportions of landholdings over ten hectares.[25] The economic gap in the countryside
has widened.

Not only has land reform legislation in South Asia seemed to
increase economic inequities, but rural development programs
have as well. Typically, such development programs have been
technologically oriented, involving improved varieties of
seeds, increased irrigation, increased use of fertilizer, and improved marketing infrastructure such as roads and credit facilities. A farmer's ability to benefit from such a program has
usually been directly contingent on his ability to provide the
necessary capital to purchase the improved varieties of seeds,
to pay for the fertilizer, to cover the costs of installing irrigation
facilities himself, or to pay for someone else's surplus water.
The rural development program benefits, therefore, have typically gone disproportionately to the wealthier farmers through
the "justice" of competitive market processes.

The economic inequalities in South Asia's rural areas have
been aggravated by the economic inequalities between South
Asia's rural areas and its urban centers. For example, in 1978
the Indian Planning Commission stated:

The pattern of industrial development that has emerged [in
India] obviously reflects the structure of effective demand.
. . . An unduly large share of resources is thus absorbed in
production which relates directly or indirectly to maintaining or improving the living standards of the higher income
groups. The demand of this relatively small class, not only

for a few visible items of conspicuous consumption but for the outlay on high quality housing and urban amenities, aviation and superior travel facilities, telephone services, and so on sustains a large part of the existing industrial structure.[26]

The economic inequalities in the rural areas and between the rural and urban areas have frequently been aggravated by the exercise of both legitimate and illegitimate political power by influential families, many of which own interests in both the rural and urban areas.

THE ROLE OF THE UNITED STATES IN SOUTH ASIAN RURAL DEVELOPMENT

In his inaugural address on January 20, 1949, President Truman announced his famous Point Four:

> Fourth, we must embark on a bold new program for making the benefits of our scientific advances and industrial progress available for the improvement and growth of underdeveloped areas. . . .
>
> I believe that we should make available to peace-loving peoples the benefits of our store of technical knowledge in order to help them realize their aspirations for a better life. And in cooperation with other nations, we should foster capital investment in areas needing development.
>
> Our aim should be to help the free people of the world through their own efforts, to produce more food, more clothing, more materials for housing, and more mechanical power to lighten their burdens.[27]

The subsequent Act for International Development (Title IV of the Foreign Economic Assistance Act of 1950) was a major U.S. effort to implement the policies enunciated in President Truman's Point Four. The goals of the Act for International Development including promoting economic stability and growth in all noncommunist countries, especially the less developed ones, and preventing the territorial and ideological expansion of communism. Since less developed areas were viewed as especially susceptible to communism, the attention of U.S. lawmakers was directed increasingly toward the less developed areas of South Asia.

In 1952 Point Four assistance to South Asia was launched in the form of Technical Cooperation Missions to India, Pakistan, Nepal and Sri Lanka (then Ceylon). In their early years, these missions concentrated on supplying U.S. experts to work in South Asia on development projects and on training South Asian personnel (in the United States or in third countries) in skills that were scarce in South Asia. In 1957 loans were made available to South Asia through the newly established Development Loan Fund. Eventually loans became available from the Export-Import Bank of Washington. Typically, the terms of these loans were generous. Some of them had a ten-year grace period and a total repayment period of forty years at interest rates varying between 0.75 and 2.5 percent. Commodity aid under various sections of Public Law 480 began to flow into South Asia—food grains, fertilizers, machinery, and steel. The United States offered particularly generous terms to India and Pakistan, whereby India and Pakistan could pay for those commodities in Indian and Pakistani rupees that were not permitted to leave the country, thereby avoiding an excessive drain on their respective foreign-exchange reserves. By 1966 total U.S. assistance to India alone had reached the $6.4 billion figure. During the same period, Soviet aid to India came to $1.6 billion.

Once the United States had committed itself to providing aid to South Asia, it had to choose precisely how to channel that aid. The Soviet Union, in line with its interests in encouraging "national democratic" and "noncapitalist" tendencies in South Asian nations, chose to funnel its aid primarily into the nations' public sectors. For example, it supplied substantial assistance to the publicly owned Bhilai and Bokaro metallurgical complexes in India.

By contrast, the United States, in line with its interests in encouraging "free enterprise" and nonsocialist "market forces," chose to direct its assistance primarily toward the private sector of South Asian economies. United States assistance to South Asian agriculture took the form primarily of developing transport, power, and educational infrastructures and of encouraging U.S. and other capital to invest in South Asian industrial projects. The overall strategy of U.S. aid was to increase the Gross National Product of various South Asian nations and, while doing so, encourage each nation's additional wealth to "trickle down" through market processes to benefit all sectors of the population. The problems of equity were hardly considered. In fact, equity and growth were frequently defined as "opposites"; if one wanted rapid growth, one could not have equity—and vice versa.

The United States, within its overarching decision to try to increase the Gross National Product of South Asian nations through commodity assistance, infrastructural development, and private sector investments, made a subordinate strategic decision: to encourage the increase in those nations' Gross National Products by macroeconomic policies (rather than by institutional change or structural reform). This subordinate strategic decision, like its predecessor, was also in line with U.S. interests in encouraging "free enterprise" and nonsocialist "market forces." In selecting its macroeconomic policies, the United States chose to focus in each recipient country on the proportion of net investment to national income (or to Net National Product or to Gross National Product). The United States saw as crucial the increase in a nation's net investment rate. This increase could come about through a variety of ways, such as internal voluntary savings, internal compulsory savings, external capital assistance (e.g., foreign loans), or external trade. Regardless of the specific way, each South Asian nation's net investment rate would have to increase.

In South Asia, India and her Five Year Plans were seen as a sort of test for macroeconomic policies. In the words of Walter Rostow:

The Indian Planning Commission estimated investment as 5% of [Net National Product] in the initial year of the plan, 1950–1. Using a 3:1 marginal capital/output ratio, they envisaged a marginal savings rate of 20% for the First Five Year Plan, a 50% rate thereafter, down to 1968–9, when the average proportion of income invested would level off at 20% of NNP . . . the Indian effort may well be remembered in economic history as the first take-off defined *ex ante* in national product terms.[28]

One of the most important contributions the United States could make to India's development, according to Rostow's strategy, was to provide the kind of foreign assistance that could be utilized by India as investment capital. The U.S. approach to Pakistan was much the same as that to India. In the words of Gustav Papanek:

Over the [next decade in Pakistan] foreign loans and grants are projected to provide more than one-third of total investment funds. According to present plans, foreign resources are not expected to decline in absolute amounts until 1975. At least over the next decade, an end to loans and grants would stop any substantial increase in per-capita income under Pakistan's present economic and political system.[29]

Were there alternative policies the United States might have adopted? Yes, there were. The United States could have adopted a policy aimed at maximizing the capacities of South Asian economies to function autonomously with ultimate goals of "national self-sufficiency." Such a policy would almost certainly have called for *reduced* U.S. loans and grants to South Asian nations. It would also have called for *increased* insistence by the United States that each South Asian nation develop its own resources for feeding its population and providing them employment, with minimum assistance from, or involvement with, external sources of funding, foodstuffs, or manufactured products. Such a U.S. policy would almost certainly have produced charges of "insensitivity" and "lack of concern" for the immediate plight of South Asian nations. Furthermore, such a policy would almost certainly have been seen in Washington as opening the door to increased Soviet hegemony over South Asia, something Washington viewed as not in its best interests. Nonetheless, a case might be argued that, had the United States adopted the policy of "national self-sufficiency" for South Asian nations, South Asia might be better off today as a result.

Another alternative policy the United States could have adopted would have aimed at reducing the most severe income inequalities in South Asia. The United States could have insisted that certain basic institutional changes and structural reforms be enacted in South Asian countries before U.S. assistance could be available. This would have been done in the belief that unless income inequalities were reduced *before* substantial economic growth began, economic growth would generate undesirable, and perhaps eventually intolerable, levels of inequality within the South Asian nations. Such a policy by the United States would have almost certainly produced charges of "interference" in the internal affairs of South Asian nations. Nonetheless, such a policy might have had the effect of avoiding some of the complex difficulties now facing South Asian nations.

The fact is that the United States chose a macroeconomic strategy of providing capital and (to several nations) commodity aid, directing this largely toward those nations' private sectors, and leaving it up to "market forces" to distribute the benefits. The opinion has often been expressed in the United States that providing capital and letting market forces "take their course" involved less "interference" in the internal affairs of other nations than direct assaults on established institutions and structures.

What are some of the accomplishments that might be traceable to the U.S. decision to pursue macroeconomic policies rather than national self-sufficiency of institutional change and structural reform policies in South Asia? One can point to the fact that famines have been averted, a considerable amount of technological knowledge has been "transferred," literacy rates have risen, as have indices of mass media participation. Near self-sufficiency in food grains has (at least temporarily) been achieved.

But behind the visible accomplishments, one can identify other consequences of U.S. aid policies. The macroeconomic strategies have consistently led the governments of South Asia to overvalue their currencies and subsidize domestic interest rates. This policy has encouraged industrialists and large farmers to take advantage of their governments' cheap-money policies and to import sophisticated technology. As a result, one finds dual economies in most South Asian nations—economies including a modern sector employing capital-intensive methods in large-scale economic units co-existing with a nonmodern sector involving small-scale units and labor-intensive methods. In dual economies, the impact of the capital-intensive sector on the labor-intensive sector is, typically, severe and destructive.[30]

Capital-intensive growth has, in some South Asian countries, forced marginally employed farm laborers to migrate to the cities in search of work. There, because of the capital-intensive urban industries, it has been difficult for many such migrants to find steady jobs. These displaced workers have frequently become a floating population, shuttling between temporary employment in the cities and temporary employment back in their villages.

Capital-intensive growth has also frequently occurred in the arena of import substitution. Foreign luxury products no longer available on the local market (often because of high import tariffs) are replaced by their indigenously produced substitutes, including air conditioners, photographic film, cars, and refrigerators. Only the wealthiest of the indigenous classes can afford these substitutes. The scarce productive resources of the economy are, more often than one might wish, employed to produce commodities that are both unnecessary and beyond the reach of most citizens of the country.

The existence of these luxury commodities and the industries that produce them can aggravate existing inequalities. If group tensions arise and scapegoats are needed, they can be found almost anywhere in South Asia—among religious minority groups, migrant groups, tribal groups, low-caste groups, high-caste groups. In 1971 South Asia was wracked by a major war stemming at least in part from aggravated inequalities. East

Pakistan, resenting the inequities between it and West Pakistan, declared itself an independent state: Bangladesh. Within virtually every nation in South Asia there have been—or currently are—political movements demanding a more equitable share of the nation's wealth and threatening autonomy or secession if their demands for greater equality are not met. To the extent U.S. assistance policies have intentionally or unintentionally contributed to the existence of these inequalities, the United States *has* "interfered" with the internal affairs of South Asian nations.

Criticisms have been leveled against the United States for the manner in which its assistance policies have led nations of South Asia to become indebted to the United States (or to other international agencies the United States supports). For example, between 1963 and 1971 India's total foreign debt rose from $4.7 to $13.2 billion, with the United States being the largest single creditor ($3.4 billion).[31] Not only did these foreign loans saddle India with a heavy debt, they also forced India into heavy debt-servicing repayments ($260 million in interest in 1970–71). Funds that could have been used for domestic development programs were being credited to countries far richer than India. Although the United States "gave back" to India some $2.2 billion worth of Indian currency in 1973, the United States still retained some $1.0 billion worth of rupees for its own further expenditures in India.

One of the least visible aspects of U.S. assistance in South Asia has been the manner in which the United States, by providing direct shipments of food grains, may have enabled South Asian governments to postpone necessary steps toward achieving national self-sufficiency in food grain production. Bangladesh is a case in point. In 1976 the U.S. embassy in Dacca cabled that:

> The incentive for Bangladesh government leaders to devote attention, resources, and talent to the problem of increasing domestic foodgrain production is reduced by the security provided by U.S. and other donors' food assistance.[32]

As a result of some of these initially unanticipated effects of U.S. aid to South Asian nations, the question has been raised: If the United States and other nations had *not* provided external assistance (or had they provided external assistance in a different manner), might the nations of South Asia be better off today?

The case of Sri Lanka may be illustrative. Of the five nations we are including in our boundaries of South Asia, Sri Lanka stands in a "success" category by itself. Although its $100 to $150 per capita income does not set it far apart from India, Bangladesh, Pakistan, and Nepal, other of its indices put it in a category of much "more developed" nations. Thus, the life expectancy in Sri Lanka is sixty-eight years, the death rate is 6.4 per thousand, and the literacy rate is 76 percent. Furthermore, Sri Lanka has achieved some success in reducing the income gaps of its citizens. Between 1963 and 1973 the country's lowest decile *increased* its average per capita real income by 105 percent; the highest decile *reduced* its average per capita real income by 15 percent.[33] This is not the place to go into detail regarding the Sri Lanka government's subsidized grain supplement, high social service budget expenditures, package of programs, and low military budget. From the point of view of this work, one interesting feature regarding Sri Lanka's relative success is that Sri Lanka is one of the few countries during the past thirty years to have U.S. aid cut off for multiyear periods of time. In this case, the *absence* of U.S. assistance appears to correlate with relative national economic success.

SOME IMPLICATIONS FOR THE UNITED STATES OF SOUTH ASIAN LAND REFORMS AND RURAL DEVELOPMENT PROGRAMS

In many sectors of South Asia the phenomenon of decreasing economic equality has been accompanied by a heightened interest in the *concept* of economic equality—especially in rural areas.[34] Although the vanguard of this interest has often been occupied by self-consciously Marxist political groups, a wide range of other parties and persons have also expressed this interest.[35] Is there something we might call economic equality that is conceptually parallel to political equality (national independence, universal franchise, basic civil liberties)? If so, is there a basic minimum of economic equality that can be considered a fundamental right of citizenship, just as there is considered to be a basic minimum of political equality (one person-one vote, fundamental civil rights)?

There is some movement in the direction of identifying such a basic minimum of economic equality in various statements made by the United Nations and its agencies. Thus, the 1948 UN General Assembly-approved Universal Declaration of Human Rights includes the rights to food, shelter, health care, and education. The International Covenant on Economic, Social, and Cultural Rights (which took effect in 1976 after ratification by thirty-five governments) includes provisions regarding freedom from hunger, the right to work, the right to an adequate standard of living, favorable working conditions, and the right to an education.[36] The Tripartite World Conference on Employment, Income Distribution and Social Progress, and the International Division of Labor (an outcome of initiatives from the International Labor Organization), held in Geneva in 1976, adopted a declaration that national development policies should include "explicitly as a priority objective the promotion of employment and the satisfaction of the basic needs of each country's population." The basic needs included "certain minimum requirements of a family for private consumption: adequate food, shelter and clothing, as well as certain household equipment and furniture." The declaration further stated that in all countries "freely chosen employment enters into a basic-needs policy as a means and as an end."[37]

From time to time the U.S. government, or its representatives, have made similar sorts of pronouncements. The U.S. 1973 Foreign Assistance Act instructed AID to direct its attention to the rural poor of developing countries. U.S. delegates at the World Food Conference in 1974 proposed, and other nations at the conference accepted, the objective "that within a decade no child will go to bed hungry, that no family will fear for its next day's bread, and that no human being's future and

capacities will be stunted by malnutrition."[38] The Right to
Food resolution—which the U.S. Senate passed on September
16, 1976[39] and in which the House of Representatives con-
curred on September 21, 1976[40]—reaffirmed the right of every
person throughout the world "to food and a nutritionally adequate diet" and stated that the United States should expand its
assistance among the world's poorest people, "with particular
emphasis on increasing food production and encouraging more
equitable patterns of food distribution and economic
growth."[41] The case could be made that a general consensus is
emerging in many sectors of the world that a basic minimum of
economic equality *is* a fundamental right of all individuals in
the same way as is a basic minimum of political equality. If that
basic minimum of economic equality does not exist,
then—according to the emerging framework of legitimacy—the
situation is unjust regardless of the competitive market
mechanisms.

If such a new framework of legitimacy is emerging, what
implications does it have for the legitimacy of those land reform
and rural development policies currently being pursued by
countries in South Asia that increase economic inequalities? In
view of the past thirty years of experience in South Asia, one
would be hard-pressed to make the case that market forces, if
allowed to run their course, will do anything other than increase inequalities. According to David Morawetz:

the *initial* distribution of assets and incomes [in a nation]
may be an important determinant of the *trend* in inequality. Such a hypothesis makes some intuitive sense. People
who own assets—whether physical or human capital—are
best placed to profit once growth begins. Furthermore,
both historical and simulative evidence suggests that the
most powerful determinator of income distribution is the
underlying structure of the economy; once growth is taking place it seems to be difficult to effectively redistribute
income through the use of "marginal" instruments such as
taxation and public employment. . . . These combined
observations have potentially powerful implications: in

particular, if equality is to be a short- to medium-term goal, it simply may not be possible to "grow first and redistribute later." Rather, it may be necessary to tackle asset redistribution as a first priority by whatever means are at hand.[42]

What implications does this observation have for the legitimacy of U.S. assistance to the countries of South Asia, if U.S. assistance helps to increase the proportion of their populations below some basic minimum of economic equality? Should the United States adopt economics rights guidelines to accompany its general human rights guidelines when it debates its foreign appropriations bills? What stance might this lead the United States to take regarding "market forces" and "land tenure policies" in South Asia particularly and developing countries generally, when those "market forces" and "land tenure policies" consistently widen the gap between rich and poor and increase the proportion of the population deprived of basic economic rights? What stance might this lead the United States to take regarding international "market forces" when those forces also can be seen consistently to increase the gap between rich and poor and to contribute in their own way to increasing the numbers, as well as the proportions, of the world's impoverished?

There is a need today to articulate clearly both in the United States and in South Asia what economic and/or political "equality" and economic and/or political "inequality" is to mean, as well as what social "justice" is to mean. Some general concepts seem to be emerging, although they still appear to be somewhat incoherent and inconsistent. As these concepts become clearer, they may have far-reaching policy implications for the United States, South Asia, and the rest of the world.

NOTES

1. For purposes of this paper, South Asia will be considered to include: India (population, 625 million); Bangladesh (population, 80 million); Pakistan (population, 73 million); Sri Lanka (population, 14

million); and Nepal (population, 13 million). Population figures are from *Asia Yearbook 1978* (Hong Kong: Far Eastern Economic Review, 1978).

2. Asian Development Bank, *Asian Agricultural Survey* (Tokyo: University of Tokyo Press; Seattle: University of Washington Press, 1969).

3. Asian Development Bank, *Rural Asia: Challenge and Opportunity*, (Singapore: Federal Publications, 1977; New York: Praeger, 1978), pp. 2 and 3.

4. Cited in David Morawetz, *Twenty-Five Years of Economic Development, 1950 to 1975*, (Washington: World Bank, 1975).

5. Ibid., p. 3.

6. Ibid., p. 64.

7. Ibid., p. 98.

8. International Labor Office, *Poverty and Landlessness in Rural Asia*, studies by S. M. Naseem et al. (Geneva: International Labor Office, 1977).

9. For the Bangladesh figures, see F. Tomasson Januzzi and James T. Peach, *Report on the Hierarchy of Interests in Land in Bangladesh* (Austin, Tex.: Center for Asian Studies and Department of Economics, University of Texas at Austin, September 1977), p. 40. For the India figures, see India, Ministry of Information and Broadcasting, *India, 1967* (Delhi), p. 144.

10. See, for example, Badrinath (of the Indian Administrative Service), *A Report on the Implementation of the Tamilnadu Agricultural Lands Record of Tenancy Rights Act, 1969* (Chepauk, Madras: Director of Tenancy Records, 1971).

11. Robert McNamara, in his 1973 Nairobi speech as World Bank president, stated: "The politically privileged among the landed elite are rarely enthusiastic over the steps necessary to advance rural development." But McNamara gave no hardheaded recommendations about what countries should do about their unenthusiastic rural landed elites. (Quotation from *International Policy Report* [Washington: Center for International Policy, May 1978], vol. 4, no. 1, p. 12.) Escott Reid, a former senior official for the World Bank, who generally endorsed McNamara's goal of increasing the national share of goods and services going to the poorest two fifths of a nation's population, wrote: "In many very poor countries the governments will have to help the poorer farmers, the underemployed artisans and the landless laborers to organize themselves against those who hold power in the villages." ("McNamara's World Bank," *Foreign Affairs* 51, no. 4 [July 1973]: 802–3). But Reid provided no blueprint for how the governments of such poor countries were supposed to organize the weakest sectors of their societies to challenge the power of the strongest sectors of their societies. The Asian Development Bank's 1977 report concludes with the statement: "Governments can no longer afford to

constrain the productive potential of their economic systems by catering to the felt needs of the privileged few. Poverty must be reduced, and it must be accomplished by providing productive jobs for the hungry rural masses." (*Rural Asia,* p. 320). However, the report provides no tried-and-true methods for governments to follow in *avoiding* catering to the privileged few or in generating productive jobs for the rural masses.

12. For purposes of this paper "equality" will be held to mean "condition of being exactly the same, or holding the same things, in measure, quantity, status, or position." To this extent "equality" is capable (in principle) of being measured by "objective" means such that observers could agree that two or more phenomena are or are not "equal," or are becoming "more equal" or "less equal." Similarly, for purposes of this paper "justice" will be held to mean a "claim for fair treatment within some particular framework of legitimacy." Different people at different times have subscribed to different "frameworks of legitimacy." Since "justice" is linked to different "frameworks of legitimacy," what appears "just" at one time or from one perspective may appear "unjust" at another time or from another perspective.

13. See, for example, Edgar Owens and Robert Shaw, *Development Reconsidered* (London: D.C. Heath, 1972); J. Adelman and Cynthia Morris, *Economic Growth and Social Equity in Developing Countries* (Stanford: Stanford University Press, 1973); and Hollis Chenery et al., *Redistribution with Growth* (London: Oxford University Press, 1974).

14. For a discussion of some of the sentiments and political pressures that contributed to this congressional mandate, see R. A. Packenham, *Liberal America and the Third World* (Princeton: Princeton University Press, 1973).

15. H. N. C. Stevenson, "Status Evaluation in the Hindu Caste System," *Journal of the Royal Anthropological Society of Great Britain and Ireland* 84 (1954): 45–65; Louis Dumont, *Homo Hierarchicus: The Caste System and Its Implications,* trans. M. Sainsbury (Chicago: The University of Chicago Press, 1970).

16. McKim Marriott and Ronald B. Inden, "An Ethnosociology of South Asian Caste Systems," unpublished manuscript, University of Chicago, 1973.

17. For discussions of the difficulties the British faced in trying to structure South Asian landholding patterns to enable the British to assign and collect land taxes, see Robert E. Frykenberg, ed., *Land Control and Social Structure in Indian History* (Madison: University of Wisconsin Press, 1969). See also Robert E. Frykenberg, ed., *Land Tenure and Peasant in South Asia* (New Delhi: Orient Longmans, 1977).

18. It is important when studying historical records to keep levels

of comparison clear. Thus, one must contrast British statements of abstract principles with indigenous statements of abstract principles, and one must contrast actual British practices with actual indigenous practices.

19. Louis Fischer, *The Life of Mahatma Gandhi* (London: Jonathan Cape, 1951), p. 164.

20. Mohandas K. Gandhi, *Trusteeship* (Ahmedabad: Navajivan Publishing House, 1960), p. 17.

21. Ibid., pp. 39 and 40.

22. For a discussion of the manner in which the Indian Supreme Court has dealt with the issue of private property since India's independence, see Rajeev Dhavan, *The Supreme Court of India: A Socio-Legal Critique of Its Juristic Techniques* (Bombay: N. M. Tripathi, 1977), chap. 3, "The Supreme Court and the Right to Property." For general information on constitutional aspects of landownership in India, see H. C. L. Merillat, *Land and the Constitution in India* (New York: Columbia University Press, 1970).

23. A considerable literature now exists regarding land reforms in South Asia. The following titles represent only a small sample of the total literature: P. C. Joshi, *Land Reforms in India: Trends and Perspectives* (Bombay: Allied Publishers, 1975); Institute of Economic Growth, *Studies in Economic Growth,* no. 19 (Delhi: Institute of Economic Growth); Januzzi and Peach, *"Report on the Hierarchy of Interests"*; Government of Pakistan, *Pakistan Economic Survey 1976–77* (Islamabad: Economic Adviser's Wing, Finance Division, 1977), esp. table 12.1, p. 191; H. N. S. Karaunatilake, *Economic Development in Ceylon* (New York: Praeger, 1971); and Mahesh Chandra Regmi, *Land Tenure and Taxation in Nepal,* 4 vols. (Berkeley: University of California, 1963–68).

24. See, for example, Joseph W. Elder, with Mahabir Ale, Mary A. Evans, David P. Gillespie, Rohit Kumar Nepali, Sitaram P. Poudyal, and Bryce P. Smith, *Planned Resettlement in Nepal's Terai: A Social Analysis of the Khajura/Bardia Punarvas Projects* (Kathmandu: Tribhuvan University Press, 1976).

25. Asian Development Bank, *Rural Asia,* p. 98.

26. Government of India Planning Commission, *Draft Plan for 1978–83 (the Sixth Five Year Plan),* selections reprinted in *International Development Review* 20, nos. 3/4 (1978): 25.

27. Quoted in S. Chandrasekhar, *America's Aid and India's Economic Development* (New York: Praeger, 1965), pp. 59 and 60.

28. Walter W. Rostow, *The Stages of Economic Growth: A Non-Communist Manifesto* (Cambridge: Cambridge University Press, 1960), p. 45.

29. Gustav F. Papenek, *Pakistan's Development: Social Goals and Private Incentives* (Cambridge, Mass.: Harvard University Press, 1967), p. 240.

30. For a more detailed assessment of this point, see Hla Pyint, *Economic Theory and the Underdeveloped Countries* (New York: Oxford University Press, 1971).

31. *The Statesman Weekly,* Calcutta, July 17, 1971.

32. Betsy Hartmann and James Boyce, "Bangladesh: Aid to the Needy?" *International Policy Report* (Washington: Center for International Policy, May 1978), vol. 4, no. 1, p. 5.

33. James P. Grant, "A Fresh Approach to Meeting Basic Human Needs of the World's Poorest Billion: Implications of the Chinese and Other 'Success' Models," manuscript prepared for delivery at the annual meeting of the American Political Science Association, Chicago, 1976, pp. 9 ff.

34. See, for example, Paul R. Brass and Marcus Franda, eds., *Radical Politics in South Asia* (Cambridge, Mass.: M.I.T. Press, 1973).

35. See, for example, "The Rural Challenge," *Seminar: The Monthly Symposium,* no.227 (July 1978), for a range of views on rural economic "inequalities" and an extensive bibliography on South Asian rural development.

36. As of 1977 the United States has not signed this international covenant, finding difficulties with such clauses as Article 6's "right to work," Article 7's "women being guaranteed conditions of work not inferior to those enjoyed by men," and Article 10's right to a paid leave for a "reasonable period" before and after childbirth. (*The UN and Human Rights* [New York: United Nations Association of the U.S.A., April 1977] p. 2.)

37. Hans Singer, *Technologies for Basic Needs* (Geneva: International Labor Organization, 1977), p. 112.

38. *The Right to Food Resolution* (New York: Bread for the World: A Christian Citizens' Movement in the USA, n.d.).

39. S. Con. Res. 138.

40. H. Con. Res. 737.

41. *The Right to Food Resolution.*

42. David Morawetz, "Twenty-Five Years of Economic Development," *Finance and Development* (September 1977): 10–13.

Chapter 8

HUMAN RIGHTS QUESTIONS IN SOUTHEAST ASIAN CULTURE: PROBLEMS FOR AMERICAN RESPONSE

STEPHEN B. YOUNG

Many Americans seem to believe that the constitutional pattern of governance in the United States today—as formalized in the Declaration of Independence, the Constitution, and the Bill of Rights—is a necessary prerequisite for protecting human rights. Thus, they evaluate the performance of other countries in the field of human rights by comparing their conduct with the standards of American politics. This tendency is somewhat unfortunate. Human rights are universal rights and must therefore reflect universal concerns. Although the Anglo-American political and legal tradition has been a forceful expositor of human rights causes, it is not the only basis upon which to build a political system that respects individual dignity.

One important aspect of the Anglo-American tradition has been the role that the Protestant tradition has played in its evolution. Although there are many respects in which the two systems of thought—one religious, the other legal-political—developed autonomously, the Protestant ethic helped to modify the scope of collective, governing society. Because Protestantism is based in part on the authority it vests in the individual to experience the purposes of the Almighty directly, the ends of society for most Protestants are not to be imposed

187

upon its members by either secular or religious authorities. God alone provides the standards by which the measure of government can be taken; and the wisdom and purposes of the Almighty can be understood by each and every individual. To the extent that this sense of moral independence fostered a concomitant political view in the United States, it has meant that the individual can measure his political system and leaders by the norms—derived from the original sources of moral purpose—that his religious experience provides.

Furthermore, these standards are not determined by those who occupy positions of civil authority. Instead, the standards are derived independently, so that they limit political activity by creating a demand for proven legitimacy, thereby reducing the range for the exercise of arbitrary power. These, then, are constraints on government; they can give rise to constitutional regimes.[1]

For the purposes of the following analysis, human rights will be defined as constraints on a political system, where those constraints are derived either by reference to a set of rational principles, or by the operation of social mechanisms.[2] Such conceptual bases can be found in social and religious traditions far removed from America or the American way of life, in such diverse places as traditional China, Vietnam, and Thailand. Not only do the perceptions of these cultures offer intriguing and consistent ways to interpret the relationships between individuals and political societies, but they also provide the bases for indigenous democratic developments in those societies.

As the following analysis will demonstrate, the fact that these cultural traditions provide independent validity to the notion of human rights in Southeast Asia and China is important for at least two separate reasons. First, because the traditions of these three Asian nations have their own functional analogies to the Protestant challenges to the purposes and actions of governments. (That these Asian standards have not served to date as catalysts for political forces producing genuine democracies is a historical fact that will be noted but not discussed in this paper.) And second, because Americans too often see traditional cultures in Asia as the principal obstacle to the emergence of enlightened democratic rule there. Derivatively, this has meant that Western observers have let their own interpretations of the power of both cultural relativism and cultural conceptions condition their expectations of political change in Asia inappropriately. These two reasons, taken together, should direct American political behavior in Asia in different directions from those that current perceptions have allowed.

CHINA

Some features of the Chinese tradition define an external standard for individuals to evaluate government performance; these are counterparts to those American beliefs that place restraints on political authority. In China one standard for evaluating governmental performance is a kind of natural law that both permits individual autonomy and commands obedience to the state. This is a function of the cosmology of yin and yang, a philosophic gloss on the natural science of ancient China that was both an analytic method and an understanding of the physical world (which gave rise to acupuncture as well as to geomancy and a form of astrology).[3] "Being" to those ancients was flux, moved by breath or energy—chi. Chi was thought to exist in two modes—yin and yang. Positing only one mode would have meant stasis or imposing an absolute on nature—an intellectual position at variance with the ceaseless changes of the observable world. So the ancients built their symbolic universe on an objective reality resulting from alternations between and combinations of two modes of a moving force. The dialectical interaction of yin and yang and their mutual evolution were said to produce all things and all movements. Yin and Yang made space, time, and number possible.

Under this theory every inanimate and animate object consisted of a combination of yang elements and yin elements. Thus, each individual human was naturally unique: a person was not the product of a family, a class, or a society so much as the incorporation in animate form of a unique combination of energy and potential. Under this scheme, parents deserve gratitude for one's conception, nourishment, and rearing, but they were only agents in a large scheme. This claim to individual autonomy has remained an important part of the little tradition in China until the present day. That little tradition had at its core the cosmology of yin and yang and was supplemented by Buddhist beliefs in the power of good deeds and bodhisattvas to manipulate fate, and as interpreted from time to time by Taoist teachings and mystics. As a counterpoint to social and family pressure for self-effacement, much of Taoist cult practice centered on prolonging individual life and using spirits to achieve selfish individual aims. Orthodoxy in China has never been able to eliminate a more unruly sense of individual moral worth.[4]

At one time the theory of yin and yang was explicitly used by the Chinese to limit political power. According to legend, King Wen, founder of the Chou dynasty, used the *I Ching* or *Book of Changes* as a guide to politics and rule. By showing him revolutions in the mandate of heaven, it indicated that the then ruling Shang dynasty had outlived its possibilities for rule and could be replaced by one whose ideas and projects resonated more correctly with the new prevailing balance of yin and yang. By embodying the prevailing balance of yin and yang. By providing the prevailing balance of yin and yang indicated by the *I Ching,* an individual could rise to supreme authority. What the *I Ching* taught politicians, therefore, was submission to the flow of yin and yang.[5] Under this ancient theory, good politics can be reduced to obedient humility before the flux of cosmic change. Laws and official appointments, for example, should follow the natural disposition of the people affected or the individuals appointed and not the whim of the ruler. Rule arises, not from imposing one's power or will, but from linking one's efforts to preexisting powers and wills.

A commentary to the *I Ching* reads as follows:

> The *I* was made on a principle of accordance with heaven and earth, and shows us therefore, without rent or confusion, the course of things in heaven and earth.

The Superior Man, in accordance with the *I*, looking up, contemplates the brilliant phenomena of the Heavens, and, looking down, examines the definite arrangements of the earth:—thus he knows the causes of darkness and light. He traces things to their beginning and follows them to their end:—thus he knows what can be said about death and life. He perceives how essence and breath form things, and the wandering away of spirit produces the change of their constitution:—thus he knows the characteristics of the anima and animus.

There is a similarity between him and heaven and earth, and hence there is no contrariety in him to them. His knowledge embraces all things and his course is intended to be helpful to all under the sky;—and hence he falls into no error. He acts according to the exigency of circumstances without being carried away by their current.[6]

Such a man in government looks beyond himself for his sense of direction. Moreover, he is bound to respect the cosmic essence and breath embodied in the people around him: he should not become a tyrant. The image of self inherent in the *I Ching* is individualistic; however, this individualism is tempered by the need to harmonize with other surrounding powers and forces.[7]

The role of external circumstances as a constitutional standard for government also appears in a pre-Confucian work, the *Shu Ching*. Here, the notion of the individual as a social component implies that rulers must acquire support from those whom they rule. To gain this support they must demonstrate a mastery of circumstances and harmonious regulation of different currents. In *The Canon of Yao* we read that the emperor Yao arranged to be succeeded as sovereign not by his own son who was "insincere and quarrelsome" but by another whose demonstrated merit showed that he was "equal to the exigency" of affairs.[8] As in the *I Ching*, the desire for a Superior Man as leader expressed itself in a search for efficacy and competence. Mastery of forces was the precondition for rule, and such mastery arose from movement in accordance with natural laws. Nature, not political opposition, was to constrain the government.

Mencius followed Confucius in looking back to older patterns for guides to present behavior. In the work of Mencius we find the following long comment on the political system of the ancient China of Yao and Shun where rulers based their power on the consent of others:

> After the death of Yao, when the three years' mourning was completed, Shun withdrew from the son of Yao to the south of South river. The princes of the kingdom, however, repairing to court, went not to the son of Yao, but they went to Shun. Singers sang not the son of Yao, but they sang Shun. Therefore I said, *"Heaven gave him the throne."* It was after these things that he went to the Middle Kingdom, and occupied the seat of the Son of Heaven. If he had, *before these things,* taken up his residence in the palace of Yao, and had applied pressure to the son of Yao, it would have been an act of usurpation, and not the gift of Heaven. Shun presented Yu to Heaven. Seventeen years elapsed, and Shun died. When the three years' mourning was expired, Yu withdrew from the son of Shun to Yangch'ang. The people of the kingdom followed [Yu] just as after the death of Yao, instead of following [Yao's] son, they had followed Shun.[9]

Mencius concluded that rulers were to serve their people and that those who failed to live up to that standard could be driven from power. When King Hsuan of Ch'i asked if a minister could put a sovereign to death, Mencius replied that:

> He who outrages the benevolence proper to his nature is called a robber; he who outrages righteousness is called a ruffian. The robber and the ruffian we call a mere "fellow." I have heard of the cutting off of the "fellow" Chou

[last king of the Shang dynasty] but I have not heard of the putting of a Sovereign to death, in his case.[10]

Under Mencius' theory, those who lived up to the role of king could not be assailed, but those who failed to act as a king should have no claim to power and could even be executed as a mere "fellow" for his wrongs.[11]

Punishment is a constraint on behavior, and ancient China also had a theory that bad rulers should be punished. Yu's son, Ch'i, said when commencing a military campaign to reduce the lord of Hu:

> The Lord of Hu wildly wastes and despises the five elements (composed of *yin* and *yang*) that regulate the seasons and had idly abandoned the three acknowledged commencements of the year. On this account, Heaven is about to destroy him and bring to an end his appointment to Hu. I am now reverently executing the punishment appointed by Heaven.[12]

Clearly, failure to conform to the flow of yin and yang requires punishment and corrective action by another political leader acting as heaven's agent.

Like kings, who could be punished if they strayed from what was right, the people, too, could be punished, but such punishments were not to be inflicted wantonly. Shun once told his minister of punishments that "through punishment there come to be no punishments and the people to be in accord with the Mean."[13] Acts requiring punishment were thought to be driven by self-assertion of human desire, a yang force; punishments were applications of a yin, restraining force.[14] Thus, administering punishments meant using yin energy by the government to counterbalance an excessive flow of yang—keeping society to the mean of what the *I Ching* itself intended. Balance was sought: too much or too little punishment would not keep the government to the mean; therefore, punishments must fit crimes. The word "mean" used in connection with punishment refers not to the Confucian work called the Doctrine of the Mean but to the attainment of a natural equilibrium among the myriad thrusts and pulls of yin and yang. Attaining the mean was an analytic standard by which government could be judged. The standard of the mean used to regulate state power was external to the government. Shun also counseled Yu to be discriminating, "be undivided in the pursuit of what is right that you may sincerely hold fast the mean."[15] What is right can be defined by what will maintain the mean.[16] Keeping to the mean avoids excessive individualism among the citizenry.

The alternating modes of elemental power, yin and yang, were thought to create a natural order independent of man's choosing. However, the interaction of such forces could be followed by discerning individuals who consulted the *I Ching* or other signs. The action proper to the circumstance can therefore be decided by many; improper action can also quickly be seen by the people as an incorrect application of human energy and resources. This power of analysis and prediction gives each person an ability to judge for himself or herself whether or not the government had indeed conformed to the due mean. Criticism of rulers is intrinsic to this cosmology of nature and individualism.

For this reason, free speech was a value to be pursued.

A man of Cheng rambled into a village school, and fell discoursing about the conduct of the government.

[In consequence] Jen-ming proposed to Tsze-ch'an to destroy [all] the village schools; but that minister said, "Why do so? If people retire morning and evening, and pass their judgment on the conduct of the government, as being good or bad, I will do what they approve of, and I will alter what they condemn—they are my teachers. On what ground should we destroy [those schools]? I have heard that by loyal conduct and goodness enmity is diminished, but I have not heard that it can be prevented by acts of violence. It may indeed be hastily stayed for a while, but it continues like a stream that has been dammed up. If you

make a great opening in the dam, there will be great injury
done—beyond our power to relieve. The best plan is to
lead the water off by a small opening. [In this case] our
best plan is to hear what is said, and use it as a medicine."
Jen'ming said, "From this time forth I know that you are
indeed equal to the administration of affairs. I acknowledge my want of ability. If you indeed do this, all Ch'ing
will be benefited by it, and not we two or three ministers
only."[17]

This sense of individualism recognizes each individual's direct tie to the ultimate, functioning similarly to the Protestants'
direct communication with God. In both traditions, individuals
held moral culpability for their deeds as determined by an
ultimate power. It was said in the *Shu Ching* that "Good and
Evil do not wrongly befall men; Heaven sends down misery or
happiness according to their conduct."[18] The *I Ching* similarly
said, "Good fortune and ill are continually prevailing each
against the other by an exact rule."[19] Such a rule necessarily
regulates any government if it is to be good.
This quasi-religious conception of a power higher than government that directly rewards and punishes individuals also
permeates the Taoist popular tradition. The *T'ai Shang Kan
Ying P'ien*, a book of moral maxims, has been distributed
widely in China since the fifteenth century, though not sanc-
tioned by the neo-Confucian norms of China's ruling elite. It
teaches that: "Curses and blessing do not come through gates
but man himself invites their arrival" and "those who are thus
good: people honor them; Tao gives them grace; blessings and
abundance follow them; all ill luck keeps away." Evildoers are
those who "Beyond their due lot . . . scheme and contrive."[20]
Common morality in traditional China imposed an equilibrium
of good/reward and evil/punishment. The mean is part of nature, a natural law that governments must obey if they are to be
just. These elements of individualism and natural law are
central to the popular symbolic universe of traditional China.[21]
The question remains why popular conceptual patterns conducive to democratic forms of political rule remained a coun-

terpoint of tension and contrast to the state Confucian cult and did not motivate institutional reforms. In traditional China the tentative pulls toward individualism and limits on arbitrary government were more than counterbalanced by other subjective forces produced by the dynamics of a patrilineal culture. Paternal authority is central and gives rise to family patterns that encourage children to feel themselves most comfortable in a social hierarchy of clearly defined roles and responsibilities. Adults raised in such a culture will be less likely to resist a strong state and will not consistently press their individualistic impulses against the exertion of state power. Thus, in China the state Confucian cult took the family under the father's autocratic rule as the model for political rule.

Lucien Pye has said that among Chinese "there are powerful psychological anxieties about challenging authority, first, because of the cultural heritage of filial piety, and second, because of the individual's basic need for dependency on authority and order."[22] In a study of China's political culture, Richard Solomon wrote: "A pervasive concern with social disorganization and interpersonal conflict gave enduring meaning to the authoritative institutions of Chinese society, and an individual's early-life experiences with family authority prepared him for commitment to these social institutions as an adult."[23] Crudely put, dominant fathers created habits of dependency in Chinese citizens, habits which then had their effect on political behavior.

Authoritarianism triumphed with the Han dynasty (202 B.C.–220 A.D.), consolidating the centralizing achievements of the first emperor of all China, Chin Shih Huang Ti, whose dynasty had collapsed soon after his death. The Han dynasty made empire prevail over China as the mandarinate, a central bureaucracy and the state Confucian cult were erected to create the pattern of government known in China until this century and even copied in many ways by the successor communist regime. In this pattern of empire a bureaucratic structure became both the government and the political process along the lines advocated by the legalists who had seen in the natural law of yin and yang a device to manipulate people through rewards and punishments and, by so doing, to establish order. But this legalist structure was empire draped in Confucian robes. Confucian notions of loyalty, filial piety, and self-cultivation were put to good use in giving legitimacy to bureaucratic orthodoxy. The expression of the Han dynasty synthesis fusing legalism with a Confucian rationale was *Yang Ju Yin Fa,* or "ceremonies for the active, apparent element and law for the hidden element."[24]

With the creation of the empire, authority in China became autocratic, and constraints on government were difficult to impose effectively. The base for popular liberties was eroded.

VIETNAM

The Vietnamese have remained closer than the Chinese to the individualism of the *I Ching,* both in cultural norms and in practices. I have found that the Vietnamese have preserved geomancy and face-reading, techniques based on yin and yang, more extensively than the Chinese have.[25] And consequently Vietnamese are less prone abjectly to accept authority and are more willing to emphasize individual self-assertion. They will assert themselves to avoid rule they find intolerable. Vietnamese politics has always had an anarchist quality, with factions and interpersonal rivalries taking precedence over programs and social cohesion.

To analyze Vietnam as a Sinicized, Confucian state as so many have done is misleading. Vietnamese society, though formally organized into patrilineages, is dominated by its women. Prior to the Chinese conquest in 110 B.C. the Vietnamese were matriarchal. In the Le dynasty law code (1428–1788) women still had equality with men in family property rights and enjoyed other benefits unknown by their sisters in China.

Vietnamese history is one of struggle against foreign invaders and domestic rulers. Factionalism plagues their religious and political organizations. The Cao Dai sect developed at least eleven branches. More recently, the Buddhist struggle movements against Ngo Dinh Diem and Generals Nguyen Khanh, Nguyen Cao Ky and Nguyen Van Thieu were well publicized. Less well known but equally real were substantial democratic developments in South Vietnam's villages and National Assembly from 1968 to 1975. This development grew out of Vietnamese preferences for frequently changing their leaders and in having control over those on whom they must depend. President Nguyen Van Thieu, a dedicated believer in the powers of fate, ruled during those years primarily through compromise, coalition, and manipulation and not by force.

The Western notion that only repression and political imprisonment made Thieu's sway possible is false. When Hanoi conquered the South, no massive pool of political prisoners was found. Those who were jailed were incarcerated largely for their procommunist activities and in most instances according to minimal due process protections.[26] Thieu fell from power as the consequence of an armed invasion of his country by an outside power, not as a result of domestic opposition. There was no evidence during February and March 1975 of significant popular support in South Vietnam for Hanoi's invasion. Corruption was widespread under Thieu, and money, not force, was the nexus holding together his ruling group, partly because money could acquire political allies when their support could not be otherwise coerced. But Thieu was constantly subject to popular criticism if his actions failed to conform to an external standard of acceptable performance. Protests against corruption in 1974 forced him to sack many generals, cabinet ministers, and province chiefs.

Restraint on government often arises when people withdraw their support from a leader. Vietnamese invest true authority only in those individuals who possess the quality of *uy tin* (moral legitimacy).[27] They know who they will support and when such support should be forthcoming. Most Vietnamese do not have *uy tin* and are therefore ineffective leaders, leaving the country subject to the evils of faction and abuse of power by all those who hold power only briefly. The communists have used Ho Chi Minh's *uy tin* to keep the party together.

Uy tin has three components: *tai, duc,* and *so. Tai* (ability) reflects the intelligence and skill necessary to master any situation one might encounter. But to acquire complete *uy tin,* one must use *tai* to advance and promote *duc* (virtue). Moreover, a leader with *uy tin* must possess personal *duc* as well. *Duc* is a complicated word, used with different meanings as the central concept of Confucianism, Taoism, and Buddhism. In the pre-Confucian China of the Shang and Chou dynasties, *duc* meant "power," the energy of one who has mastered fate; it was the quality of sage kings such as Shun and Yao, who were given authority because they had already demonstrated competence.

Today, the Vietnamese use the term *uy tin* much as *duc* was once used, and *duc* now primarily means moral and ethical righteousness. In Buddhism, *duc* is the quality of self-sacrifice that brings us ever closer to extinction of the ego. It determines our karma, or destiny. The more *duc* one displays in this life, the more felicitous one's existence becomes in the next reincarnation. In Confucianism, *duc* has nothing to do with the afterlife. It means propriety, self-cultivation, and filial piety. It is an obligation and is the external sign of the gentleman. In the Vietnamese concept of *uy tin*, a leader gathers *duc* for himself by helping those around him promote their own *duc;* the leader with *duc* does not use this power exclusively to maximize his own personal notion of virtue. To do so would be selfish, and a selfish person would lose *duc*.

Finally, *tai* used to promote *duc* will not result in *uy tin* unless fate permits. The third component of *uy tin*, then, is *so* (destiny). An accepted leader must be blessed with a fortunate horoscope or favorable facial features (*tuong so*), or his birth-site and his ancestors' graves must be well placed according to principles of geomancy. Vietnamese are fatalistic and need to be convinced that one who seeks leadership has already received heaven's mandate.

Knowledge of *uy tin* permits understanding of Vietnamese politics. Under leaders of *uy tin* Vietnamese will achieve great things. Each Vietnamese defeat of invading Chinese or Mongol forces came under the leadership of a man of *uy tin*. In 1078 it was Ly Thuong Kiet; in the thirteenth century Tran Hung Lao defeated the Mongols; in the fifteenth century Le Loi drove the Ming troops out after their twenty-year rule; and in 1789

Nguyen Hue defeated a Ch'ing expeditionary corps. More recently the mass organizing success of the Hoa Hao sect was due to the *uy tin* of its founder, Huynh Phu So. Communist power was in no small way built after September 1945 around the personal *uy tin* of Ho Chi Minh. Ngo Dinh Diem tried to solidify his rule over South Vietnam with an ideology of personalism that echoed the Vietnamese belief that leaders need *uy tin* and *duc*. Yet the people ultimately decided who did and who did not have *uy tin*.

It is not surprising that Vietnamese politics, unless repressed by a dictatorship, turns more on personality than on ideology, party loyalty, or class interest. For example, rulers in South Vietnam, knowing themselves to be without significant *uy tin*, were more interested in keeping rivals and potential rivals at bay than in building a cohesive national political movement. This gave rise to coups and countercoups.

The concept of *uy tin* is one motif in a wider Vietnamese cultural pattern of mutually supporting values and rational explanations that has brought the Vietnamese essentially unchanged through centuries of oppression, wars, and other vicissitudes. The core philosophic principle supporting the Vietnamese cultural pattern is the notion of *phuc duc*, which is the "superego" of their ethnic experience. *Phuc duc* is an amalgam of Buddhist and Confucian notions, with pre-Confucian origins, stressing individualism and private economic incentive in the context of family, which is the collective repository of good and bad karma. The theory of *phuc duc* is best expressed in the vernacular poem *Gia Huan ca*. Vietnamese want to be free to rise as high as the *phuc duc* of their families will let them, and they want to enjoy whatever material prosperity that same *phuc duc* brings their way.

In order for Vietnamese to enjoy the benefits of their *phuc duc*, it is important for them to have a government of *uy tin*, for such a government will be competent out of its ability (*tai*) and good fortune (*so*), and it will leave the people alone in order to promote its own virtue (*duc*) by restraining its selfish, aggressive, and arbitrary tendencies. Thus, a liberal bourgeois democracy as was evolving in South Vietnam after 1968 found substantial support among, and attracted participation from, the majority of the people.[28]

Belief in *uy tin* and *phuc duc* gives the Vietnamese grounds for accepting principles of democratic rule. Inherent in their traditional culture are norms that can justify a political structure that reduces arbitrary authority and leaves great freedom to individuals. Self-images of individuals as the recipients of *phuc duc*'s benefits produce citizens who desire a benevolent and restrained government.

The Vietnamese national traditions of *uy tin* and *phuc duc* are perpetuated from generation to generation by a structure of family life and personality development that molds Vietnamese to feel comfortable with these intellectual concepts. One generation, believing in *phuc duc* and reliving as adults the patterns of its youth, raises a succeeding generation to follow the same ways. It is a testament to the aptness and flexibility of the Vietnamese cultural dynamic that it has stood the batterings of centuries essentially unchanged. Individuals may come and go, dynasties rise and fall, but "Vietnameseness" remains.

To rear their children, Vietnamese families usually call upon arbitrary authority and conditional love ties to punctilious obedience of parental whims. This gives Vietnamese children a strong feeling that those with power should not be trusted, that power is unaccountable and must be placated by conformity.

Parents tend to believe that their children's fate has already been decided by heaven; therefore, there is little for them to do except keep the children fed and disciplined. Children are treated as independent adults who have to be restrained from the moment of birth. Although this gives Vietnamese a winning sense of alertness and individuality, they are in fact rather dependent on others. A childhood need for authority figures evoking dependency and emotional reliance—for limits within which children could feel secure—was never met. Thus, few Vietnamese develop effective personal autonomy or a sense of mastery over their futures.

The result of this family experience is a tension between the need to depend on someone and the conviction that no one is trustworthy becase all are selfish—indeed, that one could not even take a chance on trusting others because if they should gain power one would not have the inner strength to protect one's position. Only a person with *uy tin* can be trusted and depended upon; others are to be manipulated as much as possible. Here, concepts of self set patterns for political behavior.

The tension within this Vietnamese ethic pits a sense of individualism leading to a need to resist those in authority against a perception of one's weakness leading to dependence on those whom one mistrusts. The success of authoritarian governments in Vietnam has arisen from manipulation of the need for dependence over the contrary desire for individual autonomy. Resistance to such authority, set in motion by individualism that always looks for leaders of *uy tin,* has been constant but has been hindered by the very individualism that brings forth opposition in the first place. The desire to protect one's self that makes Vietnamese critical of a government also makes them suspicious of each other. Without leaders of *uy tin,* Vietnamese will not coalesce into the unified forms of political action that bring down centralized administrative regimes. The cultural basis for individualism in Vietnam has thus contributed to a structure hostile to the compromises necessary for united action and also for democracy.

THAILAND

In China and Vietnam there are cultural bases for individualism and moral constraints on government. In Thailand, notions of Buddhist karma give rise to a patron-client social organization that could provide a similar basis for institutions of limited government in that country.

Thai Buddhists have created a cosmology whereby the universe from animals below to demons, spirits, gods, and Buddhas above, is a ranked hierarchy of beings possessing more or less efficacy. The driving force in this cosmology is karma, which rewards the good merit (*bun*) in one's acts through elevation and punishes the bad (*baap*) through degradation and suffering. In this symbolic universe progress is made by increasing the amount of merit one has access to.

Social structure outside of the kin network arises in Thailand as persons attach themselves to patrons. Patrons are those individuals blessed with the consequences of having substantial merit. A religious concept rationalizes a social structure. If one's station in life is fixed by the quantum of merit accumulated in the past, one can still progress toward greater security, wealth, and status (and so gain resources with which to make more merit on one's own) by partaking of the merit that has accrued to a patron and is displayed in his political, social, and economic power.

Just as a client can gain by sharing in the merit accumulated by his patron, a patron can aggregate the lesser merits of his clients and add them to his own merit in order to become more efficacious.[29] A patron's obligation to foster effectively the interests of his clients causes him to share the beneficial results of his merit with them. As Hank states, "The crowning moment of happiness (for a Thai) lies in the knowledge of dependable benefits distributed in turn to faithful inferiors."[30] During long periods of cultivating such a relationship, gifts flow from clients to patrons on various occasions in exchange for a patron's services.

Patrons are those with relatively greater ability to be successful in life. They have status, power, and economic resources, all of which Thais believe to be rewards in this life for the Buddhist merit (*bun*) accumulated in past lives. The essence of a patron is his *wasanaa* or *baramee*, which is his power to protect and assist his clients. The individual with the most *wasanaa* in Thailand is the king. He is the supreme patron. Below him are lesser patrons, a patron to clients who in turn are patrons to others of lesser power and achievement. A patron must also become client to an even more efficacious senior patron to partake of that greater power to sustain his own following. Further, a patron uses his client base in order to offer the services of his clients to his senior patron.[31] The crossing currents of demands rising up from clients to a patron and from a junior patron as a client to his senior patron, and of benefits flowing down from the senior patron to lower levels of clients, create a structure of predictable reciprocal relationships as long as each patron can keep the currents flowing in both directions. The flow is constantly monitored by all in the structure to test its speed, size, and viscosity. Should a patron falter, his clients will desert him and bring their services elsewhere.

The Thai patron-client hierarchy is not immutable. It contains an inner tension in the concern of clients over the extent of their patrons' efficacy. The function of a patron is to use his efficacy (*wasanaa, barimee*); if his efficacy should ever shrink or expire, he will no longer be able to serve as a patron to his clients. A patron's position must be constantly affirmed through demonstrations of success. This is a constraint on a patron's authority.

Based on a desire for hierarchy and structure, the Thai patron-client system gives rise to a contradictory pressure for flexibility. Both willingness to submit and the ability to shift loyalties derive from the single cultural dynamic justifying the patron-client structure—the drive to maximize the good aspects of karma as it rolls out the mutual destinies of all beings. Fear of being chained to an inadequate patron lies behind the Thai concept of freedom. The word *Thai* means "free" as opposed to *Kha*, or "slave." A free man can always switch patrons; a slave is condemned to suffer the fate of his master, for richer or for poorer. As Tambiah has described, the traditional Thai polity reflected the Buddhist cosmology of a mandala, where there is a core of power or merit and an enclosing perimeter of dependent recipients of the power.[32] Beyond the edge of the mandala, the force of the central core does not reach. The circumference of the perimeter varies with the force radiated from the center. A powerful center has far-flung dependencies; a weak core has a minimal buffer between it and the outside. The ancient kingdom of Sukhothai could claim an empire reaching down to the Malay states under a strong king like Ramkamhaeng (1215–98), but under a weak king like his son even neighboring principalities no longer accepted its sovereignty and gave their allegiance to Chiengmai in the North or to Ayudhia to the South. The Thai kingdom of Ayudhia showed the same historical pulsating pattern. When defeated by the Burmese, the kings of Ayudhia lost their outlying dependencies, but when a strong king had an effective army, a rich treasury, and just plain "moxie," smaller states, overlords, and princes would seek to become clients of Ayudhia once more, sending annual tributes of gold and silver trees. The traditional Thai state resembled a galaxy in which dependent social or political entities circled around the king and his capital.[33] Even today, the Thai word for politics—*gan muang*—means "things that take place in or involve the city" reflecting the continued presence of an attitude that analyzes politics as the outreach of a central focal point.

The sway of traditional monarchs over the people and land closest to them also reflected these changing patterns. Under a formal legal hierarchy indivduals as commoners were assigned to serve some lord (*phrai som*) or perhaps the king (*phrai luang*). Persons assigned to lords also owed services to government agencies or departments (*krom*). Commoners in turn could be patrons to a circle of serfs. Depending on their rank or function, a *sakdi na* system assigned to lords and princes a number of commoner "clients." The dignitaries needed a powerful king who would extend his sway, collect more people within his galaxy, and parcel them out to his lords and officials. In turn, the king depended on his entourage to pass on some portion of the taxes and produce from their clients. Land taxes did not go to a central treasury but passed up through a hierarchy of lords, each of whom would skim some amount, leaving the residue for the king. A king's resource base, then, depended most on the wealth of his capital, the value of foreign trade passing through that city, and the productivity of the commoners directly dependent on him (*phrai luang*).

Such a system of independent, descending patron-client entities (smaller solar systems within the king's galactic polity) produced as much disorder as obedience. Tambiah has said that a galactic polity based on patron-client interlocks laid the ground for "the kind of volatile factional struggles and aggrandizing exploits that produced an intermittent chain of usurpations and rebellions."[34] The king himself was insecure. The potential of clients deserting a structure that would no longer succor them was a real restraint on royal absolutism. The great King Narai was deposed by Phra Petchachart in the rebellion of 1688. King Taksin was dethroned and executed by one of his generals, Chao Phaya Chakri, who then founded the Chakri dynasty as Rama I. Rama IV, known to the West as Mongkut and one of Thailand's greatest monarchs, wrote that "when the king [meaning I] makes such an order, the persons who are of great power and high position in the land do not agree to it and refuse to obey. . . . They refuse to do so because they are important persons and so not have to fear to offend the king. Therefore they do what they like."[35] In 1887 under Rama V (King Chulalongkorn), it was proposed that Thailand become a constitutional monarchy. In rejecting the proposal, King Chulalongkorn said that powerful ministers would resist such changes, and if it developed that they could not perform effectively as European-style administrators, they might resign in large numbers, creating a crisis for Thai politics.[36]

The tension between submission and opting out inherent in the patron-client hierarchy was a permanent part of the galactic structure of traditional Thailand. Here the subjective belief in karma resonated with an institutional arrangement where arbitrary power was checked by real constraints existing in the possibility of loss of support. Contemporary Thailand provides fewer opportunities for changing patrons and has fewer constraints on power than did the traditional polity. Modernization has introduced more rigidity into Thai politics, exacerbating the tension engendered by the desire to opt out. Three factors are important here. Thailand has become a territorial state instead of a hegemonic galactic one—boundaries are now fixed. Governors of Udorn or Nan no longer can look to Luang Prabang, Burma, or Vientienne for overlordship if the central Thai authority is not sufficiently supportive. Second, functional administrative departments limit the extent to which an individual with *wasanaa* can expand his network of clients. Third, under rule by an authoritarian clique composed of a few generals, aristocrats, high civil servants, and their associates, the play of politics now is to reduce the number of competitors for highest power. This diminishes the channels through which the benefits of efficacy can flow down to nourish patron-client substructures. With fewer senior patrons, there are fewer opportunities for subpatrons and underclients to leave their current patrons and attach themselves to new ones. Wilson described the political system (in 1962) as dominated by ten or fifteen individuals, with only six or eight in power at any one time. These few divided up about one thousand second-level clients who were generals, top-ranked civil servants, parliamentarians, princes, and powerful businessmen. This second tier in turn set up followings among a ruling class of commercial or white-collar people estimated at only 1 or 2 percent of the adult population.[37] The situation is not significantly different today.

A fixed bureaucratic hierarchy has another limitation. Under the old galactic system the outer perimeter of the system was very flexible. New agglomerations of people could easily be added to the chains of patronage leading up to the monarch in his central city. Now, however, the points of contact with the top of the structure are limited. As new groups arise—intellectuals, unions, tenant farmers—they have no easy way to find a patron. These groups resent being at the ordered-about end of an authoritarian hierarchy. Their demand is for "democracy" or the freedom to find their own patrons without regard for the bureaucratic structure.

This new institutional structure has introduced more anxieties by grating against an older individual desire to accumulate merit and get "free" of inadequate patrons. This new anxiety has produced political movements calling for democracy. Cultural perceptions seem to have a direct bearing on both the direction and the momentum of political change. The Revolution of 1932 ended the absolute monarchy and expanded the patron-client system to include the military and the civil service. Student-led demonstrations in October 1973 brought down a military regime; since then, Thai political leaders have moved, though fitfully at times, toward a more democratic political structure. In the spring of 1979 another parliament was elected in yet another attempt to establish and maintain democracy.

Parliamentary democracy has not yet succeeded in Thailand because it has not been based on an open-ended patron-client structure. Administrative centralization of government has meant that any patron-client relationship must tap into the central power structure to be effective. There lie status, economic leverage, and access to the resources with which to nourish a network of clients. The revolution of 1932, which ended absolute monarchy, merely expanded access to the top of the central patron-client structure from the royal family to senior military men and civil servants. In no sense was this event a popular or mass revolution changing traditional patterns of social and political life.

On a few occasions since 1932 when more thorough parliamentary democracy was attempted, it led quickly to breakdown and anarchy. Each time the political process would open up, a military group would, after a coup, reassert the primacy of the central administrative patron-client hierarchy. Such experiments with democratic procedures threatened existing patrons without providing the newly elected politicians with the means to set themselves up as new but dependable patrons and so provide a democratic structure of still predictable and mutually advantageous relationships. These electoral experiments did not provide a basis for the order that Thais also seek in a patron-client system. Flexibility quickly became anarchy.

However, pressures within Thailand for "democracy" are real. The military leaders now recognize this. These pressures reflect indigenous needs for flexibility within a patron-client structure. Thus, one has the modest hope that electoral mechanisms can be designed in a Thai fashion to provide this flexibility and, by so doing, to limit the arbitrary authority of the senior members of the central administrative hierarchy. Such a system must provide patron-client links to groups now excluded from the hierarchy and must give political parties and elected officials the resources with which to become patrons.

CONCLUSION

These traditional patterns have not become institutionalized in political structures based on popular representation and constitutional checks and balances. China, Vietnam, and Thailand have had no procedures to insure that government will abide by the norms of self-restraint.

To help create new political arrangements that would be more responsive to popular impulses in these countries, it would be best to ground new structures on those existing values that have meaning for most members of those societies. Otherwise, changes will be short-lived. Progress protecting human rights can best be made by building procedures and institutions out of traditional values. Governmental restraint leaves room for political expression to grow. The task for human rights advocates is thus to understand the dynamics of other societies so that progressive changes can be suggested, introduced, and supported. Success can come best from reform, not from revolution. Communist revolutions in China and Vietnam preserve perhaps the worst features of old authoritarianism with only marginal gains made by adding Western technology.[38]

Americans have not been very effective at grafting progressive political procedures on traditional societies. The U.S. client regime in Vietnam collapsed once aid was cut; the Kuo Min Tang in China was neither progressive nor successful, even with U.S. aid. In Thailand the United States has been at best a bystander during democratic experiments and at worst a patron of the central bureaucratic hierarchy. It would be too hasty to conclude that these failures, so often based on ignorance and misperception, mean that indigenous traditional forces cannot motivate democratic rule. It is not clear that the idea of democracy is destined to fail in Asia; nor is it clear that socialism will provide prosperity and liberty. The U.S. human rights effort should not demand wholesale change in the social and political orders of foreign countries. At the same time, however, the United States should not accept failure to protect rights as "all that can be expected" of Asians. Between these two extremes lies a mean of greater use and value.

Understanding others in their own terms has not been the strongest American suit. Too often, therefore, American officials and scholars find it terribly hard to predict changing events in foreign countries. Sinologists were unprepared for the interest in democracy and rights expressed by wall posters in China during 1978; the Carter administration was unprepared for the volatile Islamic fundamentalism that toppled the Shah of Iran in the same year. Even at home, cultural traditions at variance with the dominant Protestant culture of "Americanism" have been discouraged and disparaged. The "melting pot" was supposed to fuse immigrants into Americans. Its failure became apparent in the late 1960s, as the unmeltable ethnics became the subject of commentary and political appeals.

The central concepts of other cultures are probably the most important facts for Americans to learn. They have a power to shape the self-images and emotions of whole populations. These core concepts become, in Daniel Bell's words, "axial principles" that create a primary logic for the "organizing frame around which the other institutions are draped."[39]

NOTES

1. This is similar to the checks on the power of the magistrates in Rome by the Senate and Assemblies, and by appeals to tribunes and other officials. Arbitrary power was the corruptor of commonwealths, as described in Bernard Bailyn in *The Ideological Origins of the American Revolution* (Cambridge, Mass.: Belknap Press, 1967). In the Anglo-American context, the purpose of constitutional arrangements was to restrain the will of those in power.

2. The definition of human rights is an often contested problem. For the purposes of this discussion, this functional definition seems to offer the broadest and most effective handle for comparing societies. For another discussion of similar issues, see E. Mabry Rogers and Stephen B. Young, "Public Office as a Public Trust," *Georgetown Law Review* 63, no. 5 (May 1975).

3. Manfred Porket, *The Theoretical Foundations of Chinese Medicine,* M.I.T. East Asia Science Series, vol. 3 (Cambridge, Mass.: M.I.T. Press, 1974). My views on this point have been profoundly shaped by Mr. Duong Thai Ban, a Vietnamese geomancer and physiognomist.

4. Wm. Theodore de Bary, "Individualism and Humanitarianism in Late Ming Thought," in *Self and Society in Ming Thought,* ed. de Bary (New York: Columbia University Press, 1970), pp. 145–48.

5. Examples of how the *I Ching* was so used can be found in James Legge, trans., *The Chinese Classics,* vol. V, "The Ch'un Ts'ew with

the Tso Chuen" (Hong Kong: Hong Kong University Press, 1970), pp. 439, 514, 541.

6. Raymond Van Over, ed., *The I Ching* (New York: New American Library, 1971), p. 380.

7. Ibid., p. 326.

8. Clae Waltham, *Shu Ching, Book of History* (Chicago: Gateway, 1971), pp. 3–7.

9. Legge, *Chinese Classics*, vol. II, *The Works of Mencius*, bk. V, pt. I, chap. 5, pp. 357–58.

10. Ibid., bk. I, pt. II, chap. 8, p. 167.

11. Unfortunately, Confucian thought emphasized conformity of the self to external standards, understood as the submission of selfish impulses before paternal and political authority. Ceremonies and propriety became corsets of rectitude surrounding the inner person dedicated to self-cultivation. This kind of Confucianism could become a rationalization for all formal authority and fall away from Mencius' insistence on reciprocity between ruler and ruled. Autonomous individual action was out of favor as Confucian teachings were used as a state cult. Yet in the eleventh and twelfth centuries, under the Sung dynasty, Confucian thought flowered anew by borrowing the theory of yin and yang from the *I Ching* and explaining it in Confucian terms.

12. Waltham, *Shu Ching*, "Documents of Hsia: The Speech at Kan," pp. 55–56.

13. Ibid., "The Counsels of the Great Yu," p. 22.

14. F. Max Muller, ed., and James Legge, trans., *Sacred Books of the East*, "The Le Chi" (Oxford: Oxford University Press, 1927), pp. 283–96.

15. Waltham, *Shu Ching*, "The Counsels of the Great Yu," p. 23.

16. We find other references in the *Shu Ching* linking punishment with good government and the Mean; a king of the Shang dynasty was admonished to "set up the standard of the Mean before the people" (Waltham, "Documents of Shang, The Announcement by Chung Hui," p. 7). Also, "persons of artful tongues should not determine criminal cases, but really good persons whose awards will hit the Mean," and "examine carefully the penal code and deliberate well all about it that your decisions may be likely to hit the Mean and be correct" (Waltham, "Documents of Chou, The Marquis of Luan Punishment," p. 235).

17. Legge, *Chinese Classics*, vol. 5., *Tso Chuan*, Duke Seang, 31st year, 3d comment to par. 7, p. 555.

18. Waltham, *Shu Ching*, "Document of Shang, The Common Possession of Pure Virtue," p. 83.

19. Van Over, *I Ching*, p. 399.

20. D. T. Suzuki and Paul Canis, trans., *Treatise on Response and Retribution* (LaSalle, Ill.: Open Court, 1973), pp. 51–56.

21. The concept of a symbolic universe is discussed in Peter Berger

and Thomas Luckman, *The Social Construction of Reality* (New York: Doubleday, 1966).

22. Lucien Pye, *The Spirit of Chinese Politics* (Cambridge, Mass.: M.I.T. Press, 1971), p. 108.

23. Richard Solomon, *Mao's Revolution and the Chinese Political Culture* (Berkeley: University of California Press, 1971), p. 105.

24. The first political philosopher to set forth this synthesis of law and Confucian morality was Hsun Tzu, who lived before the Han dynasty. Under the Han, Tung Chung Shu rationalized the Confucianized state cult as part of the imperial system of rule after many others had added their thoughts to the composite.

25. I have derived my analysis of Vietnam's political culture from my own research in Vietnamese materials. Earlier articles of mine supplement this presentation: "The Law of Property and Elite Privileges During Vietnam's Le Dynasty, 1428–1788," *Journal of Asian History* 10, no. 1 (1976); "Unpopular Socialism in United Vietnam," *ORBIS* 21, no. 2 (1977); "Vietnamese Marxism: A Transition in Elite Ideology," *Asian Survey* (August 1979). My approach to the Vietnamese materials has been informed by certain cultural anthropologists, especially Ruth Benedict and by psychodynamics in the works of Erik Erikson and Harry Stack Sullivan. My work is of the same genre as Lucian Pye's studies of political culture in Burma and China and Richard Solomon's work on Chinese concepts of authority.

26. Guenter Lewy, *American in Vietnam* (New York: Oxford University Press, 1978).

27. The notion of *phuc duc* and the concept of *uy tin* are not understood in the West. Upon their arrival in Vietnam, French colonists formulated an incorrect analysis of Vietnamese society that has been taken as the basis for every succeeding Western commentary. The French, looking at the mandarinate of the Nguyen dynasty (centered at the imperial court in Hue), concluded that the Vietnamese had a Chinese Confucian, class-stratified society. Most contemporary studies of Vietnam, communist and noncommunist, adopt the erroneous French image of Vietnamese reality. Frances FitzGerald in her book, *Fire in the Lake*, does so, and so do historians such as Joseph Buttinger and David Marr.

But Vietnam's nineteenth-century Confucian elite has rather recent origins in Vietnamese history. A scholar-gentry class using the neo-Confucian norms of China's classic mandarin state and society began to form in northern Vietnam only in the mid-1600s. Then Vietnam's nineteenth-century mandarins under the Nguyen dynasty extensively imported neo-Confucian ideology from China as the norm for their political structure, because they possessed neither *uy tin* nor *phuc duc* and sought a new basis for their moral authority. For example, in 1812 Emperor Gia Long, who had founded the dynasty that would acquiesce to the French conquest, adopted the Ching dynasty law code from China, while the villages continued to live by the Vietnamese Le dynasty code of the mid-fifteenth century. The Nguyen dynasty did not embody the basic ethnic values of *phuc duc* and *uy tin*. Therefore, it could not successfully mobilize the people to resist French colonial expansion as Vietnamese in prior centuries had defeated Chinese and Mongol invasions.

28. Democratic developments in South Vietnam are discussed in *Electoral Politics in South Vietnam,* ed John C. Donnell and Charles A. Joiner, (Lexington, Mass.: Lexington Books, 1974).

29. Lucien Hanks, "Merit and Power in the Thai Social Order," *American Anthropologist* 64, no. 6 (1962): 1247–61, and "The Thai Social Order as Entourage and Circle" in *Change and Persistence in Thai Society,* ed. William Skinner and A. Thomas Kirsch (Ithaca: Cornell University Press, 1975); see also A. Thomas Kirsch, "The Thai Buddhist Quest for Merit," 1969 (mimeograph).

30. Hanks, "Thai Social Order."

31. Ibid.

32. Stanley Tambiah, *World Conqueror, World Renouncer,* Cambridge Studies in Social Anthropology, no. 15 (Cambridge: Cambridge University Press, 1977), pp. 102–16.

33. Ibid., pp. 132–58.

34. Ibid., p. 212.

35. Akin Rabibhadana, *The Organization of Thai Society in the Early Bangkok Period, 1782–1873,* Data Paper no. 74 of Cornell Thailand Project Interim Reports Series (Ithaca: Cornell University Press, 1969), p. 146.

36. David Engle, *Law and Kingship in Thailand During the Reign of King Chulalongkorn,* Michigan Papers on South and Southeast Asia, no. 9 (Ann Arbor: Center for South and Southeast Asian Studies, University of Michigan, 1975), p. 15.

37. David Wilson, *Politics in Thailand* (Ithaca: Cornell University Press, 1962).

38. Simon Leys, *Chinese Shadows* (New York: The Viking Press, 1977).

39. Daniel Bell, *The Coming of Post-Industrial Society* (New York: Basic Books, 1976), p. 10.

SECTION III

It is difficult to discuss meaningfully the notion of human rights in the abstract, and it is even more difficult to assign and develop a place for human rights in the regular operations of international politics. To an extent, useful precedent has been set by international organizations, which have attempted to set standards of behavior for national governments toward their own citizens. Some of these standards (and subsequent policy recommendations) have been incorporated into treaties; others have appeared in a variety of forms in national foreign policies.

This section includes two chapters that are concerned with the multilateral and bilateral dimensions of a human rights policy. Sidney Weintraub explores the ways in which foreign aid policies have been used to further human rights; John Barton investigates the possible uses of the American Convention on Human Rights for multilateral and bilateral purposes. Because these two dimensions so often are related to one another—because bilateral and multilateral policy must so often be coordinated—the issues of assistance and international law have become coordinates for almost any human rights policy. For the United States in particular, immediate choices will be necessary as it weaves its way through the intricate maze of competing pressures and needs in both areas. Although these essays are in a strict sense policy analyses, they take their foci from the questions posed in the first two sections of this volume: that the results and recommendations of these different essays differ serves to demonstrate the complexities with

215

which the foreign policy community—and indeed, an informed electorate—must contend in the years to come.

One of the most pervasive problems in implementing human rights policies has been measurement: which violations do we examine, how do we measure violations of rights, how do we calibrate policy actions and determine their success or failure? The answers to these questions are themselves subject to debate and question, for they are based on one of several possible views of polity and society. However, these queries are statistically as well as politically important. The appendix included here introduces some of the problems which policy has posed for political actors, and discusses the kinds of research and clarification which will be needed in the future.

Chapter 9

HUMAN RIGHTS AND BASIC NEEDS IN UNITED STATES FOREIGN AID POLICY

SIDNEY WEINTRAUB

INTRODUCTION

The two moral pillars of U.S. foreign policy are the promotion of human rights and the effort to help the world's poor satisfy their basic needs. Together they represent the nobler content of what is otherwise mostly an exercise in *Realpolitik*. They are linked not only in their innate decency but also explicitly in U.S. foreign aid and related legislation. Our laws prescribe that we can give aid to poor countries only if they do not blatantly violate the human rights of their people; and if they do, our aid must be seen as directly satisfying basic needs of the poor majority.

Both policies are products of the 1970s, launched with fanfare and now hobbling along because of pressures of competing domestic and foreign policy interests. The United States helps to meet basic needs with one of the lowest aid programs of the noncommunist industrial world, measured relative to GNP, and even this poor record relies heavily on admittedly political programs in the Middle East (i.e., programs motivated primarily by reasons other than satisfying basic human needs).[1] We are selective in our advocacy of human rights depending on our other interests in countries. Violation of human rights in the People's Republic of China, to cite just one topical example, is obviously a peripheral issue in total U.S.-China policy.

217

These are familiar themes and it would serve no public purpose to rehearse them once again merely either to criticize or praise policy. Both praise and criticism may in fact be warranted in that a sense of morality now does exist in U.S. foreign policy, even if this morality is inconstant. The object of this essay is to analyze how the tandem policies actually work and to suggest improvements.

The two policies are highly experimental. No country ever has developed from poverty to reasonable affluence by deliberately giving priority both to participatory democracy and meeting the basic needs of the majority of its people. On the other hand, countries have made this transformation by emphasizing growth of GNP. In some cases distributive justice has followed, and in other cases it has not. Despite this, U.S. foreign aid policy has opted for stressing equity and participation.[2] The United States rarely has chosen the beneficiaries of its aid among the developing countries based on the morality of their leadership. The location of the country, and the anticommunism of its leadership, have been far more significant. It is by no means a settled issue that a human rights starting point for aid policy maximizes U.S. self-interest. What we have, therefore, are untested policies with uncertain outcomes stimulated by a sense that doing right not only is self-ennobling but may even make for effective foreign policy.

The next section of this chapter will describe the evolution of the two policies. This will be followed by a discussion of the linkages between human rights and various aspects of foreign economic policy. These linkages transcend aid, but aid is the cutting edge. This will be followed by an analysis of how the twin policies have worked in practice, including some attempt to assess accomplishments of U.S. actions. The final sections will examine options to the current approach and make recommendations for future policy.

THE EVOLVING POLICIES

A. HUMAN RIGHTS

The human rights policy grew out of candidate Jimmy Carter's concern that the United States often was perceived in the world as a supporter of the status quo, an ally of right-wing nondemocratic regimes and an opponent of left-wing governments intent on change. The emergence of this issue in U.S. foreign policy has been described as a historical happening.[3] Opportunities, often fortuitous, presented themselves, and were exploited for reasons that were a mixture of good domestic politics, international image making, and President Carter's own sense of what was right and moral.[4] Some of the accidents of timing were the events surrounding the Vietnam war, the revelations regarding U.S. opposition to the Allende regime in Chile and the emergence of the right-wing Pinochet government, and the realization of excesses against human and civil rights by both the CIA and the FBI. Perhaps the crucial happening was the Helsinki agreement of 1975, which contained Basket Three and Principle VII, a sort of human rights afterthought to a conference that otherwise dealt with political boundaries in Europe, and the fact that a conference was to be held in Belgrade in 1977–78 to review compliance with these provisions. The establishment of groups in the USSR, Czechoslovakia, Poland, and East Germany to monitor national compliance with these provisions of the Helsinki agreement gave particular prominence to the human rights issue in East-West affairs.

On North-South issues, the emergence of human rights took a different path. Here the initial leadership was taken by the Congress within the framework of the foreign aid program. Both sides of the ideological aisle had misgivings about U.S. foreign aid programs. The liberals were concerned that aid too often went to repressive regimes and the conservatives that aid was as large as it was, and both groups were able to agree not to give assistance to a government "which engages in a consistent pattern of gross violation of . . . human rights . . . unless such assistance will directly benefit . . . needy people."[5] This human rights provision for bilateral aid has since been extended, usually in less peremptory form, to the PL 480 or food aid program, assistance provided through multilateral agencies, security assistance, the lending and guarantee programs of the Export-Import Bank, and the programs of the Overseas Private Investment Corporation (OPIC). In a sense, this was not a completely new departure for the bilateral aid program, since over the years since the enactment in 1960 of the current legislation, just about everybody's pet prohibition or limitation on aid giving had been included. Most of these provisions were motivated explicitly by self-interest. The best example was the Hickenlooper amendment, which forbade aid to countries that expropriated property of U.S. citizens or corporations without taking steps for just compensation or arbitration. The human rights provisions were different; they were Hickenlooper with morality.

At the outset of the Carter administration, the new policy was pursued vigorously, indeed zealously. On the East-West level, the White House criticized the Soviet Union directly for its violation of human rights while at the same time asserting that this criticism should have no effect on the SALT negotiations. The president responded directly in early 1977 to the letter sent to him by Andrei Sakharov. Major countries like Brazil were cited for keeping political prisoners. Human rights seemed almost to be *primus inter pares* among U.S. foreign policy interests and pursued with the naive belief that pinpointed outspokenness on this issue would not affect other bilateral relations. A new and inexperienced administration had come to power with an ideological reaction against the old and hostility to what seemed to be the crassness of the earlier foreign policy. (This reaction of rejecting all that had gone before was similar to that in other areas of foreign policy. For example, step-by-step diplomacy in the Middle East initially was rejected in favor of trying for a comprehensive solution.)

In time, this zeal gave way to caution. Both in the White House and the State Department, there was realization that other U.S. interests often take precedence over human rights issues.[6] The most dramatic manifestations of this shift were toning down critical public statements about the Soviet Union in order not to prejudice the SALT talks, being less overtly obstreperous with Brazil as our relations progressively deteriorated, continuing military assistance to South Korea even as we cut such assistance to Argentina and Uruguay, sending Vice-President Mondale to the Philippines despite its abysmal human rights record and after what was evidently a less than fully democratic election, and expressing public support for the Shah of Iran in late 1978 when the mass demonstrations against him erupted and U.S. concern was greater for noncommunist stability in that country than for the Shah's previous human rights record.

What now remains is what one would expect in policymaking toward any country, namely, to consider human rights issues along with other issues. In this sense, as in many others, the Carter administration has reverted to traditional diplomacy. However, there has been some change. Human rights issues rarely entered into policy deliberations in previous administrations unless they could be used to promote anticommunism. They now enter regularly, and a procedure exists for this entry. (The danger does exist that the reaction to the initial overkill will be a resynthesis around a policy of cynicism. Indeed, there is evidence that this already has occurred. President Carter sent a letter to President Anastasio Somoza in the summer of 1978 praising him for the improvement of human rights in Nicaragua at the very moment that country was about to explode because of the Somoza regime's persistent denial of its citizens' human rights.[7])

B. BASIC HUMAN NEEDS

The basic-human-needs strategy of development antedates the Carter administration, and here, too, the initiative came from the Congress and not the executive.[8] Like the human rights issue, the content of the strategy (aid to the poor to help them meet minimum requirements for such elemental needs as food, clothing, shelter, and education) fit the tone that the Carter administration wished to project, and it was therefore wholeheartedly embraced.

And, again, as with the human rights stress in foreign policy, there was a tendency to overstate. From the thesis that "GNP isn't everything," many of the basic-human-needs advocates moved to a position that "GNP isn't anything." This latter theme lends itself to arguments that growth is not synonymous with progress, since higher levels of GNP can lead to disruptive societal changes and usually involve environmental degradation. These arguments, however, were mainly the intellectualizing of people from rich countries and not the stated objectives of spokesmen from the poor countries.

The U.S. bilateral aid program moved with complete abandon in line with the new philosophy. Infrastructure projects, such as roads, dams, and communications networks, were no longer to be financed; funds were allocated almost exclusively to agriculture, education, health, and population projects. The U.S. bilateral aid program became a series of mostly unrelated development projects, usually small (averaging between $2 and $3 million per project), because that is how the poor are most effectively reached directly, with only secondary concern for national or sectoral development. Small became beautiful,[9] even if the results were picayune. One consequence of this initial overdrawn policy was that the Agency for International Development (AID) actually was unable during several fiscal years to commit all the funds allocated for Africa because of the narrow definition given to the "new directions" philosophy and obligated the money instead in Latin America, generally the best off of the world's developing regions. There is an interesting byplay in a report of the Senate Appropriations Committee as to whether a farm-to-market road network is bad because it is infrastructure.[10] Rural cooperatives among the inexperienced poor, most of which have failed, were encouraged because they involved direct cooperation (participation) of the poor. Despite its misgivings, the Inter-American Development Bank (IDB) was pressured by the United States into giving more assistance to cooperatives, since this was deemed to be proper development. However, none of the multilateral development banks pushed the basic-human-needs concept to the limits that prevailed in the U.S. bilateral program, although U.S. pressure was exerted on the IDB to expand the scope of its explicit basic-needs lending. For example, in its *World Development Report*, the World Bank stressed the importance of large infrastructure projects in Asia, both for their own sake and as technique for employment creation.[11]

There was an inevitable reaction to this oversell. AID, which in the first exuberance of its basic-human-needs (or new directions) approach eliminated its economic analysis capacity (on the grounds that this was no longer needed in the kind of reactive program that was contemplated and that instead reliance could be placed on planning and analysis done in the country itself and by the multilateral development banks), later sought to reconstitute this by new hiring. Instead of isolated projects of opportunity, current AID policy statements stress country analysis and planning and cross-sectoral approaches. Even more important, there is now a recognition that "to meet the basic human needs of one to two billion people obviously requires a vast expansion in the production of goods and services."[12] That is, GNP does count. That it does has once again become a familiar theme.[13] In its 1977 report the United Nations Committee for Development Planning stated its unease that new ideas like "basic needs" were getting too sloganized; these ideas were fine for getting attention but incomplete as a development strategy.[14]

The evolutionary parallelism with human rights is reasonably exact. An inherently laudable objective, in this case of seeking to use tax funds paid by citizens of the United States for the benefit of the disadvantaged majority in the aid-receiving countries, was pushed to the point that distribution per se was defined as development. This strategy also found support from both "bleeding hearts" and "hard-nosed realists" in the Congress, the former on the grounds that aid should help those who most need it and the latter because, at least at the outset of the new policy, it implied lower aid levels.[15]

What seems to be emerging out of this ferment on development policy is that distribution (of income, education, health, and other services) will take its place alongside growth as an objective of U.S. foreign aid policy and international aid policy generally.

There undoubtedly are some verities that helped to determine the bureaucratic unfolding of these twin policies in the United States. In each case there was some revulsion to what had gone before (crassness in foreign policy, and growth without justice in development policy), a rediscovery of old concepts (of the need for the United States to stand in the world for decency), and then taking these without nuance beyond their sustainable carrying power. The ultimate syntheses are as yet undetermined but seem likely in each case to involve retention of a significant element of the newer concerns for human rights and basic needs while not thoroughly casting away the older concerns for other U.S. foreign policy objectives and for growth as an important feature of development policy.

LINKAGES BETWEEN THE TWO POLICIES

The human rights policy of the United States is carried out through many more instruments than the granting or withholding of foreign aid. With respect to the Soviet Union, for example, the main instruments are diplomatic representation, public statements, and publicity regarding human rights violations. The use of economic coercion is generally anathema to the executive branch in the U.S.–USSR relationship. The previous administration opposed the Jackson-Vanik amendment to the trade legislation linking the granting of most-favored-nation tariff treatment and loans and guarantees from the Export-Import Bank to freer emigration from the Soviet Union and other communist countries. The present administration apparently feels the same way. There is a significant difference in the approach to equals, such as the Soviet Union, and to countries that are evidently considered to be unequal, such as those to whom the United States gives concessional aid. The executive branch does not hesitate to practice economic coercion on the latter. President Ferdinand Marcos presumably had this kind of coercion in mind when he used the term "moral imperialism" to depict U.S. human rights policy.[16]

One of the most frequent criticisms launched against the human rights policy of the Carter administration is that it punishes friends and allies and not adversaries. This is inevitable if the major coercive instrument is the aid program or other governmental programs that provide some form of subsidized benefit to another country.[17] President Carter deplored the violation of human rights in Cambodia before the government was overthrown by invasion from Vietnam, but he had no military or economic aid program to remove; he could both deplore and act to remove benefits in the case of, say, Uruguay. The direct linkage between the human rights and basic-needs policies must be with aid-receiving client states.

The United States often uses measures of economic coercion other than development assistance for foreign policy purposes. A trade embargo was applied against Communist China, Cuba, and other communist states. The United States agreed with others to not purchase chromium from Rhodesia. There is a limit on the kinds of transactions that the Export-Import Bank can engage in with South Africa. U.S. trade legislation prohibits the granting of tariff preferences to less developed countries that have expropriated property of U.S. citizens without providing for just compensation. However, there is a difference between using trade as a coercive instrument, since this involves a deprivation for some U.S. trader and perhaps the country as a whole, and using aid, which is essentially an unrequited benefit (except in the abstract sense that development in poor countries will eventually raise incomes in the United States).

Different degrees of U.S. government subsidization are involved in different instruments. A grant of aid to a less developed country is, by definition, 100 percent grant or subsidy. A concessional loan by AID, because of its low interest rate, grace period for repayment, and long repayment terms, may amount to about 90 percent grant. An Export-Import Bank loan, which carries market or near market interest rates, has some subsidy element resulting from the official government involvement, but the amount is small. The same is true for a credit from the Commodity Credit Corporation to facilitate foreign purchases of U.S. agricultural commodities. The purpose of the Export-Import Bank is to foster U.S. exports, and denying export credits on noneconomic grounds obviously frustrates the very purpose of the institution. Withholding concessional aid, on the other hand, means the reallocation of a grant or near grant to some other country.

U.S. legislation and executive branch policy distinguish

among instruments, although there is a body of opinion that argues that a principled human rights policy should extend through the entire continuum from purely market-directed transactions, to those involving slight government subsidization, to near grant, and to full grant.[18] One of the most internally divisive and externally vitriolic disputes over the administration's human rights policy erupted in mid-1978 following the withholding of credits and guarantees of the Export-Import Bank of almost $300 million for hydroelectric turbine and papermaking machinery sales to Argentina by U.S. companies. The decision later was reversed but only after the companies exerted considerable pressure.[19]

The legislative provisions for development assistance administered by AID and for food aid are essentially identical. In each case, aid may not be granted to governments that engage in a consistent pattern of gross violations of human rights "unless such assistance will directly benefit needy people."[20] The legislation regarding U.S. participation in the international financial institutions is similar but adapted to the fact that the United States is only one of many members; the executive is required to use the voice and vote of the United States to advance the cause of human rights.[21] The provision regarding security assistance is less stringent; it forbids such aid if it directly assists the government of the recipient country to "repress the legitimate rights of the population . . . contrary to the Universal Declaration of Human Rights."[22] OPIC is enjoined in its programs in a country "to take into account" that country's respect for human rights. OPIC is further subject to the same provisions as AID in its bilateral program, but with an additional escape from this limitation on national security grounds.[23] The limitation on the Export-Import Bank is that it may deny support of exports to a given country only when this would "clearly and importantly advance U.S. policy" with respect to human rights (and other objectives).[24] There is a rough progression from less to more stringency the greater the degree of government grant or subsidy involved. Trade with countries following a consistent pattern of gross violations of human rights is not affected by the foregoing provisions unless some form of government financing, guaranty, or insurance is involved. (U.S. experience with the unilateral imposition of trade sanctions can hardly be considered a rousing success. At a time of pressure on the value of the dollar, it is most unlikely that the United States would impose human rights impediments on trade such as those now imposed on subsidized financing.)

The definition of human rights used as the basis for decisions under these legislative provisions rests on the Charter of the United Nations, the Universal Declaration of Human Rights, and other international agreements and covenants. In a carefully drafted speech seeking to define U.S. policy, Secretary of State Cyrus Vance delineated three categories of human rights: those relating to the integrity of the person (freedom from torture and other cruel, inhuman, or degrading treatment; from arbitrary arrest or imprisonment; from denial of a fair public trial; and from invasion of the home); economic rights (the right to food, shelter, health care, and education—in other words, the right to fulfillment of basic human needs); and civil and political liberties (freedoms of thought, religion, assembly, speech, press, movement within and outside one's country, and to take part in government). Vance warned against any "hubristic attempt to impose our values on others." He stated that there were no automatic answers to meet all country situations.[25] What the foregoing implies is that there is a reasonable definition of human rights violation at the extreme, say, in Uganda under Amin, but considerable ambiguity in most other cases. If decisions are to be made on a case-by-case basis, as Vance stated and as seems inevitable, some machinery is needed to make these decisions.

For economic assistance, this is done by an Inter-Agency Committee on Human Rights and Foreign Assistance, chaired by Deputy Secretary of State Warren Christopher (hence, the Christopher committee), and that includes representatives from the Departments of State, Treasury, Defense, and Agriculture, the National Security Council, AID, the Export-Import Bank, and the other agencies as appropriate. The committee itself has a subordinate group that meets more frequently. In their required annual report to the Congress in 1978 on U.S. efforts to advance the cause of human rights through the multilateral development banks, the Departments of State and Treasury described the information coming to the Christopher committee as reports from U.S. embassies and from international human rights organizations. Other criteria cited in the decision-making process were: recent human rights trends in a country; the effectiveness of possible U.S. actions; the extent that the assistance being reviewed promotes basic needs; other U.S. interests in the country; and preserving the integrity of the multilateral development banks.[26]

The standards for making judgments are evidently less than precise. Other than general guidelines of the type cited, the government has never published detailed information on how and on what grounds Christopher committee decisions are made.[27]

However, a human rights policy apparatus, even if flawed, is in place.[28] It rests on legislation and there is an effort at congressional oversight, and it is supported by a regular review procedure for economic assistance. If one believes that human rights considerations are relevant for granting or withholding foreign aid, this is a contribution of the Carter administration.

THE HUMAN RIGHTS–BASIC-NEEDS POLICIES IN PRACTICE

A. PRAISE AND CRITICISM

There is an extensive literature praising and criticizing U.S. human rights policy. The administration is able to cite some general and many specific instances of successes of the policy. The key general contribution claimed is the awareness that now exists in the United States and elsewhere of human rights violations. It is also asserted that the U.S. image has been altered from identification with repression to one of concern for victims of repression. The willingness of dissidents to come forth publicly in the Soviet Union and Eastern European countries undoubtedly stems in part from their awareness of the U.S. posture. One can argue whether this matters in promoting the security and well-being of the United States—it can be argued that promotion of human rights is a sideshow compared with more fundamental international power relationships—but even those who take this position presumably would welcome a perception of the United States as a country that has some concern for decency.

On a more specific level, the administration is able to cite scores of examples when U.S. actions helped to promote human rights. To cite just a few: political prisoners have been released in more than a dozen countries; international bodies have been permitted to make on-site investigations of prisons and human rights violations; the American (i.e., hemispheric) Convention on Human Rights is now in force; and a peaceful transition to a new president took place in the Dominican Republic in 1978, which almost certainly would not have occurred had the United States stood idly by. For whatever reason (Jackson-Vanik, to get rid of dissidents), permitted emigration from the Soviet Union increased to an annual rate of about thirty thousand in 1978 compared with an average of sixteen thousand a year in the preceding three years.

There have been failures. Yuri Orlov and Anatoly Shcharansky were imprisoned precisely because they sought to monitor the Soviet Union's compliance with the human rights provisions of the Helsinki agreement. (Or should this be deemed a success since it epitomized Soviet concern?)

Because of the inevitable inconsistency of actions resulting from balancing human rights with other national considerations, cynicism has developed regarding U.S. sincerity.[29] For example, many Uruguayans are convinced that economic and military assistance to them can be cut off because they are a throwaway country from the U.S. strategic standpoint and that this explains the different treatment accorded South Korea or the Philippines.

Perhaps the most severe genre of criticism is that of Aleksandr Solzhenitsyn:

And decline in courage is ironically emphasized by occasional explosions of anger and inflexibility on the part of

the same bureaucrats when dealing with weak governments and weak countries, not supported by anyone, or
with currents which cannot offer any resistance. But they
get tongue-tied and paralyzed when they deal with powerful governments and threatening forces, with aggressors
and international terrorists.[30]

If the leading instrument of U.S. human rights policy is to be
the economic aid program (which, together with military aid, is
the case), then it is inevitable that punishment will be meted out
to poor countries, since they are the potential recipients of this
aid. However, it does not follow that because other national
considerations lead the United States to be more circumspect
with the powerful, the government should therefore ignore
human rights considerations in dealings with the weak.

B. THE BASIC-NEEDS ESCAPE FROM THE HUMAN RIGHTS SANCTION
The human rights legislation as it pertains to bilateral development and concessional food aid has two parts: first, a prohibition of aid when there is a consistent pattern of gross violations of human rights; and, second, an escape from this on
basic-needs grounds. In the case of the multilateral development banks, there is also a third element, namely, that the
United States has a vote but not a veto in these institutions
(save for the soft-loan facility of the Inter-American Development Bank, where the United States does have a veto).[31] How
have these three elements been handled in practice?
First, consider the bilateral development assistance program. AID, early in the Carter administration, asked the State
Department which countries were likely to be turned down for
concessional assistance on human rights grounds. The State
Department was reluctant (and still is) to provide what came to
be known as a "hit list." However, AID, even if it was not
given a list, was given a notion of troublesome countries. This
can be important to AID because of the basic-needs escape
from the human rights prohibition. AID has reported the following to Congress:

Wherever there is a serious question whether the statutory conditions exist (that there is a consistent pattern of gross violations of internationally recognized human rights) in an A.I.D. recipient country, activities proposed for that country are reviewed to ensure that proposed country programs benefit needy people. A.I.D. does not wait for final determination that a particular government is a violator.[32]

In other words, even though AID projects are normally designed to directly help the poor majority, special attention is paid to insuring that this is the case for countries that are human rights violators. Loan documents must be drafted with particular care in these cases. Some countries are beyond the pale, and AID does not even make the effort, as in Uganda under Idi Amin, and apparently also in Chile and Uruguay. However, aid was continued in other countries with oppressive regimes, such as Nicaragua, El Salvador, and Honduras.

It takes two or more years from the conception of a loan idea until obligation of funds. It is thus possible to tailor projects so that they can qualify under the statute. Since bilateral aid is within the sole control (or joint control, counting the recipient country) of the United States, the country selection probably does not differ very much from what would be the case without the statutory provisions of human rights prohibition/basic-needs escape. It is hard to believe that the United States would have given concessionary development assistance to Uganda under Amin even without the law, and it is hard to see why relatively high-income countries such as Chile and Uruguay should be receiving scarce concessionary aid, human rights violations or not. (The United States has not stopped Title II food aid, such as milk for infants, to Chile.)

At one point, AID argued that its projects should be exempt from review by the Christopher committee, since AID could make certain that there was a basic-needs escape in every case. Although this blanket exemption was not granted, AID projects rarely are held up on human rights grounds.

Assistance granted by multilateral development institutions

of which the United States is a member rarely are prevented either, but the process is much more complicated. As of the end of June 1978 the United States had abstained or voted no on thirty-five loan projects in the multilateral development banks involving twelve countries (see Table 9.1). Twenty-five other loans to countries with serious human rights problems (usually the same countries for which the United States opposed or abstained on loans) were supported over the same period because they were deemed to meet basic human needs (see Table 9.2).

Tables 9.1 and 9.2 deserve some commentary. In defining U.S. human rights policy, the Department of State refers to it as "calibrated and sequential."[33] By this is meant that there is an escalation in the severity of action: unpublicized communication to governments about U.S. concern over human rights violations; the use of other diplomatic instruments, even including public statements; and differentiating votes in multilateral development institutions between outright opposition and abstention. For example, the United States abstained on two loans to Argentina and voted no on a third between June and October 1977. Then the president of Argentina indicated in October that some improvements would be made in his country's human rights situation, and the United States supported a substantial IDB loan in November, using the basic-needs escape. When the president's indication was not followed by meaningful action, the United States reverted in December to 2 no votes. In the case of Benin, the 2 abstentions in May 1977 were followed in June by U.S. support for a loan on the grounds that some political and religious prisoners were released. (In fact, what occurred was a change in the assessment of the human rights situation in Benin from that which prompted the two abstentions.) While there had been opposition earlier to an IDB loan to Chile, the abstentions of May 10, 1977 on two Ethiopian loans were the first clear actions by the Carter administration under the legislation relating to the multilateral development banks (and actually came at an awkward time for AID, which had some loans ready to go that were to be complementary to the IDA loans); in October the United

States supported a loan to Ethiopia on basic-needs grounds and then in April 1978 shifted back to an abstention.

It is difficult, without having been present at the meetings where the issues were discussed, to understand the series of votes on loans to South Korea. The United States abstained on two small loans in October and December 1977; this might have been a significant action in view of the close U.S.-Korean relationship. However, at about the same time, the United States was supporting four more substantial loans. In the case of Nicaragua, the United States repeatedly voted yes on loans using the basic-needs escape. In the case of the Philippines, the intermixture of abstention and support defies analysis without access to the internal records of discussion. Trends, sometimes unperceived by outsiders because undertakings were entered into in secrecy, and at other times evident to outsiders (such as the release of prisoners, lifting martial law, or permitting the visit of an international human rights group to investigate local conditions) explain the calibrations back and forth between support, abstention, and outright opposition. The Department of State, and the Treasury through its interaction with representatives in the multilateral institution of the country receiving the loan, can make sure that any U.S. signal is received.

The U.S. voting pattern in the multilateral development banks generally has been received with hostility, not only by the countries whose loans were opposed, but also by the management of the institutions. The reasoning is that the insertion of the human rights issue by the United States, which necessarily is subjective to some extent, brings political considerations into institutions that are enjoined by their charters to eschew politics in their support of economic development (e.g., the World Bank Charter states that "only economic considerations shall be relevant to . . . decisions").[34] The U.S. view on this point is that enhanced respect for human rights *is* part of the development process. The United States has been supported in its voting opposition on human rights grounds by virtually no other country, with the rare exception of the United Kingdom and even the rarer exception of some Scandinavian countries, and occasionally Venezuela in the IDB. (This

TABLE 9.1

Projects of Multilateral Development Banks Opposed by the U.S. on Human Rights Grounds, May 1977–June 1978

	Country	Action (A or N) a/	Amount ($ millions)	Date	Institution b/	Project
1.	Argentina	A	100.0	6/16/77	IBRD	Industrial credit
2.	Argentina	A	9.0	6/16/77	IFC	Soybean processing
3.	Argentina	N	36.0	10/27/77	IDB	Gas pipeline
4.	Argentina	N	53.9	12/ 1/77	IDB	Cellulose
5.	Argentina	N	105.0	12/ 8/77	IDB	Petrochemicals
6.	Argentina	A	105.0	2/21/78	IBRD	Grain storage
7.	Argentina	A	9.0	3/24/78	IFC	Cement plant
8.	Argentina	A	5.0	4/25/78	IFC	Pulp and paper
9.	Argentina	A	60.0	5/ 9/78	IBRD	Agricultural credit
10.	Argentina	A	10.0	5/30/78	IFC	Polyethylene
11.	Benin	A	1.7	5/26/77	IDA	Regional Development
12.	Benin	A	5.5	5/26/77	IDA	Roads
13.	Central Afr. Empire	A	6.3	10/20/77	AFDF	Education
14.	Chile	N	25.0	12/ 8/77	IDB	Roads
15.	Chile	N	16.5	3/ 2/78	IDB	Rural health
16.	El Salvador	A	23.0	5/18/78	IBRD	Telecommunications
17.	Ethiopia	A	25.0	5/10/77	IDA	Irrigation
18.	Ethiopia	A	32.0	5/10/77	IDA	Roads
19.	Ethiopia	A	24.0	4/ 4/78	IDA	Grain market and storage
20.	Guinea	A	5.5	11/23/78	AFDF	Kenaf production
21.	Korea, South	A	0.2	10/31/77	ADB	Power generation
22.	Korea, South	A	1.7	12/22/77	ADB	Mineral exploitation
23.	Paraguay	N	33.0	3/ 7/78	IBRD	Highway
24.	Paraguay	N	12.6	3/23/78	IDB	Highway
25.	Paraguay	N	32.5	5/25/78	IDB	Power transmission

Table 9.1 (Continued)

Country	Action (A or N) [a]	Amount ($ millions)	Date	Institution [b]	Project
26. Philippines	A	35.0	11/29/77	ADB	Development bank
27. Philippines	A	29.0	12/ 9/77	ADB	Hydropower generatn.
28. Philippines	A	80.0	4/25/78	IBRD	Priv. investment fund
29. Philippines	A	15.0	5/18/78	IBRD	Development Bank
30. Philippines	A	80.0	6/27/78	IFC	Shipyard
31. Uruguay	N	3.7	12/21/77	IDB	Coastal roads
32. Uruguay	N	26.0	12/21/77	IDB	Dam
33. Yemen, PDR	N	5.2	2/14/78	IDA	Irrigation
34. Yemen, PDR	A	5.0	6/13/78	IDA	Power generation
35. Yemen, PDR	A	1.2	6/28/78	IDA	Water supply

Source: U.S. Departments of State and Treasury.

Note

[a] A=abstention; N=no vote.
[b] IBRD—International Bank for Reconstruction and Development (the World Bank).
  IFC—International Finance Corporation.
  IDA—International Development Association. (The first three together make
    up the World Bank Group.)
  IDB—Inter-American Development Bank.
  ADB—Asian Development Bank
  AFDP—African Development Fund

TABLE 9.2

Projects of Multilateral Development Banks Supported by the U.S. on Basic-Human-Needs Grounds, May 1977–June 1978

	Country	Amount ($ millions)	Date	Institution a/	Project
1.	Argentina	81.0	11/ 3/77	IDB (FSO) b/	Water supply
2.	Benin	5.6	6/27/77	AFDF	Health services
3.	Cent. Afr. Empire	6.4	11/23/77	AFDF	Health services
4.	El Salvador	9.0	5/18/78	IBRD	Ind. and agr. training
5.	Ethiopia	6.3	10/20/77	AFDF	Transportation
6.	Korea, South	41.5	10/31/77	ADB	Secondary roads
7.	Korea, South	30.0	12/20/77	ADB	Reg. water supply
8.	Korea, South	36.0	12/22/77	IBRD	Agricultural development
9.	Korea, South	55.0	12/27/77	IBRD	Industrial bank
10.	Nicaragua	3.0	11/29/77	IBRD	Rural sanitation
11.	Nicaragua	10.1	11/29/77	IBRD	Managua water supply
12.	Nicaragua	20.0	11/17/77	IDB (FSO)	Rural health
13.	Nicaragua	32.0	5/25/78	IDB (FSO)	Highway
14.	Paraguay	7.6	11/10/77	IDB (FSO)	Grain storage
15.	Paraguay	6.2	11/ 3/77	IDB (FSO)	Rural water supply
16.	Paraguay	6.0	12/13/77	IBRD	Rural water supply
17.	Philippines	8.0	12/22/77	IBRD	Sm. tree farming
18.	Philippines	30.0	1/31/78	IBRD	Priv. development corp.
19.	Philippines	65.0	2/28/78	IBRD	Irrigation
20.	Philippines	2.0	3/21/78	IBRD	Education
21.	Philippines	60.0	4/ 9/78	IBRD	Rural electrification
22.	Philippines	28.0	4/11/78	IDA	Rural infrastructure
23.	Philippines	23.5	5/11/78	ADB	Irrigation
24.	Philippines	150.0	5/18/78	IBRD	Multipurpose dam
25.	Uruguay	9.7	6/13/78	IBRD	Vocational training

Source: U.S. Departments of State and Treasury.

a/ See Table 9.1 note for meaning of abbreviations.
b/ Refers to the Fund for Special Operations of the IDB. The United States must approve an FSO loan for it to be implemented, since approval requires a two-thirds vote and the United States has 34 percent of the weighted vote.

is not to say that other countries have not themselves at times injected political considerations into votes; the European countries that had socialist governments did so after Allende was overthrown in Chile.) The United States has never been on the winning side when opposing a loan on human rights grounds in the executive boards of the multilateral development banks.

Some sessions of the executive board, where loans are approved, were quite stormy when the United States first introduced its voting practice on human rights. The procedure has become more routinized and orderly with experience. When the U.S. executive director is instructed to vote no or abstain on a loan, the country seeking the loan is warned in advance, and there may be cases when this had led to the withdrawal of a loan. If the issue comes to the board, the U.S. director is normally silent and at the very end of the procedure merely states that he is abstaining on or opposing the loan under instructions, and that generally is that. The U.S. action is usually quietly received as a political statement. A vote is not taken unless one is requested, and the U.S. director rarely does that now.

The loneliness of the sole naysayer on human rights grounds obviously is uncomfortable. U.S. legislation contains the following provision on seeking allies:

> The Secretary of State and the Secretary of the Treasury shall initiate a wide consultation designed to develop a viable standard for the meeting of basic human needs and the protection of human rights and a mechanism for acting together to insure that the rewards of international economic cooperation are especially available to those who subscribe to such standards and are seen to be moving toward making them effective in their own systems of governance.[35]

Consultations with other countries have been extensive, including Great Britain, Germany, Sweden, Denmark, France, Belgium, the European Commission, Japan, Australia, Canada, India, Venezuela, Colombia, and Trinidad and Tobago, at various levels of the governments. Many reasons are given by other countries for their lack of support for the U.S. voting position. The most frequent is that the injection of the human rights issue into deliberations of the multilateral development institutions could ultimately destroy the institutions as each country used its vote to stress its political priorities.[36] The Nordic countries have indicated that their role as a bridge to the developing countries would be damaged if they joined the United States on human rights votes. Germany seems to argue that its human rights policy must be universally applicable (to include East Germany as well as the developing countries) and that more is accomplished by its unobtrusive pragmatic approach. As a result, the United States stands mostly alone, following its principles (selectively) and uniformly not preventing loans on human rights grounds in the multilateral development banks.[37]

In contrast to bilateral aid, the formal go–no go decision on specific projects in the multilateral institution comes about two to three years after the loan project is first conceived. Voting in the executive boards occurs after the international staffs have done all the preparatory work. These staffs, not U.S. officials, put together loan projects. U.S. officials receive monthly reports of loan projects in preparation and, in theory, could seek to frustrate or shape the projects well in advance of executive board action. However, this would require two considerations that do not now exist: that among the weighted majority of voting power there was an agreed "hit list" of proscribed countries; and that other countries making up this majority were prepared to join with the United States in taking into account human rights considerations in their actions. If these two considerations did exist, the management of the multilateral banks might feel constrained to consult at an earlier stage of project preparation, either to give up particular projects or to shape them so that they met basic human needs criteria, in order not to spend three years working on loans that ultimately would be rejected.

As a result of the lack of control during the project preparation process (and the lack of a consensus that would provide control), the visible actions of the human rights–basic-needs policy take place mainly in the multilateral development institutions. The bilateral program, where the United States has control, goes on almost as though the human rights policy did not exist because of the basic-needs strategy on which the entire program rests. The battleground has become distorted; the United States has been slugging it out in an arena where it has least control and cannot win (if winning is defined as preventing loans).

OTHER OPTIONS FOR U.S. POLICY

One basic question worth asking is whether the aid program is a good instrument for carrying out the U.S. human rights policy. Development of very poor countries (e.g., those with per capita incomes of $500 a year or less, with birthrates exceeding 25 or 30 per thousand, infant mortality exceeding 50 per thousand, illiteracy in excess of 33 percent, life expectancy of less than 60 years) requires a sustained effort, year in and year out, and not a tap that is turned on and off at the prerogative of the aid giver. Does a commitment to a sustained development assistance program dovetail with a "calibrated and sequential" response to human rights trends in poor countries?

The essential answer to this line of questioning is that development aid and human rights policies can be consistent if aid is used affirmatively to reward those countries with good human rights records. Such aid programs can be durable. Stopping aid to punish countries violating the human rights of their nationals, and then temporarily renewing it again if a few prisoners are released, and then stopping it again when more persons are arrested, makes a mockery of the development motive of aid.

In addition, a foreign aid program has viability as a development program only if it supplements a domestic effort. Failing that, it may be useful for the limited group of people who directly receive the benefits of U.S. assistance, or it may be pure charity. These may be desirable objectives, but they are not national development programs. If the aid recipient country is itself seeking to promote distributive justice or to encourage participation in societal processes, then foreign aid can enhance these efforts. If the country does not have such a program, the small projects engaged in by the United States can hardly be crucial to development.

Looking at the bilateral program, would it not be a more productive use of scarce U.S. resources to have development aid programs only in countries whose overall policies are designed to meet the basic needs and promote the rights of their citizens? Such programs would be both durable and supplementary to the country's own effort. To use the basic-needs criterion as a case-by-case justification in countries where there are consistent human rights violations enhances neither human rights nor basic needs to any significant extent. (Charity in the form of food aid might be an exception in that its cessation in countries with bad human rights records might lead directly to starvation and certainly would worsen malnutrition.) A policy change that aimed at directing bilateral aid only to countries that have good human rights–basic-needs records would require a "hit list" of another type—a positive list of countries to which our bilateral aid would go and for which a basic-needs escape from the human rights sanction would not be needed.

That the United States has many interests other than the promotion of human rights is only marginally relevant as a criticism of this proposed policy. Concessional development assistance should, as a rationing device, be limited to, or at least heavily concentrated in, very poor countries, and only a few of these are strategically important to the United States. (Indonesia is the outstanding exception.) Middle-income countries (Brazil, Mexico, Argentina, the Philippines, South Korea, to name some important ones) where the United States does have major interests other than the promotion of human rights do not need bilateral concessional aid. Their economic relations with the United States are centered primarily on trade and investment issues. They are also the principal recipients of loans from the multilateral institutions at market-related interest rates.

Devising viable options to supplant current human rights policy in the multilateral institutions, where the United States cannot go it alone, is difficult. The United States could, if it wished, deal with loan projects much earlier in the preparation process; and if it were supported by enough other countries so that loans could be prevented at an earlier stage on human rights grounds, this would be a viable policy. It would politicize the multilateral institutions (if inserting human rights considerations were deemed to be politicizing), but it could be effective if the weighted majority supported this. This option would require consultations with other countries far more precise than the consultations thus far carried out in order to reach agreement on proscribed countries and on the procedures for making views known about projects long before they come to the executive boards. However, this approach to human rights policy is most unlikely to succeed because it is doubtful that many countries would support the United States.

If such an approach were tested and failed, the options remaining to the United States are to continue with the status quo or to abandon the effort in the multilateral banks to prevent loans on human rights grounds. (Another conceivable option is to shift some concessional aid away from the multilateral institutions back to the bilateral program where the United States can control the aid giving, but to cripple the multilateral aid effort in order to prevent loans to a few countries would be human rights overkill.) Each alternative has its disadvantages: maintaining the status quo because it has proved to be divisive and generally ineffective; and abandoning any human rights effort in the multilateral banks because it would sacrifice an important element of decency in U.S. foreign policy.

CONCLUSIONS

The twin policies of promoting human rights and seeking to satisfy the basic needs of the world's poorest people have had similar evolutions: genesis of each in decency; zealousness in initial execution that called into question their very foundations; subsequent backtracking; and now groping about their roles in the future.

Some of the criticisms of the policies seem excessively perfectionistic. For a country that has as many interests as the United States, there will be inevitable inconsistencies in carrying out a human rights policy. Uganda will not be treated on an equal footing with China, sovereign equality notwithstanding, nor will policy considerations be the same for U.S. actions in Uruguay as in Iran. The argument of inconsistency, if it asserts that all countries must be treated alike, is really a red herring. This does not mean that the United States cannot have a human rights policy in both the Soviet Union and Nicaragua but rather that pursuing these policies will take different forms.

This type of reasoning can be carried one step further. Not only will there be inconsistency in action depending on the importance of countries, but there will also be differences in the use of policy instruments. The best tool in some cases is diplomatic pressure. The United States can control where its bilateral concessional aid will go; it cannot control how other countries will act in the multilateral development banks. Trade cannot be turned on and off to reward and punish countries in pursuing human rights policy; and even if it could, it would be an exercise in futility, since other countries would provide the goods and alternative markets. To assert that all economic instruments can be used equally in the pursuit of human rights is to reject reality.

It was this general logic that led to the use of aid programs as the primary instruments of economic coercion in the promotion of human rights. The logic broke down in the multilateral development institutions when others refused to join with the United States.[38]

Aid (like trade) cannot serve its primary function if one cannot count on consistency. Similarly, aid cannot be a significant supplement to promoting a development program incorporating distributive justice unless the recipient country's own program stresses this. This is particularly true if the aid program is small, as is the U.S. bilateral program in most countries. These considerations argue against turning aid on and off—as punishment when people are arrested and as a reward when others are released—but rather to pursue what has always been a basic tenet of foreign aid, to supplement a developing country's own efforts.

This reasoning leads to the following conclusions on aid given bilaterally and through multilateral channels.

(1) In scheduling concessionary bilateral aid, do this positively. That is, do not use aid as a variable stick and carrot; rather, plan several years ahead (the time it takes to develop projects) to give aid only to countries with good human rights records and good programs to promote distributive justice, and do not seek to justify projects in countries with bad records on the grounds that the aid will reach poor people.[39] This policy cannot be absolute. Human rights practices of countries can change rapidly, and aid plans may have to be altered for some countries. The United States will also wish to provide aid on

political grounds (say, in Egypt as part of the peace process) regardless of human rights considerations.

(2) The human rights policy can work more effectively in the multilateral development banks if enough other countries are prepared to join with the United States in preventing loans for countries with bad human rights records at an earlier stage in the project preparation process. An effort at seeking allies for such a procedure is worth making, even though it is likely to fail.

Should this assessment (of failure) prove correct, the United States must then make a choice between continuation of the current practice or quietly abandoning the human rights policy in the multilateral development banks. My own preference is to continue the present practice, as frustrating as it may be, because it does permit the United States to express the political judgment that promotion of human rights is a feature of development.

I would like to conclude on a note about U.S. sincerity. This will be questioned as long as the United States pursues its human rights policy in the poorest countries with an inadequate aid program. This is about as credible as a monopolist preaching the virtues of free enterprise as he gouges the public. The United States must re-earn the right to be taken seriously in its human rights policy in the poor countries.[40]

NOTES

1. U.S. official development assistance (ODA), according to data of the Development Assistance Committee (DAC), was 0.22 percent of GNP in 1977, placing the United States fourteenth of the seventeen DAC countries. The average ODA/GNP ratio for all the DAC countries in 1977 was 0.31 percent. The essentially political assistance that qualifies as ODA was 43 percent of all U.S. ODA in that year (i.e., supporting assistance, mostly to Middle Eastern countries).

2. The Agency for International Development has described its policy in A Strategy for a More Effective Bilateral Development Assistance Program, AID Policy Paper (March 1978). The so-called New Directions of AID were initiated by the Congress in the Foreign Assistance Act of 1973. At about the same time (1973), the World Bank initiated ''new-style'' projects with the similar intent of benefit-

ing the absolute poor, although it did not abandon old-style projects as completely as did AID.

3. Thomas W. Wilson, Jr., "Human Rights: A Bedrock Consensus," 1977 (mimeograph).

4. Elizabeth Drew, "A Reporter at Large: Human Rights," *The New Yorker,* July 18, 1977, pp. 36–62, discusses the evolution of the human rights policy of the Carter administration.

5. Section 116 of the Foreign Assistance Act of 1961, as amended.

6. This seems so self-evident to diplomatists that it hardly requires mentioning. Yet official statements repeat it endlessly, almost apologetically. For example, Patricia Derian, the Assistant Secretary of State for Human Rights and Humanitarian Affairs, told the House Committee on International Relations on August 9, 1978, that "human rights objectives cannot be determinative of each and every foreign policy decision." Department of State *Bulletin* 78, no. 2020 (November 1978): 52. Roughly the same phrase is contained in a Derian speech of October 15, 1978, in Nashville before the National Association of Human Rights Workers.

7. The existence of this letter was reported in the *Washington Post,* August 1, 1978. The letter was not made public.

8. The restructuring of U.S. foreign aid dates from the Foreign Assistance Act of 1973. This legislation owed much of its intellectual content to the pioneering work of the Overseas Development Council, a private research foundation in Washington, D.C. Robert McNamara's speech in 1973 to the annual meeting of the World Bank Group also developed the emphasis of directly attacking absolute poverty. Hollis Chenery of the World Bank and others authored a seminal book, *Redistribution with Growth* (London: Oxford University Press, 1974), which combined the twin themes of growth and income distribution. Once the dam gates were opened, the world seemed to rediscover an age-old theme of distributive justice. Intellectual underpinning for organizing development strategy around the fulfillment of basic human needs also came from the World Employment Conference of 1976 (see *Employment, Growth and Basic Needs: A One-World Problem* [New York: Praeger Publishers for the Overseas Development Council, 1977]), and the International Labor Organization has since done considerable quantitative analysis of exactly what is required to meet basic human needs in different places.

9. Indeed, copies of the book by E. F. Schumacher, *Small Is Beautiful* (New York: Harper and Row paperback, 1975 [1st ed., 1973, hardback]), were distributed to all senior AID officials.

10. Minority views of Senators Brooke, Young, Hatfield, Bellmon, Case, Burdick, Stevens, and Bayh, *Foreign Assistance and Related Programs Appropriation Bill, 1978,* Report no. 95-352, Committee on Appropriations, July 18, 1977, pp. 153–54.

11. The World Bank, *World Development Report, 1978* (Washing-

ton, 1978): "It is in this context [of insufficient employment] that the potential of large-scale public works programs, which can provide employment in rural areas while at the same time constructing assets to enhance economic growth, must be developed" (p. 45).

12. *A Strategy for a More Effective Bilateral Assistance Program*, p. 27.

13. For example, see Paul Streeten, "The Distinctive Features of a Basic Needs Approach to Development," a paper prepared in the World Bank, August 10, 1977 (mimeograph), which cites the need to define a basic-needs strategy "as one supplementing or complementing existing strategies" (p. 1).

14. Committee for Development Planning, *Report on the Thirteenth Session (11–21 April 1977)* (New York: United Nations, 1977), p. 3. The Development Assistance Committee's publication, *Development Cooperation, 1978 Review* (Paris: Organization for Economic Cooperation and Development, November 1978), also discusses the possibility that the basic-human-needs strategy was oversold (p. 11).

15. As one congressman central to the AID appropriation process put it, there is merit in experimental projects so small as to be beneath contempt.

16. *Washington Post*, August 29, 1978.

17. When asked about the disparity of treatment between Cuba and Argentina, Mark L. Schneider, Deputy Assistant Secretary of State for Human Rights, responded: "We obviously have many more bilateral relations with Argentina, therefore human rights-related actions occur more often in terms of those assistance relationships." U.S. Congress, House, *Human Rights and United States Foreign Policy: A Review of the Administration's Record*, Hearings before the Subcommittee on International Organizations of the Committee on International Relations, October 25, 1977 (Washington: U.S. Government Printing Office, 1978), p. 13.

18. This view is expressed by Sandra Vogelgesang, "What Price Principle?—U.S. Policy on Human Rights," *Foreign Affairs* 56, no. 4 (July 1978): 819–41.

19. The incident was reported extensively in the U.S. press, e.g., *The Wall Street Journal*, September 27, 1978.

20. Section 116 of the Foreign Assistance Act of 1961, as amended, and Section 112 of PL 480.

21. Section 701 of the International Financial Institutions Act.

22. Section 113 of the Foreign Assistance Appropriations Act of 1971.

23. Section 239 of the Foreign Assistance Act of 1961, as amended.

24. Section 2(b)(1) (B) of the Export-Import Bank Act of 1945, as amended. Before November 10, 1978, the Export-Import Bank was required to "take into account" a country's respect for human rights in its support of exports.

25. Speech before the University of Georgia's Law School, April 30, 1977.

26. Report submitted to Congress in Response to Title VII, Public Law 95-118, Fall 1978 (mimeograph).

27. Since decisions made in this atmosphere tend to be as much political as moral, and based on partial information on current trends, one participant in Christopher committee meetings has likened the proceedings to a kangaroo court. There were, in fact, some early decisions that must have been based on inadequate information, but participants now seem agreed that the mechanical process is efficient.

28. The locus of deliberation for arms transfer policy is the Arms Export Control Board. The functioning of the board, including the procedure for review of human rights issues, can be found in a series of statements in the Department of State *Bulletin* 78, no. 2012 (March 1978): 42–53.

29. Stanley Hoffmann, "The Hell of Good Intentions," *Foreign Policy*, no. 29 (Winter 1977): 3–26, discusses this.

30. Address to the Harvard University graduating class, *Harvard Gazette*, June 8, 1978.

31. The multilateral development banks in which the United States participates are the World Bank Group, the Inter-American Development Bank, the Asian Development Bank, and the African Development Fund.

32. Report to the Congress under Section 116(d)(2) of the Foreign Assistance Act of 1961 (as amended 1976).

33. Report submitted to Congress in Response to Title VI, Public Law 95-118, Fall 1978 (mimeograph).

34. Article IV, Section 10 of the Articles of Agreement of the World Bank. The other multilateral banks have similar provisions in their articles.

35. Section 703(b) of Public Law 95-118.

36. This theme is stressed in a brief article by Arnold H. Weiss, "Human Rights in World Bank–IMF Lending," *American Banker*, September 25, 1978, p. 21.

37. This essay has not discussed the pursuit of human rights objectives in the International Monetary Fund because of the substantive difference of that institution from the multilateral development banks. The IMF is not primarily a dispenser of aid. Its functions relate to the international exchange-rate system, helping countries deal with balance-of-payments deficits by providing short- to medium-term financing, and helping thereby to facilitate world trade. Support in the fund for the U.S. human rights policy would undoubtedly be even less than in the banks.

38. In addition to the multilateral development banks, the U.S. assistance going through multilateral channels goes through the intermediary of United Nations institutions, such as the United Nations

Development Programme. Since these bodies operate on the one-country, one-vote principle, rather than weighted voting as in the banks, the United States has even less control over decisions in them than in the banks.

39. A practical question arises as to whether this should be done legislatively, that is, remove the basic-needs escape from the current legislation on bilateral aid, or leave the legislation as it is and permit some discretion to the executive. The advantage of rigidity is that the policy will be followed; its disadvantage is that it forecloses rescheduling aid when a trend toward a better (worse) human rights record is emerging. My own preference would be to permit the flexibility but to make clear in the legislative record that the intention is for the executive branch not to use the basic-needs escape unless an improving trend of human rights concern has shown some persistence over a reasonable length of time.

40. There is a relevant line in Bertolt Brecht, *The Threepenny Opera:* "Erst kommt das Fressen; dann kommt die Moral" (roughly: "eating comes first, then preaching").

SELECTED BIBLIOGRAPHY

1. AID Policy Paper. *A Strategy for a More Effective Bilateral Development Assistance Program* (March 1978).

2. Birnbaum, Karl E. "Human Rights and East-West Relations." *Foreign Affairs* (July 1977).

3. "Charter 77." A translation of the Czech human rights manifesto reprinted in the *New York Times*, January 27, 1977.

4. Chenery, Hollis. *Redistribution with Growth* (London: Oxford University Press, 1974).

5. Conference on Security and Cooperation in Europe: Final Act (signed in Helsinki on August 1, 1975). Department of State *Bulletin*, September 1, 1975.

6. Development Assistance Committee publication. *Development Cooperation, 1978 Review* (Paris: Organization for Economic Cooperation and Development, November 1978).

7. Drew, Elizabeth. "A Reporter at Large: Human Rights." *The New Yorker*, July 18, 1977.

8. Dworkin, Ronald. *Taking Rights Seriously* (Cambridge, Mass.: Harvard University Press, 1977).

9. Fraser, Donald M. "Freedom and Foreign Policy." *Foreign Policy* (Spring 1977).

10. Hoffmann, Stanley. "The Hell of Good Intentions." *Foreign Policy* (Winter 1977): 3–26.

11. International Labor Organization. *Employment, Growth and Basic Needs: A One-World Problem* (New York: Praeger Publishers for the Overseas Development Council, 1977).

12. Rawls, John. *A Theory of Justice* (Cambridge, Mass.: Harvard University Press paperback, 1971).

13. Schlesinger, Arthur. "Human Rights and the American Tradition." *Foreign Affairs* 57, no. 3 ("America and the World 1978").

14. Schumacher, E. F. *Small Is Beautiful* (New York: Harper and Row paperback, 1975 [1st ed. 1973, hardback]).

15. Streeten, Paul. "The Distinctive Features of a Basic Needs Approach to Development," August 10, 1977 (mimeograph).

16. Vance, Cyrus R. "Human Rights and Foreign Policy." Department of State *Bulletin,* May 23, 1977.

17. Vogelgesang, Sandra. "What Price Principle?—U.S. Policy on Human Rights." *Foreign Affairs* (July 1978).

18. World Bank. *World Development Report,* 1978 (Washington, D.C., 1978).

Chapter 10

THE LIKELY EFFECTS OF THE NEW AMERICAN CONVENTION ON HUMAN RIGHTS

JOHN H. BARTON

Since World War II a number of multilateral human rights conventions have been negotiated. Although the United States is not yet a party to any of the major conventions, President Carter has submitted four of the most important to the Senate: the International Covenant on Civil and Political Rights, the International Covenant on Economic, Social and Cultural Rights, the International Convention on the Elimination of All Forms of Racial Discrimination, and the American Convention on Human Rights.[1]

These treaties are a novel development in international law. International law has traditionally served to regulate international disputes; the new covenants, however, are designed to affect disputes arising within a single nation. The force that usually supports international law is reciprocity between governments—each government restrains itself in return for the benefits of restraint by other governments. Yet this reciprocity, exemplified in such areas as trade interests and treatment of prisoners of war, is nearly absent in the human rights area. The way a nation treats its own citizens rarely affects other nations. Thus, the political force of these new conventions derives from mechanisms quite different from those at work in traditional international law.[2]

To understand the mechanisms underlying this new international law of human rights and the capabilities and limitations of those mechanisms, it is useful to examine the enforcement procedures built into the new agreements. These procedures fall into three general categories: judicial, diplomatic, and legislative. In evaluating each of these mechanisms, it is also useful to consider the experience gained under previous multilateral arrangements, particularly the European Convention on Human Rights (ECHR),[3] which has been the most effective of the post–World War II human rights conventions. As a regional convention, it is especially helpful in evaluating the new American Convention (ACHR), the most significant of the new conventions laid before the Senate.

JUDICIAL ENFORCEMENT

Courts have a special legitimacy and authority. Thus, the ECHR and the ACHR each create an international court, which can be reached after an elaborate screening procedure.

Only the European Convention has used this full judicial approach. The European Court has declared, for example, that the Austrian government should pay damages to a criminal defendant who had been held too long before trial.[4] It has held that the United Kingdom violated the convention in prohibiting the Sunday *Times* from publishing an article on the thalidomide tragedy while civil litigation on thalidomide was pending.[5] In other cases, the court or related institutions decided against the petitioner—for example, in claims that the German Constitutional Court's decision against liberalization of abortion[6] and the German wiretap laws[7] were in violation of the convention. The ECHR institutions are thus already acting as an international supreme court, enforcing and interpreting a bill of rights that restrains the governments of the member nations.

Just as U.S. law responds to the U.S. Supreme Court, compliance—which occurs in the individual cases almost as a matter of course—is supplemented by broader legal change to accord with the logic of the decisions. In response to full or partial ECHR procedures, Austria has reformed its laws on detention before trial.[8] Belgium has created a hearing procedure for vagrancy detentions,[9] the United Kingdom has created hearing procedures for certain immigration issues[10] and for certain claims by prisoners.[11] Perhaps most dramatically, the United Kingdom has committed itself internationally not to use the five controversial interrogation techniques it had used in Northern Ireland and in a number of preceding colonial conflicts.[12] Thus, a petition to the ECHR institution has become a nearly routine tool for law reform. If a petition is admissible, the ECHR institutions will focus on the problem posed and lead politicians—anxious to avoid an adverse court decision—to concentrate on the problem as well. Reform often follows.

International conventions can be applied by national courts as well as by international courts. National court jurisdiction often receives less attention in the negotiations than does the international court jurisdiction; therefore, it rarely has the same restrictions or constraints. For the ordinary litigant, national courts are likely to be more easily available and broadly useful than the elaborate international processes.

Sometimes, domestic enforcement rests on the treaty itself, for treaties automatically become domestic law in some nations. In France, for example, even though the nation has not accepted the jurisdiction of the European Court of Human Rights, domestic courts are authorized and obliged to apply the convention.[13] This implicit adoption of judicial review is novel particularly since France has traditionally looked to the democratic parliament rather than to the aristocratic judiciary as the protector of human rights. The details of direct application are complex, varying from jurisdiction to jurisdiction.[14] In some nations there is a difference between "self-executing" and "non-self-executing" treaties or clauses. Only the former can be directly applied. The latter are interpreted as the nation's international commitment to enact conforming legislation; domestic courts are restricted to applying whatever consistent or inconsistent legislation has been enacted. In a federal system the treaty may directly bind federal but not local governments. In some nations later inconsistent legislation overrules a treaty; in others it does not. And, even when domestic courts have authority to apply an international bill of rights, they may interpret that bill in a way that places little restriction on the national government. Each year's *Yearbook of the European Convention on Human Rights* presents excerpts from national court cases in which the convention was considered. No one can leaf through that section without being struck by the dreary preponderance of cases in which the convention-based argument was rejected. But even with all these limitations, domestic enforcement is more ordinary and more frequent. In the long term, it is likely to prove more significant than international enforcement in giving ordinary litigants the benefit of an international bill of rights.

The existence of international bills of rights has undoubtedly contributed to a broader move toward judicial review. For example, in response to a highly controversial German decision that German constitutional rights take priority over European Economic Community law,[15] the EEC stated that it would consider itself bound by ECHR norms.[16] According to the Community's European Court of Justice, the EEC must respect fundamental rights; in at least one case the court specifically cited the ECHR.[17] In a different arena, the Indian Supreme Court has tried to protect human rights from constitutional amendments that would limit those rights. Relying heavily on U.S. and Commonwealth interpretations of human rights, the Court has held formally that constitutional amendments, although enacted by a formally correct procedure, must be struck down if they violate the spirit or framework of the Constitution.[18] As a final example of this pattern, the force of the ECHR and of the broad international movement toward judicial application of human rights norms are leading the United Kingdom to consider the adoption of a formal bill of rights.[19] The outcome of the U.K. debate is still unclear, for such adoption would modify the central constitutional concept of parliamentary supremacy and transfer significant power from administrators to lawyers. Whether or not the United Kingdom acts now on this issue, there is a clear trend among many nations toward judicial review to protect human rights.

An international bill of rights can also help domestic courts that are placed in the position of reviewing foreign judicial systems, a task they usually avoid. For example, courts do not generally review the fairness of a foreign trial procedure before permitting the extradition of a suspect for trial abroad.[20] They are also hesitant to apply an exclusionary rule against evidence seized abroad illegally.[21] The courts are concerned about infringing on the executive, about potential judicial imperialism, and about the effectiveness of their judgments on foreign police conduct. Even when a bill of rights is explicitly written into an international agreement, as in a military status of focus agreement, U.S. courts have generally been reluctant to enforce it judicially; it has been assumed that diplomatic action is likely to be a more effective means of redress.[22] This is an area in which courts might usefully play a greater role.

Taken together, these developments suggest one way to enforce human rights—evolution of judicial review. National and international courts would cite bills of rights and one another's opinions to apply a body of common principles against governments. The international human rights movement would become a judicial review movement reflecting this contagious concept of using the prestige of courts to restrain governments.

The approach is good, but it does have limitations. It works only in nations in which there is already respect for the rule of law and in which courts already have effective and independent power. Judicial approaches are ways to help law-oriented societies remain fundamentally free and improve, not ways to change repressive governments. The notion of the rule of law and the notion that a court is a proper interpreter of a bill of rights are Western ideas, presuming a sharp distinction between law and either morality or politics—ideas that would be very difficult to apply in, say, a Confucian society. For strong human rights institutions to evolve, it may also be necessary for them to be part of a more broadly based politics of unification, as has happened to an extent in Europe. The ECHR may have been negotiable only because Europeans recoiled at the horror of Nazism and felt a need to reassert a tradition of freedom in the face of the Soviet giant. Whether Latin America can be equally successful is unclear. The countries of Latin America share traditions of law and a sense of freedom shaped by the shared histories of revolution. However, there has been less pressure there for integration. In addition, it is often the military rather than the courts that shape not only constitutional change[23] but the entire structure of human rights abuses. Even in Europe, when politically charged issues arise—for example, the Belgian school language legislation[24]—the ECHR institutions have avoided giving affront to powerful political forces.

One may also question the strength of the international standards themselves. The international conventions are negotiated by governments in relatively ordinary times and are therefore usually weaker than those documents, like the U.S. Bill of Rights, that derive from revolution. The ECHR and ACHR bills of rights, for example, permit preventive detention under emergency conditions and further permit public order restrictions on freedoms such as those of the press. The international conventions may also lose specificity because of the need to respond to different traditions such as Anglo-American and continental approaches to criminal trial procedures and liberal and socialist views of the right to property. International bills of rights may offer only a least-common-denominator level of protection.[25]

Most important, judicial review has inherent limitations. It is antidemocratic. It works well for the eighteenth-century rights that protect criminal procedure from political influence or impose direct limitations on government, even a democratic government. But the judicial approach is much less effective for the nineteenth-century equal protection and affirmative rights. The United States is discovering this problem as courts move in to areas such as school and prison reform. The court becomes a substitute administrator operating in a uniquely cumbersome manner. It loses public respect, and its decisions lack both democratic control and democratic mandate.

In spite of these limitations, judicial review is probably the most effective international mechanism available for enforcing many of the most important human rights. Yet, despite this effectiveness and despite the facts that the United States is the source of the concept and is steeped in the judicial review tradition, the United States has refused to permit application of international judicial review to itself. Perhaps some Americans judge that their own domestic human rights protections are better than any international protection that might be invented or operated by foreign governments. Some Americans give the U.S. Supreme Court a symbolic position that admits of no review by a higher court. Whatever the reason, the United States has imposed limitations (the Connolly amendment) on its acceptance of the jurisdiction of the International Court of Justice;[26] and in choosing among the optional clauses and protocols of the new human rights conventions, the president has avoided close analogues to international judicial review.[27] Even more seriously, in the negotiation of the ACHR, the United States has consistently—and rather successfully— pressed to insure that the convention would nowhere be directly applicable as national law without enabling national legislation.[28] Thus, although some nations might, on their own, make the convention directly applicable, the United States has significantly decreased the chance that the domestic judicial mechanisms so successful in Europe can also be effective in the Western Hemisphere. Moreover, it has refused to accept the supervision it hopes others will accept.

DIPLOMATIC ENFORCEMENT

Nations have also negotiated state-to-state diplomatic mechanisms to seek to enforce human rights. These state-to-state mechanisms respond to domestic political pressures to do something about foreign repression and can be applied against recalcitrant governments that refuse to accept judicial supervision. The diplomatic criticism that is the heart of this approach can easily be criticized itself. It is often ineffective, especially as compared with quiet private diplomacy. It often seems to respond to a prophetic instinct rather than to the conditions for reform in the criticized nation. Nevertheless, it is sometimes all that is available and has, in some contexts, produced worthwhile results.

There is a wide variety of frameworks for such action. The covenants and other UN treaties, the ECHR, and the ACHR all establish formal procedures by which one nation can complain of another's violation of the covenants' bills of rights. In the latter cases, the dispute may ultimately lead to a judicial decision, provided the parties have accepted the necessary optional jurisdictions. (President Carter has indicated his intention to adhere to the ACHR's interstate procedure but presumably not in a way that could be referred to the court.) Whether or not such specialized institutions are available, nations can bring human rights complaints to the General Assembly or the UN Commission on Human Rights. And complaints can be made in regular diplomatic frameworks as were President Carter's criticism of the Soviet Union and congressional moves to limit trade with the Soviet Union and aid to repressive regimes.

The most successful applications of the institutions are those where there is already an international dispute and the dispute has human rights overtones. When, for example, Greece complained to the ECHR about the United Kingdom's treatment of Greek individuals in Cyprus during the 1950s,[29] the ECHR investigation became a series of negotiations in which the two nations moved closer and closer to each other's positions. The negotiation was successful, and the issue was resolved (for the short run) by the Zurich and London agreements creating a new political structure for Cyprus. In another example, Austria complained of Italy's judicial treatment of a defendant in the mixed nationality of Bolzano/Bozen area.[30] The ECHR institutions recommended clemency for the individual and probably helped to defuse transborder minority tensions arising from the incident.

The roles for international action in such contexts are broad and varied. Proceedings may be initiated as a bargaining chip in negotiations. The proceeding may be used by the parties to resolve specific subissues, to make a politial concession easier, or to provide a statement whose expected impact is already factored into a broader political compromise. The international proceeding can offer enough confidentiality to become a negotiating forum, but its existence is public knowledge and can assist in satisfying public demands for action.

In the preceding examples, there was an international dispute that happened to have human rights aspects. If, however, the issue is more centrally one of human rights criticism of another nation, the process develops quite differently, for it raises more severe issues of foreign interference. Nevertheless, these state-to-state proceedings sometimes help as well. For example, no formal ECHR proceeding was brought in response to the Greek military coup of 1967 until after the Consultative Assembly, a parliamentary body associated with the ECHR institutions, expressed its dismay and asked for such a proceeding.[31] The suit, brought a few months later by Nordic and Benelux governments, produced a report condemning Greece, which was improperly leaked to the press and provoked a "you're expelled"—"no, I quit first" denouement at the end of 1969.[32] When the military government ran into difficulties in 1973 and began speaking of liberalization, the Consultative Assembly passed a new resolution encouraging the liberalization and laying down specific conditions for readmitting Greece into the Council of Europe.[33] The following year, after the regime fell, the new Greek government moved to comply with the assembly resolution, carrying out elections and establishing a new constitution and was readmitted to the ECHR institutions.[34]

It is hard to say how much Greece was responding to internal pressures (deriving from the military government's misjudgment in staging a Cyprus coup); to the Consultative Assembly's standards; or to pressures by the European Economic Community, which was stalling an association agreement pending Greek democracy. Nevertheless, the international institutions at least helped to shape a resolution that was triggered by other political forces and may have contributed to the stability of the new government.

In situations like the South-West Africa/Nambian controversies, international institutions have played a different role, helping to keep an issue alive pending multilateral political action and to make it easier for the UN and the Great Powers to take appropriate action when the politically feasible time arrived. The United Nations and the International Court of Justice had dealt with this issue essentially since they were founded,[35] but with little positive effect; at the same time, their deliberations probably helped prevent the territory's formal absorption into South Africa. When the 1974 Portuguese coup upset the strategic balance in southern Africa, the issue became ripe for new diplomacy and a 1978 resolution creating a UN Observation Force has kept alive some hope of transferring power in the near future.[36] The previous deliberations made this diplomacy more defensible politically and helped avoid an appearance of imperialism. The human rights procedures are not exclusively symbolic, and they can contribute usefully to shaping more political diplomacy.

Nevertheless, the examples also demonstrate the limits of institutions built around the diplomacy of deep diplomatic criticism. First, rather surprisingly, it is often hard to find a plaintiff. In general, one nation will institute formal enforcement procedures against another only if there is a very specific dispute or if the accused nation is already considered to be a pariah. International accusation is a highly political art. In Europe it was the good-citizen-type governments that instituted formal proceedings against Greece, and then only after urging by an assembly.

Second, such diplomacy is rarely able to make a practical difference. Even in the Greek case, in which the government was unpopular and the nation was somewhat open to foreign ideas and broadcasts, the government was not displaced until it made a major error. Especially when the criticism is ignored, it is easy to move from criticism to sanctions—typically, trade or aid sanctions. Such economic sanctions are rather artificial in the human rights area and may tend, as shown in the South African case and perhaps in the Jackson-Vanik moves against the Soviet Union, to intensify recalcitrance rather than to produce conversion.[37] In the Greek case, an affirmative incentive—denying Greece the privilege of entry into European institutions until the government changed—was much more effective.

Third, developing new institutional structures is often not important in this type of diplomacy. The extreme example is the proliferation of UN human rights institutions, which had made only a limited difference in the choice of subjects actually raised. A critic can always use diplomatic channels. The role of institutions and conventions in this diplomacy is therefore less one of providing a framework for criticism than of providing special services for particular situations. The Inter-American Commission on Human Rights, formally a nearly powerless organ set up by the Organization of American States in 1960, long before the new ACHR was negotiated, has pioneered such roles. During the 1965 Dominican Republic crisis it helped to protect political prisoners through a course of negotiations between the two competing governments. The next year, it helped to supervise an election in the same nation.[38] And it has prepared the key report on the violation of human rights in Chile.[39]

Fourth, because the barriers to executive action are so high, a parliamentary organ is often useful. The European Consultative Assembly played a central role in the Greek case. In the United States, Congress has imposed (although at times the executive might prefer not to implement them) human rights restrictions on foreign assistance[40] and has created a review procedure for the Helsinki accords.[41] A serious international human rights system can benefit from a parliamentary body. Whether or not such a body has formal power is nearly irrelevant; what is crucial is that it can express an opinion uncensored by executive limitations.

Judging from this experience, it is hard to predict the effectiveness of the state-to-state procedures in the new ACHR. Latin Americans have been readier to criticize one another's human rights violations than have Europeans—the Inter-American Commission for Human Rights has already criticized Cuba, Haiti, Brazil, and Chile.[42] Moreover, the American institutions have much greater flexibility than their European analogues in the way of jurisdiction powers to give advisory opinions and to initiate investigation on their own motion.[43] In spite of the hemisphere's great traditions, however, the status of freedom is so low that it is hard to envision hemispheric institutions holding out an ideal of human rights in the way that the European ideal was held out to Greece. The greatest importance of the ACHR in the state-to-state area may be to channel the criticisms made by the existing democratic nations—criticisms that are otherwise likely to smack of paternalism. Finally, as the new ACHR enters into force, the evolution of the old Inter-American Commission is still unclear.[44] The old commission was very imaginative in helping diplomatic enforcement; it would be unfortunate if the ACHR caused the commission to imitate the more passive and legalistic roles that its European analogue has played under a similar convention but a radically different political situation.

LEGISLATIVE ENFORCEMENT

At the domestic level, one of the most common methods of enforcing human rights is legislation. This is often the most direct approach to tasks such as improving a criminal justice system or protecting the freedom of the electronic media. As exemplified by the Civil Rights Act of 1964, it is frequently a crucial mechanism for protecting nondiscrimination and group rights.

Fostering this type of continuing reform is probably the weakest part of the international system. On a nontechnical level, human rights discussions may educate and mobilize citizens to seek reform. Some of the multilateral conventions include administration bodies that discuss legislation and can become a force for law reform.[45] In certain technical areas, such as labor, there are international institutions with expertise to help national and international constituencies pressure for law reform.[46] These approaches have been most successful in Europe, where integration is already far advanced, and on issues where nations recognize a mutual and global interest in maintaining a particular norm. Thus, each nation views the international effort to maintain labor standards as a way to help protect itself from foreign goods manufactured under unfair labor conditions. But even these mechanisms are probably not developed to their full potential; ironically, they are least developed for those human rights issues that are intrinsically international.

There are a number of such intrinsically international developments that have human rights implications: refugee movement, international data banks, international police cooperation, international broadcasting. Formal or de facto international agreements on such issues automatically affect human rights. On some of these issues, such as refugee movement, national legislatures are usually dominant but are likely to ignore the rights of nonnationals. Such issues may be unresolvable until contact between legislatures leads to a change in viewpoint. On other issues, such as police cooperation, executives cooperate beyond the control of any nation's legislative or judicial review processes. Here, it is necessary to define new ways to cooperate to pursue human rights; for example, perhaps to create an international analogue of a police review board. Legislatures themselves may have to cooperate with each other to define such arrangements and to impose them on executives that are reluctant to give up any power, especially in the sensitive foreign policy area.

The global affirmative rights are a special example of this problem. If the developing world's demands for social and economic opportunity are ever conceivably to be met, there will have to be a parallel effort to achieve equality within the developing nations themselves. Even then, the disadvantaged of the developing world compete with the disadvantaged of the developed world. To see this problem in the Western Hemisphere, one need only consider the issue of illegal immigration from Mexico to the United States. Its economic sources and implications in the two nations and its overtones of discrimination and U.S. patronization are beyond the ability of any judicial system to control or reverse. They may be beyond the ability of any combination of international diplomacy and politically feasible domestic legislation.

Thus, there is need for a new type of international human rights institution—a multinational legislature, parallel to the international judiciary and the executive-controlled institutions that are already under construction. In the short term, such an institution could help national legislatures control the international activity of executives in areas like police cooperation. In the longer term, it might help legislatures find compromises to problems posing direct conflicts of interest such as refugee problems. Europe has moved in this direction with the European Economic Community's Parliament, which discusses issues such as a fund for depressed regions throughout the EEC, and the Council of Europe's Consultative Assembly, which played an important role in the Greek case. The new ACHR includes no parallel institutions, but its commission can formulate recommendations suggesting new steps toward realizing human rights. Moreover, the Organization of American States has long demonstrated great flexibility and can conceivably and usefully create a parliamentary organ, even if only on a purely consultative level.

CONCLUSION

The politics of international human rights is radically different from that of previous international law and organization. Traditionally, international law and organization have been a way for the executives of different nations to reach accommodations that are beneficial to their societies. On the relevant issues, executive interest is usually quite close to societal interest, but the accommodation risks favoring executives at the expense of the societies. Executive representatives dominate most international organizations—and legislatures understandably fear that international organization is a way to place the focus of decision making beyond their control.

The concept of international human rights, to be more than mere propaganda, must build on a different form of international law. It has already built on radically different principles: on the international esprit de corps of jurists, on the goodwill of some executives, and on the near self-contradiction of condemnatory diplomacy. These principles are even weaker than those of traditional international law; international human rights mechanisms become most effective when least needed and a captive of more cynical politics when most needed.

If the concept of fulfilling international human rights is to gain greater strength, it must build on principles more congenial to its character. The heart of human rights is continuous revolution—continuous fear of the potential tyranny of any government and continuous effort to reshape government to protect and assist the individual or disadvantaged group. When courts are weak or lack jurisdiction, these tasks fall to legislatures. The next international human rights task is to help legislatures cooperate to meet the fundamentally international human rights issues that are just beginning to be raised. This approach upsets the traditional preeminence of the executive in foreign policy. Yet, underlying any interest in international human rights is the fact that foreign violations of human rights have become part of domestic politics. The international human rights movement cannot help but be an attempt to reshape and control executive-dominated diplomacy.

NOTES

1. International Covenant on Civil and Political Rights, adopted by the General Assembly on December 16, 1966, entered into force March 23, 1976; International Covenant on Economic, Social, and Cultural Rights, adopted by the General Assembly on December 16, 1966, entered into force January 3, 1976; International Convention on the Elimination of All Forms of Racial Discrimination, adopted by the General Assembly on December 21, 1965, entered into force January 4, 1969, 660 U.N.T.S. 195; American Convention on Human Rights, adopted by the Organization of American States on November 22, 1969, entered into force July 18, 1978, OAS Doc. OEA/Ser. K/XVI/1.1 (1970). In addition, President Truman submitted the Genocide Convention, Jan. 12, 1951, 78 U.N.T.S. 271 (1951), which the Senate had failed to accept under the Eisenhower administration. That convention, however, lacks the type of elaborate enforcement structure that is the focus of this paper.

2. In emphasizing the novelty of the new international human rights covenants, I do not deny that there are historical predecessors, e.g., the British foreign policy response to the Holy Alliance, cooperation to suppress the slave trade, humanitarian intervention, or the minorities protection system of Versailles. Nor do I wish to deny that there were important humanitarian motivations in much traditional international law such as the law of war. Nevertheless, it is accurate to note that an international bill of rights is politically different from a domestic revolutionary bill of rights and that the pressures for compliance and enforcement are politically different from those at work in much of international law.

3. Convention for the Protection of Human Rights and Fundamental Freedoms, entered into force 3 September 1953.

4. Ringeisen v. Austria, Euro. Ct. of H.R., Judgment of 22 June 1972, Eu. Ct. H.R. Publ. Series A., No. 15 at 4 (1972).

5. Times Newspapers Ltd. v. U.K., Application No. 6538/74, Euro. Ct. of H.R., April 26, 1979.

6. Bruggemann and Scheuten v. F.R.G., Application No. 5959175, Committee of Ministers, Resolution DH (78) 1 (adopted on 17 March 1978).

7. Case of Klass and Others, Euro. Ct. of H.R., 6 September 1978.

8. L. Sohn & T. Buergenthal, *International Protection of Human Rights* 1172 (Indianapolis: Bobbs-Merrill, 1973).

9. *Id*. at 1183.

10. A. Robertson, *Human Rights in Europe* (Manchester, U.K.: Manchester University Press, 1977), p. 180.

11. Appendix, Committee of Ministers Resolution (76) 35, "Summary of information provided by the Government of the United Kingdom during the examination of the 'Golder' Case before the Committee of Ministers," 19 *Yearbook of the European Convention on Human Rights* 1090 (1926).

12. J. Whale, "Irish Stand Their Ground in Strasbourg Showdown," Sunday *Times* (London), 13 Feb. 1977.

13. For the subtleties, *see* J. Rivero, "Les Garanties Constitutionelles des Droits de l'Homme en Droit Français," 29 *Revue Internationale de Droit Comparé* 9 (1977).

14. For an introduction to this problem, see "Self-Executing Treaties and the Human Rights Provisions of the United Nations Charter: A Separation of Powers Problem," 25 *Buff. L. Rev.* 773 (1976) (U.S.). A. Drzemczewski, "The Domestic Status of the European Convention on Human Rights: New Dimensions," 1977 *Lg. Issues of European Integration* 1 (1977).

15. Internationale Handelsgesellschaft mbh v. Einfuhr-und Vorratsstelle für Getreide und Futtermittel (case 2 Bvl. 52/71) 14 Comm. Mkt. L.R. 540 (German Federal Constitutional Court, 29 May 1974).

16. Joint Declaration by the European Parliament, the Council, and the Commission, 5 April 1977, Official Journal C103/1 (1977).

17. Rutili v. The French Minister of the Interior, 36/75 [1975] ECR 1219. See generally, Commission of the European Convention, *The Protection of fundamental rights as community law is created and developed* (Report of 4 February 1976), *Bulletin of the European Communities*, Supplement 5/76 (1976).

18. The leading case is *Golak Nath's Case*, AIR 1967 SC 1643, holding that fundamental rights could not be curtailed by constitutional amendment. The government responded with a constitutional amendment empowering Parliament to amend any provision of the Constitution, including those relating to fundamental rights. In Kesavananda v. State of Kerala, AIR 1973 SC 1461, the Court upheld this

amendment, but declared that the amending procedure did not "enable Parliament to alter the basic structure or framework of the Constitution" and struck down part of a subsequent amendment. (Agreed summary, *id* at 1462.) The Court followed this doctrine in striking down a constitutional amendment relating to irregularities in Mrs. Gandhi's election campaign, Smt. Indira Nehru Gandhi v. Raj Narain, AIR 1975 SC 2299, but did not go so far as to strike down an arrangement for preventive detention, Jabalpore v. Shinkla, AIR 1976 SC 1207.

19. See Lord Hailsham's Dimbleby Lecture, *The Times*, Oct. 15, 1976, p. 4; J. Jaconelli, "The European Convention on Human Rights—The Text of a British Bill of Rights." 1976 *Public Law* 226; I. Duncanson, "Balloonists, Bill of Rights and Dinosaurs," 1928 *Public Law* 391.

20. Gallina v. Fraser, 278 F.2d 77 (2d Circ., 1960); but see Beschluss von 27 Marz 1973, 37 *Entscheidungen des Bundesverfassungsgerichts* 57 (German Federal Constitutional Court restricting extradition to East Germany Under Mutual Assistance Agreement).

21. Stonehill v. United States 405 F.2d 738 (9th Circ., 1968); but see Berlin Democratic Club v. Rumsfeld. 410 FS 144 (DCDC 1976) (denying summary judgment for defendant U.S. in challenge to intelligence activities in West Berlin).

22. Holmes v. Laird 459 F.2d 1211 (DC Cir. 1972). See generally, R. Lillich, "The Role of Domestic Courts in Promoting International Human Rights Norms," 24 *N.Y.L.S. L. Rev.* 153 (1978).

23. But see D. Clark, "Judicial Protection of the Constitution in Latin America," 2 *Hastings Constit. L. Qtly.* 405 (1975).

24. Case relating to certain aspects of the laws on the use of languages in education in Belgium, Euro. Ct. of H.R., 23 July 1968.

25. For a sample of the limitations of the current conventions, see "Comment: The International Human Right Treaties: Some Problems of Policy and Interpretation," 126 *U. Penn. L. Rev.* 886 (1978).

26. *See* L. Preuss, "The International Court of Justice, The Senate, and Matters of Domestic Jurisdiction," 40 *Am. J. of Int'l Law* 720 (1946).

27. President's Human Rights Treaty Message to the Senate, 14 WEEKLY COMP. OF PRES. DOC. 395 (Feb. 23, 1978). For discussion and criticism, see D. Weissbrodt, "United States Ratification of the Human Rights Covenants," 63 *Minn. L. Rev.* 35, 66–72 (1978).

28. D. Fox, "Evaluation of the American Convention on Human Rights and Prospects for its Ratification by the United States," (unpublished 1972), reprinted in Subcommittee on International Organizations and Movements of the House Committee on Foreign Affairs, Hearings on International Protection of Human Rights, 93d Cong., 1st Sess., 683, 688–91 (1974). L. LeBlanc, *The OAS and the Promotion and Protection of Human Rights* 20–22 (The Hague: Nijhoft, 1977).

29. Greece v. U.K. Applications No. 176156 and 299157, whose

peaceful settlement was recognized in Committee of Ministers Resolutions 59 (12) and 59 (32), at 2 *Yearbook of the European Convention on Human Rights*, 186 and 196 (1958–59). Later, the Greek negotiator stated: "I think ... that this outcome has been one of the most satisfying in the framework of powers and mechanism of the Convention. ... the debates which took place before the Commission permitted the two parties to come together in the political domain, thanks to a rigorous observance of the rules of law and of fundamental rights." Ambassador Kambalouris, at the Colloque de Grenoble (25–26 Jan. 1973), published at 6 *Revue des droits de l'homme* 787 (1973) (translated by author).

30. Austria v. Italy, Application No. 788160, 4 *Yearbook of the European Convention on Human Rights* 116 (1961).

31. Standing Committee of the Consultative Assembly of the Council of Europe, Resolution 346 of 23 June 1967.

32. European Commission of Human Rights, *The Greek Case*, Report of the Commission adopted on 5 November 1969. Council of Europe, Doc. 15, 707/1 (1969), vol. 1, pt. 1, at 5–11. See Sohn and Buergenthal, *supra* n. 8 at 1074–75.

33. Consultative Assembly of the Council of Europe, Resolution 558 of 22 Jan. 1974. The conditions included the "lifting of the state of emergency and release of all political detainees ... the restoration of human rights ... including the right to organize political parties freely ... local and municipal elections, with secret ballot, held under conditions of unrestricted freedom of expression ... election of a parliament ... a genuinely democratic constitution."

34. Committee of Ministers Resolution 74 (34), 28 Nov. 1974. J. Catsiapis, "La Constitution de la Grèce de Juin 1975," 91 *Revue du Droit Public et de la Science Politique en France et a l'Étranger* 1977, 1599 (1975).

35. Sohn and Buergenthal, *supra* n. 9 at pp. 373–504.

36. Security Council Resolution 435 (1978); 29 Sept. 1978.

37. On the South African case, see T. Millar, *The Commonwealth and The United Nations* 168–69 (Sydney, 1967). On the Jackson-Vanik amendment, *see* "An Interim Analysis of the Effects of the Jackson-Vanik Amendment on Trade and Human Rights: The Roumania Example," 8 *Law & Pol. in Int'l Bus* 193 (1976).

38. Inter-American Commission on Human Rights, Report on the Activities of the Inter-American Commission on Human Rights, in the Dominican Republic, 1 June to 31 August 1965, OASOR, OEA/Ser. L/V/11.12, Doc. 14 Rev. (1965); Inter-American Convention on Human Rights, Report of the Inter-American Commission on Human Rights on Its Activities in the Dominican Republic, 1 September 1965–6 July 1966, OASOR, OEA/Ser. L/V/11.15, Doc. 6 Rev. (1966).

39. *Report on the Status of Human Rights in Chile*, OAS/Ser.L/V/II. 34, (doc. 21), October, 1974.

40. See J. Salzberg and D. Young, "The Parliamentary Role in Implementing International Human Rights: A U.S. Example," 12 *Tex Int'l L.J.* 251 (1977).

41. PL-94-304 (codified at 22 USC §§3001–08). The Department of State opposed this legislation in a letter dated Dec. 19, 1976, included as part of the House Report, HR 94-1149 (May 14, 1976).

42. LeBlanc, *supra* n. 28 at 107–63.

43. See T. Buergenthal, "The American and European Conventions on Human Rights: Some Similarities and Differences." February 1979 (Paper presented at the San Jose Conference on the Inter-American Human Rights System).

44. For a discussion of these transitional issues, arguing strongly that the Commission will retain its current authorities, see Panel Discussion, "Regional Approaches to Human Rights: The Inter-American Experience," *Proceedings of the 72d Annual Meeting, American Society of International Law, 1978* at 197, especially remarks of E. Carreno and F. Armstrong (1978).

45. See T. Buergenthal, "Implementing the U.N. Racial Covenant," 12 *Tex Int'l L.J.* 187 (1977).

46. F. Wolf, "Aspects Judiciares de la Protection Internationale des Droits de l'Homme par l'O.I.T.", *IV Revue des droits de l'homme* 773, 785–86 (1971). Although the ILO convention also includes more formal processes, the key mechanism is a Commission of Experts for the Application of Conventions and Recommendations, established rather informally in 1926. This Commission reviews reports and communications. On occasion, it also sends a representative to a nation at the latter's request. *Id.* at 779–87. Other procedures include study groups, such as one sent to Spain in 1968–69. *Id.* at 816–17.

Appendix

STATISTICAL ANALYSIS FOR IMPLEMENTING HUMAN RIGHTS POLICY

BARNETT R. RUBIN AND PAULA R. NEWBERG

Each indignity visited upon a human being, each torture, is irreducibly singular and inexpiable. Every time a human being is flogged, starved, deprived of self-respect, a specific black hole opens in the fabric of life. It is an additional obscenity to depersonalize inhumaneness, to blanket the irreparable fact of individual agony with anonymous categories of statistical analysis, historical theory, or sociological model-building. . . . But the mortal mind is so constructed that it cannot contain, in genuine individuation, more than a thimbleful of known presences. At least twenty million men, women, and children were done to death in the Stalinist purges. If we possess a vivid inward perception, we can visualize, we can number, and, in some measure, we can identify with fifty persons, perhaps a hundred. Beyond that stretches the comfortable limbo of abstraction. So if we are to understand at all, we *must* try to analyze, to classify, to put forward those reveries of reason which are called theories.

—George Steiner

The fifth paragraph of the fourth chapter of the treatise *Sanhedrin* of the Mishnah declares that, for God's Justice, he who kills one man destroys the world; if there is no plurality, he who annihilates all men would be no more guilty than the primitive and solitary Cain. ... The vociferous catastrophes of a general order—fires, wars, epidemics—are one single pain, illusorily multiplied in many mirrors.

—Jorge Luis Borges

There is something unalterably repugnant about converting information about human rights into statistics. But to avoid keeping accounts of the totality of the violations out of moral queasiness is to acquiesce before the enormity of the offense. The mass production of imprisonment and executions must at some point be grasped statistically. Insofar as the gross numbers of offenses are extremely important to understand, such statistical accumulation and analysis is a necessary task. We must also try to comprehend the meaning of this: that each violation is a tangible and discrete person suffering great indignity. Emotionally, it is extremely hard to grasp these two kinds of problems at once.

Concern over the violation of human rights in other countries has been introduced systematically into U.S. foreign policy during the last several years. Implementing this policy has been difficult and many critics assert that the policies have been applied inconsistently. Such claims have come both from states defending themselves against charges about their human rights violations as well as from people who believe that human rights have been given too little weight in the calculus of more traditional foreign policy considerations.

An American human rights policy cannot be defended against such charges unless it can identify clearly its goals and is based on information that permits comparisons among countries. This does not mean that all countries must be judged by the same inflexible standard. The needs, wealth, capacities, and past history of a country can influence the level of national and international expectations, as suggested by Heginbotham and Bite (1978:350–53). Nevertheless, the problem of comparing the extent to which countries fall short of these modified expectations remains. While the implementation of the policy must conform to the specific situation in each country, as Secretary Vance has emphasized (Vance, 1977), the nature of the policy toward each country should be determined by general criteria.

MEASUREMENT

Is it possible to measure the violation of rights? Two arguments have been offered against this possibility. The first asserts that the necessary information is unobtainable. This is a problem of practice, not principle, and will be considered later. The second asserts that these phenomena are by their nature not susceptible to measurement. This doubt may be largely based on a misconception about the meaning of measurement.

Any procedure that assigns one of a set of values of a variable (not necessarily numerical values) to each of a set of cases is a measurement. There are several types of measurement, which can be ordered from the lowest to the highest level according to the amount of information that they convey about the objects measured.

The lowest level of measurement for a variable is the classification. Nominal variables distribute cases into categories that have no relation to each other besides mutual exclusivity. Ordinal variables order or rank the cases and are transitive. For instance, classifying national presses as "free," "partly free," or "unfree" defines an ordinal variable with three levels over all national presses included in a survey.

Both nominal and ordinal variables are measured qualitatively. The higher levels of measurement apply to quantitative variables. An interval-level variable assigns numbers to the cases, but the origin and scale of these numbers are arbitrary. The ratio of the distances between two pairs of such numbers is defined, but not their absolute magnitude. These scales have different zero points and different sizes of units, but they are equivalent in the sense described above.

A numerical variable that also has an absolute zero is measured on a ratio scale. On such a scale it is possible to gauge the relative values of two cases by taking the ratio of their values. The number of political prisoners per 100,000 adult population is a ratio variable, since there is a natural zero, and it is meaningful to say that one country has twice as many prisoners proportionate to its adult population as another.

The most common phrase used by U.S. policymakers and legislators to describe phenomena that should trigger American action in defense of human rights is "a consistent pattern of gross violations of internationally recognized human rights."* This language implicitly assumes that human rights violations can be measured, at least at the ordinal level, so that they can be ordered by importance. It defines a threshold for the tolerance of particular violations. When the severity of these violations crosses the implied threshold, the statutes require the U.S. government in general to react by changing aid programs and voting against loans from multilateral agencies.

Collecting statistics about human rights violations, either by governments or by independent agencies, would not be an entirely new activity. For instance, the FBI collects data on the commission of major "crimes" all over the United States. From these data it constructs an overall index of the crime rate as well as an index for each of the standard metropolitan statistical areas. For these purposes it is possible to compare indices to determine the relative level of criminal activity in different cities.

The measurement of human rights violations is also a type of crime reporting. However, there are differences in the two activities. The violations of the law counted by the crime reports all occur within a country with a single constitution that unites the various local legal systems into a national legal system. The same law of evidence prevails to determine whether in fact a crime of a certain type has been committed.

---

*This phrase, derived from United Nations language (Resolution 1503), is used in several public laws, including: the International Development and Food Assistance Act of 1975, PL 94–161, Section 116(a); the International Security Assistance and Arms Export Control Act of 1976, PL 94–329, Section 502B(a)(2); and the Inter-American Development Bank and African Development Fund Act, PL 94–302, Sections 28(a) and 211(a).

Furthermore, government agencies report on the criminal activities of their citizens. They benefit both from the help of other citizens (such as the victims whose reports to the police provide the basis for the crime statistics) and from all the powerful attributes of sovereignty.

Human rights are for the most part violated by governments or quasi-governments such as liberation movements.These governments invoke the rights and powers of sovereignty to prevent accurate reporting of these violations. They are also often inclined to resist accusations of wrongdoing by offering alternative versions of any reported phenomena. The laws regarding respect for human rights vary from country to country, even when they share common cultural, political, or legal heritages.

More important, there is no effective international judicial system to determine by consistent rules of evidence when these widely varying laws have been violated. The standard-setting activities of multilateral organizations are only beginning to approach this task. Too often the political dimensions of multilateral discussions and negotiations overwhelm their purported goals. Ultimately, the accusatory process that typifies these processes may not necessarily be the best way to compel compliance with international standards.

It is worth noting that the violation of rights is sometimes a systemic or structural problem, particularly when the rights that are violated are economic or social ones. Governments can violate rights in certain explicit ways; the global organization and transfer of resources may either support such continued violations or independently but not explicitly allow policies that ultimately cause violations to continue. The causal lines are difficult to draw here but deserve further thought; they may be quite relevant to future studies of the unintended consequences of the use of power.

OBJECTS OF MEASUREMENT

There are internationally recognized lists of human rights that serve as the basis for most human rights reporting. Although they are not part of a legal system properly speaking, these codes establish lists of the violation of rights that we can measure. Measurement requires more variables than most lists provide, but they are the first point of departure. The list used by the State Department in its yearly human rights reports is based on the Universal Declaration of Human Rights. It also incorporates a tripartite classification of rights outlined by the secretary of state (Vance, 1977) and includes the following:

1. Respect for the integrity of the person, including freedom from:
   a. torture (Article 5)
   b. cruel, inhuman, or degrading treatment or punishment (Article 5)
   c. arbitrary arrest or imprisonment (Article 9)
   d. denial of fair public trial (Article 10)
   e. invasion of the home (Article 12)

2. Government policies relating to the fulfillment of such vital needs as food, shelter, health care, and education (Article 25 and 26)

3. Respect for civil and political liberties, including:
   a. freedom of thought, speech, press, religion, and assembly (Articles 18, 19, and 20)
   b. freedom of movement within the country, foreign travel, and emigration (Article 13)
   c. freedom to participate in the political process (Article 21)

SOME PROBLEMS OF MEASUREMENT

Measuring these variables poses three related problems: specification, level of measurement, and time scale.

A. SPECIFICATION

There are many possible ways to specify the precise variable to be measured even if we assume that it is possible to define and identify rights and violations in a standard and easy way. For example, we could count the number of arbitrary arrests and imprisonments per year in proportion to the adult population, or we could count the number of people under arbitrary detention on a given day (this is the procedure used by the census to count the population). Both of these measures, however, are insensitive to the length of imprisonment. We could compensate for this by calculating the average length of arbitrary imprisonment in addition to a measure of how many people were affected. Or we could estimate the transition rates (rate of arrest and rate of release) per time unit.

Deeper analysis of each variable to determine the specific ways that these rights are respected or infringed on would help determine how to specify and measure the variables. For instance, it is possible to measure press freedom on a three-point scale as Freedom House does, but such a scale can be quite inaccurate and misleading. A detailed examination of press freedom in various countries would, however, reveal a complex set of institutions that protect or restrain it: prepublication censorship; placing censors in all publication offices; self-censorship and post facto review by the state; constitutional guarantees supported by independent judiciary or vitiated by one-party domination; or explicit standards for censoring. Clearly, what we call "press freedom" must be subdivided into several elements before we can refine the scales of measurement. Each right has a similarly complex analytical breakdown.

B. LEVEL OF MEASUREMENT

Choosing a level of measurement is closely related to the specification of the indicator to be measured. Since the goal of the measurement is to permit ordinal comparisons, at least an ordinal variable is required in every case. In many cases a higher level of measurement is possible. All of the various indicators suggested above for the degree of arbitrary arrest or imprisonment are ratio variables. If precise numbers are uncertain, we can group the countries into deciles, quintiles, or some other set of ordered categories and treat the variable as an ordinal variable. The choice of level of measurement would also be partly dictated by the method of analysis to be used.

The higher the level of measurement, the more tools of analysis are available. As a result, many researchers often treat ordinal variables as interval variables.

C. TIME SCALE

The level of respect for rights changes over time. This presents a separate set of measurement problems, including: spacing the observations properly; choosing a base unit for variables measured as rates; choosing a scale for comparisons over time; and dealing with sudden changes in governmental policy toward rights.

Spacing the observations means deciding how often to revise the measurements for each country. Each country's human rights situation should ideally be characterized by the set of measurements on the variables at every moment, but this is impossible. For the most part, countries do not change every second or every day. Observations should be spaced to allow sufficient time for information to be gathered and analyzed, while also close enough to note the periodic changes that occur. Yearly reports have the advantage of conforming both to past usage and to the standard operating procedures of many organizations.

Some variables will be measured as rates, such as the indicators of the frequency and duration of arbitrary arrest and imprisonment. These can be measured over any time period. The best choice would be to use the sampling interval as the base unit. Thus, if indicators were updated every year, the calculated rates would be annual rates. If a smaller base unit, such as a month, were used, it would probably give a more accurate general picture of a regime to use an average monthly rate than to use a single month's figures. Once a set of variables can be identified, measuring these rates is a fairly straightforward task.

Sudden changes in the level of respect for human rights need to be analyzed separately, particularly because the indicators should reflect the period during which policy is to be implemented. Different types of variables require different adjustments for this purpose. Some variables are "global." They describe overall states of the entire social system rather than the frequency of events of a certain type. A variable describing the extent of press freedom in a given country is such a global variable. One may set a convention that if the value of a global variable for some country changes over a reporting period, the value it takes at the end of the period is the one to be used. Other variables are rates. They describe the frequency of actions of a certain type. If a regime or policy change leads to a sudden alteration of the level of a variable measured as a rate, one can use only data from after the change to calculate rates for the usual base period.

DATA ANALYSIS

The approach outlined here would yield measurements on a large number of variables for each country. It is necessary to condense the information in these measurements to make comparisons among countries. There are many different ways of doing this, and the choice would depend both on the particular purposes for which the information was used and on characteristics of the distribution of the variables.

In the few pieces of work in this area the condensing problem has been treated only as a weighting problem, and only very limited types of weighting schemes have been considered. (See Morris, 1978; Heginbotham and Bite, 1978.) There are, however, many practical ways to evaluate the data.

Sets of weights can be chosen to reflect certain characteristics of the data or to show our own beliefs about the relative importance of the variables for the purpose we have in mind. These weights are called ex post and ex ante weights, respectively, because they are determined after or before examining the data. This discussion is restricted to weights that form weighted averages, that is, that are all positive and sum to one. (Lexical ordering is an alternative to weighting and can be considered a special case of ex ante weights.) For example, in constructing the Physical Quality of Life Index (PQLI), three ex ante schemes were used to indicate equally weighted averages: infant mortality, life expectancy at age one, and the adult literacy rate. (Morris considered only ex ante weighting schemes.) After describing the inadequacy of existing data, Heginbotham and Bite note:

> There is no general agreement as to the relative importance that should be attached to the three major categories of violations that have been differentiated in this study. Even more complex is the problem of weighting different types of violations within categories. . . . When one is dealing with such emotion-laden matters as electric shock torture, years in prison without trial, and summary execution or mysterious disappearance without trial, it is difficult indeed to achieve even impressionistic consensus or relative weightings.

Determining the relative importance of these variables is a problem that arises only when the joint distribution of the variables does not show large positive correlation among them. Consider a hypothetical situation in which data have been collected on two types of human rights violations for a set of countries. If the variables are perfectly and positively correlated ($r = 1.00$), it does not matter whether they are weighted equally or used separately as the lone indicator of the level of respect for human rights. The relative distances among the countries (for quantitative variables) or the the rankings (for ordinal variables) would not be changed by any choice of weights, regardless of the estimation of the relative importance of the two variables.

The dependence among the variables will not be perfect, and it may not be entirely positive. A negative correlation might indicate the existence of a tradeoff between two variables. For instance, one view of underdeveloped countries holds that attempts to meet the needs of their poor are hindered by civil and political liberties. Were this true, one would expect to observe a negative correlation between the PQLI and various indicators of political freedom, at least within the group of underdeveloped countries. Roughly speaking, the greater the degree of positive dependence among the variables, the less important the choice of weights in determining the overall score of the countries.

The U.S. government's tripartite division reflects a statistical phenomenon. The various rights included under the rubric of respect for the integrity of the person seem to be violated or respected together. These rights are somewhat correlated with respect for civil and political rights—most countries that allow freedom to their citizens usually respect the integrity of the person. The converse is not true. There are many countries (including some socialist countries and some one-party Third World countries) where the integrity of the person is largely respected but where civil and political rights are sharply curtailed. On the other hand, government policies to fulfill vital needs such as food, health, shelter, and education seem to be independent of the other two types of human rights, except in extreme cases where brutal regimes impoverish their people as well. (Morris notes that countries with very high PQLIs for their level of GNP include Cuba, South Korea, Taiwan, and Sri Lanka.)

There are several statistical techniques available for examining the degree of mutual dependence among a set of variables. For quantitative variables there are the related techniques of factor analysis and principal components, which produce sets of ex post weights. (These weights, however, are not constrained to be positive or to sum to one.) The method of principal components analyzes how much of the variation of a set of quantitative variables measured on the same scale can be accounted for by a smaller number of underlying variables. The underlying variables are formed from weighted sums of the observed variables. If, for instance, the variables measuring respect for the integrity of the person, fulfillment of basic needs, and respect for civil and political liberties varied positively together within categories but independently among categories, there would be three significant principal components, each of which would concentrate its weights on the variables in one of the three categories of rights.

This technique is completely valid only for quantitative variables measured on the same scale. For qualitative variables the general methods for latent structure analysis developed by Goodman (1973, 1974b) make it possible to estimate parameters analogous to factor loadings for quantitative variables. Latent structure analysis tests whether the observed pattern of association among the variables can be attributed to the effects of a smaller number of underlying variables that we cannot observe directly, such as a general tendency to observe human rights.* They do not, however, allow one to determine which individual cases should be assigned to which level of the latent variables. Like so many other aspects of measuring for these purposes, this too is a subjective initial judgment.

Once the sets of human rights indicators that vary together have been determined, there are a number of alternative ways to use this information for comparisons. One is to use ex post weights to form indexes, as is done in some social science research when factor scores are used. This method has several disadvantages, however. These indexes would not be weighted averages of variables that are positively correlated. They could just as well be contrasts of variables that are negatively correlated. This method would also require the continued collection of data on a large number of variables. Further, principal components are not robust: the weights calculated from one sample always perform less efficiently in repeated applications. These methods can, however, give a good idea of what variables are the most accurate indicators of the overall level of violations within categories. These would be the variables given the greatest weight in the principal components or that had the strongest relationship to the latent variables. In the future, attention could be concentrated on these variables alone, which would decrease the amount of data needed. In the simplest case, one variable alone would turn out to be a good indicator, but such a solution would be dangerous for policy.

*The parameters analogous to the coefficients of the principal components are the conditional probabilities that a case is at a certain level of an observed variable given that it is at a certain level of the latent variable. These conditional probabilities express the strength of the relation between the latent or unobserved variables and the observed variables, as do the weights of the principal components.

Governments would learn that a particular practice alone was being monitored and could substitute some other form of repression for it. Hence, the number of indicators should not be restricted too narrowly.

A more basic problem with ex post weights is that they reflect structural relationships rather than ethical or political concerns. They are thus more useful for research than for direct policy construction or implementation. It could turn out, for instance, that the number of people murdered by the government is an inaccurate indicator of the level of the violation of other human rights. (Even a decrease in the violation of a particular right may simply indicate that such violation is no longer the most efficient way for a government to pursue its general policy goals.) It may be less important structurally than other factors that arouse our concern much less. In Zinoviev's *Yawning Heights*, the Master writes, under the title "Social Systems": "The main difficulty one experiences in trying to understand social systems is not discovering sensational facts or statistics or getting access to carefully guarded state secrets; it is finding a way to order everything that is obvious, a way to understand daily life." The Master contrasts this approach to that of Ivanburg's greatest citizen, Father Justice, whose work is devoted to exposing the secret facts and figures of mass repression.

If a foreign policy is designed to discourage individual egregious abuses rather than to transform social systems, the structural or systematic relationships that are expressed in the ex post weights may be irrelevant. We would then have to use ex ante weights that reflect the degree of concern over certain types of violations. This problem should arise only if the weights or sets of indicators suggested by the ex post analysis deal too lightly with certain types of violations that we consider important independently of their correlation with a hypothetical general level of violation of human rights or of a particular subcategory of human rights.

In this case we return to an earlier dilemma. How many reports of torture are equivalent to a murder? Or, in more basic terms: What do we care about, and how much?

One way to think about this issue is to consider what is meant by forming an index with ex ante weights. A change in one unit of each component of the index contributes to a change in the level of the index in proportion to the component's weighting coefficient. Hence, the components are considered to substitute for each other in proportions given by the ratios of their weights. For example, in an index of the production of goods and services, such as the Gross National Product, physical quantities are weighted by their prices. The relative prices of two goods express how many units of one good substitute for the other on the market, where physical units of all goods are valued through another good, the *numéraire,* money.

Some utilitarian accounts of ethical choice would evaluate these alternatives in terms of weights in a utility function. These weights could be used in constructing the index we are discussing, which could be considered a linearized utility function. But even if we accepted such a utilitarian approach and choice, we would not be in a position to specify our preferences so precisely. Some ethical positions argue strongly against applying a weighting scheme to the taking of life. The text in the Mishnah referred to by Borges in the essay cited in the epigraph expresses this argument. Because life is a necessary condition for enjoying any other right or any of the goods of this world, "he who destroys a life is as one who destroys the world." In this account, then, life has infinite value and cannot be substituted for any other good; capital punishment would therefore be a crime more heinous than almost any other.

An alternative to weighting for such situations is lexical ordering (Rawls, 1971: 43–45). A lexical ordering is an ordering like that of words in a dictionary. The words are initially ordered by their first letter. They are then ordered by their second letter within each group sharing the same first letter. Thus, we could order countries lexically, with the level of violation of the right to live in the first position. This variable could be measured as the proportion of the population killed by the government per year.

This procedure has the attraction of ethical clarity, but it would present certain practical difficulties. This variable alone would completely determine the ordering of the countries, since no two governments would kill precisely the same proportion of their population. The ordering would also be sensitive to inaccuracies in the counts and to differences in population size and age structure. Hence, it would be safer to group countries into a few ordered classes according to the approximate level of their violation of the right to life. This ordinal variable could then be the first variable in a lexical ordering. The remaining variables could then be treated in any of the other ways suggested here.

Another method of ranking countries that is rather different from all those considered thus far is the ranking coefficient. The cases are assigned ranks on each variable, and the ranks are then averaged with some set of weights to form an index. Kendall (1939) compared an index of the agricultural productivity of English counties calculated from the averaged ranks with one calculated from the principal components and found that the ranking coefficient gave very similar results with much less work. The computational effort is no longer a significant consideration, but the conceptual simplicity of the ranking coefficient is still a great attraction.

DATA COLLECTION

The preceding discussion leaves unanswered an extremely complex series of questions: Who should have the responsibility for measuring violations? Which sources should be used? How public should discovery and analysis be?

Clearly, the interests and capabilities of nongovernmental organizations, national governments, and intergovernmental organizations vary substantially. Not only do they have access to different kinds and quantities of information, but the purposes to which they put their findings resonate quite differently in the international system. In fact, each kind of organization tends implicitly to emphasize varying aspects of a problem before assessing their importance; this form of self-selection imposes a methodological bias prior to analysis that, although often comprehensible or plausible, influences the ways in which others can use the same material. Objectivity and impartiality, both in collection and in use, become fleeting prospects.

International data are collected by various international agencies, including agencies of the U.S., OECD, the ILO, and WHO. All of these organizations rely on the cooperation of member states. Because many governments, particularly the worst offenders, claim that external supervision invades their sovereignty and imposes alien standards, this remains an inadequate way to collect information.

Other international data are collected by national governments as part of their intelligence operations. The U.S. government, for instance, collects quantitative data on economic and military affairs. It can be argued that, if one seriously intends to make respect for human rights a permanent criterion for deciding on the nature of bilateral political relations, a national government should also collect data on human rights violations. (The technologies of the CIA and the NSA should be well suited for such work.) Such activity would, of course, yet more firmly establish the image of the United States and its president as a hypocritical parson peeping into bedroom windows all over town.

REFERENCES

Amnesty International Annual Report, 1975–76. London, 1977.

Borges, Jorge Luis. "A New Refutation of Time." Trans. James E. Irby. *Labyrinths: Selected Stories and Other Writings.* Ed. Donald A. Yates and James E. Irby. New York: New Directions Publishing, 1964.

Department of State. *Country Reports on Human Rights Practices: Report Submitted to the Committee on International Relations, U.S. House of Representatives, and Committee on Foreign Relations, U.S. Senate, by the Department of State in Accordance with Sections 116(d) and 502B(b) of the Foreign Assistance Act as Amended, February 3, 1978.* Washington: U.S. Government Printing Office, 1978.

Goodman, Leo A. "The Analysis of Systems of Qualitative Variables When Some of the Variables Are Unobservable. Part 2—The Use of Modified Latent Distance Models." Unpublished Manuscript, 1973.

————. "The Analysis of Systems of Qualitative Variables When Some of the Variables Are Unobservable. Part I—A Modified Latent Structure Approach." *American Journal of Sociology* 79, no. 5 (March 1974a):1179–1259.

————. "Exploratory Latent Structure Analysis Using Both Identifiable and Unidentifiable Models." *Biometrika* 61, no. 2 (1974b)2:215–31.

Heginbotham, Stanley J., and Vita Bite. "Issues in Interpretation and Evaluation of Country Studies." *Human Rights Conditions in Selected Countries and the U.S. Response: Prepared by the Subcommittee on International Organizations of the Committee on International Relations, U.S. House of Representatives, by the Foreign Affairs and National Defense Division, Congressional Research Service, Library of Congress, July 25, 1978.* Washington: U.S. Government Printing Office, 1978. Pp. 341–57.

Kendall, M. G. "The Geographical Distribution of Crop Productivity in England." *Journal of the Royal Statistical Society* 102 (1939):21–48.

Morris, Morris David. "Measuring the Condition of the World's Poor: The Physical Quality of Life Index." Unpublished manuscript. Overseas Development Council. 1978.

Rawls, John. *A Theory of Justice.* Cambridge, Mass.: Harvard University Press, 1971.

Steiner, George. "Books: De Profundis." *The New Yorker,* September 4, 1978, 97–99.

Vance, Cyrus. "Human Rights Policy." Washington: Department of State, Bureau of Public Affairs, 1977.

Zinoviev, Alexandre. *Les Hauteurs Béantes.* Trans. Wladimir Berelowitch. Lausanne: Editions l'Âge d'Homme, 1977.

INDEX